QUEEN OF THE HURRICANES

A FEMINIST HISTORY SOCIETY BOOK

QUEEN OF THE HURRICANES

THE FEARLESS ELSIE MACGILL

by

CRYSTAL SISSONS

Second Story Press

Library and Archives Canada Cataloguing in Publication

Sissons, Crystal, 1979–, author
Queen of the Hurricanes : the fearless Elsie MacGill / by Crystal Sissons.

Issued in print and electronic formats.
ISBN 978-1-927583-53-1 (pbk.)
ISBN 978-1-927583-57-9 (bound)
ISBN 978-1-927583-54-8 (epub)

1. MacGill, Elsie Gregory, 1905-1980. 2. Women engineers–Canada–
Biography. 3. Aeronautical engineers–Canada–Biography. 4. Feminists–
Canada–Biography. 5. Social reformers–Canada–Biography. 6. Hurricane
(Fighter plane)–History. I. Title.

TL540.M245S58 2014   629.130092   C2014-903986-7

C2014-903987-5

Edited by Jennifer Penney
Copyedited by Carolyn Jongeward
Typesetting by Melissa Kaita
Original design by Zab Design & Typography Inc.

Cover photos courtesy of Elizabeth Schneewind and Helen Brock/
Thunder Bay Historical Museum, Hurricane, 984.78.56

Every effort has been made to secure permission and provide appropriate
credit for photographic material. The publisher deeply regrets any omission
and pledges to correct errors called to its attention in subsequent editions.

Printed and bound in Canada

*Second Story Press gratefully acknowledges the support of the
Ontario Arts Council and the Canada Council for the Arts for our
publishing program. We acknowledge the financial support of the
Government of Canada through the Canada Book Fund.*

Published by
Second Story Press
20 Maud Street, Suite 401
Toronto, ON M5V 2M5
www.secondstorypress.ca

This book is dedicated to the memory of:

Dr. Helen Smith, Associate Professor in History and Women's Studies at Lakehead University, whose door was always open whether the topic was historical or not. Your passion for women's history and dedication to your students lives on in each of us who was fortunate enough to sit in your lectures;

My incredible grandparents Eva and George Sissons and Evelyn and Jack Smeeth;

My wonderful and much missed father-in-law, Jean-Louis Vidal, who always followed the beat of his own drummer and seized each day's new possibilities with wonder and excitement;

And, to each and every person passionate about education and making our shared world a better place. Never doubt that you can make a difference.

CONTENTS

A NOTE ON FOOTNOTES

The copious footnotes supporting the author's extensive research for this biography of Elsie MacGill can be accessed online at: http://secondstorypress.ca/resources or at http://feministhistories.ca/books

PREFACE

Here is a book that has been badly needed if we are to understand
the nature of the women's movement of the 1970s and 1980s and a
woman who inspired much of the change in the status of women
before and after those years.

Elsie Gregory MacGill was a public figure when I moved to
Toronto in 1967. Her mother had been a very famous person in my
childhood years on the west coast of Canada, but I had not met
either of them in person.

In muggy late August of 1968 at the American Sociological
Association meetings in Boston, I met Helen MacGill Hughes,
Elsie's sister, a well-known sociologist married to an even better
known sociologist, Everett Hughes. There is something special
about the people who grow up on the British Columbia coast, and
I recognized this in Helen at once – we "clicked." Helen was committed to helping women in sociology as well as more generally. She
sent me her unpublished papers and we kept in touch now and then.
She had the low-key manner, sense of irony, humour, energy, and
drive that I associate with people from the coast.

Had I met Elsie? Helen wanted to know, and was surprised I
had not. Elsie was then serving on the Royal Commission on the
Status of Women. She was working extremely hard at that and travelling across the country extensively. I was moving to Princeton for
my doctoral studies and was not often in Canada. We must have met
at some time during those years because when I returned to Toronto

in 1971 we most certainly had been introduced. Elsie had all those great British Columbian characteristics combined with long years in the tough engineering world of Ontario.

My first clear recollection is of Elsie at the April 1972 founding meeting of what became the National Action Committee on the Status of Women (NAC) in the King Edward Hotel on King Street East in Toronto. Members of all the major women's organizations and from the early women's movement had come together in the wake of the *Report of the Royal Commission on the Status of Women* in Canada. The question for all of us was how to get the recommendations of that report implemented at the federal level. Already the recommendations directed to the provinces and municipalities were taken up by provincial organizations, including some of the well-established Council of Women groups and the newly formed feminist groups. In that Strategy for Change Conference were women from a very broad range of backgrounds – unions, business, religious groups, political groups, arts, local community groups, and well-established women's organizations. Elsie had been the national president of the Business and Professional Women's Clubs and as I recall she was there in that capacity. She was in the thick of things.

It was Elsie's custom to write out – often in green ink – recommendations and notes on what should be done. She was very focused on ensuring that the work of the organization being formed should be effective. The grand gesture was not for Elsie. She was not opposed to demonstrations and picket lines if they had a chance of succeeding, but took much more pleasure in seeing women helped, their rights enshrined, and their opportunities opened up. Pie-in-the-sky resolutions brought her to the microphone to try to bring them into some shape that would actually go through the political and legislative processes of the nation.

Elsie knew those processes much better than most people, had studied them, and was interested in results in law and, even more, in regulations that would translate the ideas into action. Elsie had an astute and critical view of the legislative process. The only other person I worked with who was this knowledgeable outside Parliament was Eugene Forsey, another great quiet reformer. Elsie was not a political party person but got on well with individual Members of Parliament in all parties. She was particularly interested in Deputy Ministers and women in the federal public service who had the knowledge and skills to get things done. She went out of her way to meet these women, get to know them, and be able to call them up to try to influence them. No doubt she did.

In 1975, I was elected president of the National Action Committee on the Status of Women at a convention in Winnipeg. The first president (1972–74) had been Laura Sabia, a charismatic leader with a particularly effective style that intimidated many people and brought joy to our hearts. The second president was Grace Hartman, a deeply influential union leader who had to resign after one year when she was elected National President of Canadian Union of Public Employees, which required all her attention. Laura was a Conservative, Grace was New Democratic Party, and I was a Liberal, which no doubt contributed to my election. We had set out to cover the bases. We were aiming for major legislative changes.

I consulted Elsie before standing for the NAC presidency. She was mildly positive, but it was clear she thought I had a lot to learn. She was right. Immediately after my being elected, Elsie was in touch to give me advice. Indeed, she was in touch nearly every day of my leadership of NAC. "Now Lorna," she would say on the telephone, "have you got a pencil? Now write this down." She was a fantastic mentor and friend, always with a serious point and always with a laugh. I became friends with both Elsie, her husband Bill, and Bill's daughter, and knew they had a rich life of friendships, music, engineering, and social action. But she still found time to attend NAC executive meetings and keep the minutes, write letters and articles, and give superb advice. She pushed us into action.

Elsie wore leg braces and walked with great difficulty all the time I knew her, but it made no difference to her work, or her ideas, or her social life. She cooked at home and entertained friends. She must often have been in pain. It was that, I think, and an infection that led her to take the medicine that affected her lungs and led to her death. A family member – perhaps Helen – had called to let me know that Elsie was dying and there was nothing that could be done. It was terrible news.

But what a legacy she left! Her engineering world, her writing, her work on behalf of the advancement of women, the many people she had mentored, her music, her impact on the world – and always with those west coast jokes, manners, and diffidence. She died before she received all the honours she deserved.

Crystal Sissons has brought so much of this to light, complementing the work written about Elsie's engineering career. It is an important account of one of the most influential feminists of the 20th century, an engineer, a social activist, a knowledgeable analyst, a musician, a family person, and someone who successfully changed the lives of women in Canada for the better.

—Dr. Lorna Marsden

INTRODUCTION

As the young [aviation] industry in the late 1920s began to grow up and flex its flying muscles, Dr. MacGill was at the heart of things spreading her wings, too, along with the pilots who were to become the air vice-marshals and the designers who were later the industry's executives.[1]

—Kit Irving

Our concept of the future influences the direction and development of that future. I believe that the future of the human race depends to a great extent upon the expansion of scientific knowledge and, further, that the wise use of technology that proceeds from that knowledge is our best hope of improving the lot of people around the world.[2]

—Elsie Gregory MacGill

Aviation history captures the imagination with its engaging stories and strong personalities. The most famous woman in aviation history is Amelia Earhart, whose daring adventures in the 1920s continue to captivate. The ongoing mystery surrounding her disappearance still generates curiosity and speculation.[3] While she was breaking barriers in aviation as a pilot, another woman was starting to break new ground in the related field of aeronautical engineering.

Few Canadians know the story of Elsie Gregory MacGill,[4] a woman with a passion for preserving women's history, who made a name for herself as a trail-blazing aeronautical engineer and a prominent Canadian feminist. However, as Elsie herself found out, memories can quickly fade. This realization encouraged her, and many others to create biographical accounts of groundbreaking women from all walks of life.[5] There are several accounts of Elsie's life story, including a biography, a novel and a comic book, newspaper and magazine articles. This book draws on and adds to these narratives.[6]

Elsie's story begins in 1905 in Vancouver, British Columbia. She was the second daughter and youngest child of Helen Gregory MacGill (d. 1947), a notable professional woman and feminist in her own right. Elsie became the first woman to graduate in engineering from the University of Toronto (1927), to earn a master's degree in aeronautical engineering (1929) and then to practice professionally in her field for more than fifty years.

During the Second World War she garnered international recognition as the Chief Aeronautical Engineer at Canadian Car and Foundry in Fort William, Ontario (now a part of Thunder Bay, Ontario). Throughout her career, Elsie maintained a strong commitment to advancing the engineering profession. Before the end of the war she opted to pursue her own business as a consulting engineer in Toronto, Ontario. As she settled into her role as a business owner, Elsie – building on the feminist legacy she inherited from her mother – became active in the Canadian Federation of Business and Professional Women's Clubs of Canada, serving as a provincial and then a national leader.[7] Later she was a persuasive feminist voice on the Royal Commission on the Status of Women in Canada (1967–1970) and promoted its recommendations through new organizations such as the National Action Committee on the Status of Women and the Ontario Committee on the Status of Women, which sprang up in the 1970s. She also actively participated in the United Nations' International Women's Year in 1975.

Elsie's life provides unique insights into the history of women in the engineering profession and of professional women more generally. One of the things that makes her story so interesting is the unique twinning of her life as a professional engineer and as a feminist activist. As these parallel streams of her life developed, they often overlapped and merged, giving Elsie a methodical approach to pursuing feminist goals, and a commitment to women's progression in engineering and in the sciences. Her dedication to these goals did not render her unapproachable. In fact, most of Elsie's friends and colleagues savoured her zest for life, her passion, her laughter, and her optimism.

She earned the respect of men and women alike because the changes she advocated required equal participation by both. Her engineering colleagues valued her opinions and admired her personal strength and dedication to the field, while feminist collaborators applauded her leadership and her willingness to offer help and support to her colleagues. As fellow feminist Laura Sabia recalled, Elsie's actions and leadership took into account the nature of politics, and her calls for change were reasonable and carefully planned, and earned her wide-ranging respect.[8]

Throughout Elsie's lifetime, technology was in a rapid state of change. Airplanes had been introduced only a few years before her birth, yet during her lifetime Elsie worked on many leading-edge developments in aeronautics, witnessed the launching of the first satellite, and saw men walking on the moon. Elsie saw no reason that similar degrees of change could not occur in the status and rights of women. In her youth, Canadian women won the right to vote and were finally recognized as "persons" under the law. These events supported her lifelong conviction that radical social change was possible.[9]

· · · · · · · · ·

Biographies have always been a key means of preserving women's history. Elsie's biography of her mother was motivated by this fact.[10] At times questions have been raised about the objectivity of these accounts, but recent assessments have acknowledged that biographies have the ability to look at the intricate nature of a single life while simultaneously contextualizing it and teasing out new insights about the period in which it occurs.[11]

Elsie's life was complex. In many ways it fits the model of a 'great life' and could be told in the format of a classical biography of her achievements and continual upward movement in her profession.[12] But her strong feminist activism also challenges this model. Once she felt secure in her profession, she took up key roles in the women's movement, which led to a complicated weaving between these two diverse areas. For the most part, she was successful in this endeavour, but at times sacrifices and compromises were required. Using the lens of feminist biography it is possible to hone in on these diverse aspects and to carefully examine Elsie's strong contributions to the feminist movement in Canada.[13] This approach also allows us to tease out the challenges and contradictions she experienced.

While my research and writing on Elsie's journey has encompassed more than ten years of my own life, I am well aware of the limitations of this genre. My own background and interests have shaped the format of this biography as much as the selected approach and sources. However, in an attempt to provide as close an account as possible, I have employed a wide range of primary and secondary sources that have been augmented by interviews and written correspondence of family members and colleagues who knew Elsie personally. These latter sources have been particularly valuable in grounding Elsie for me, especially because I never had a chance to meet her. As it is her story, I have also consciously chosen to let Elsie speak for herself as much as possible instead of trying to overly paraphrase her thoughts and ideas.

· · · · · · · · ·

Until recently, the history of women engineers was largely ignored by historians, including feminist ones. However, where there once was a dearth of publications, especially in Canada, new studies demonstrate that the field is maturing.[14] Women engineers are also taking an active role in supporting and writing the history of their forerunners.[15] Part of this enthusiasm stems from a desire to assess the activism among women engineers that began to gain momentum in the later 1970s and 1980s. Unfortunately, this interest was also largely sparked by tragedy. On December 6, 1989, fourteen young women at the École Polytechnique in Montréal were shot and killed by a young man determined to rid the engineering school of "feminists." This act forced Canadians to assess the situation and try to understand its roots and causes. Reviewing the history of women in engineering, and assessing both their successes and challenges has been a part of this process.[16]

Many women engineers are eager to have access to the stories of the trail-blazing generation of women who came before them. Their support makes possible studies with more nuance and depth, moving beyond simple chronological histories to examine the careers of women in all their complexity. For instance, in Marianne Gosztonyi Ainley's last publication, *Creating Complicated Lives: Women and Science at English-Canadian Universities, 1880–1980*,[17] she cautions using the comparison between male and female career trajectories in the sciences, noting: "Initially, I too compared women's careers with those of their male colleagues, but over the years I shifted my focus to track women's life-course changes in order to emphasize their agency – the 'ability or power to make decisions based on one's own needs and desires in matters that primarily affect oneself.'[18] Indeed, she called for future scholars to "problematize the notion of a career" and recognize its complexity as important.[19]

Elsie MacGill is one of the trailblazers worth studying. What truly sets Elsie apart is not just her success as a professional engineer and her dedication to the advancement of the profession, but that she merged these with her work as a feminist activist. This combination affected both aspects of her life. At times her feminist commitments compromised her engineering career. But her engineering experience enhanced her ability to effectively lead in her feminist projects and to serve as an interpreter of the challenges and possibilities that rapid technological change presented for Canadian society.

Elsie's professional achievements were exceptional, but she was not alone in her journey. Her mother and sister were important and beloved companions. And at the age of 37, she married a partner who accepted and supported her as both a professional and a feminist.

While this biographical account recognizes Elsie's achievements, it also acknowledges her frailties. Although she does deserve recognition for her groundbreaking work in engineering and in women's rights, she was also initially blind to the struggles of others who could not follow easily in her footsteps. As she became more aware of social privilege and discrimination, she endeavoured to affect meaningful changes. However, she never became comfortable with the idea of being a "woman" engineer, she saw herself only as an engineer doing her job. In fact, she later told a reporter: 'Whatever you do, don't make me sound like a paragon.... I'm an engineer and I do what engineers do, that's all."[20] Even among her feminist colleagues Elsie made mistakes. By admitting to them she earned even greater respect from those who sought her guidance and leadership.

Elsie was a vibrant and complex individual who sought every opportunity to make a positive difference in the world around her. As her friend Lorna Marsden wrote: "She knew no fear in tackling the most difficult of the problems facing women, but she found such a gracious and humorous way of doing so that those in the most powerful offices in this country listened to her when she spoke and, from her, learned about the aspirations of all of us in the women's movement."[21]

Footnotes for this chapter can be found online at:
http://secondstorypress.ca/resources and at http://feministhistories.ca/books

Chapter 1
ROOTS AND ROLE MODELS

Unless we have a plan and a definite purpose, universities and schools will be a waste of time.

Few of us are born brilliant…we must develop our capabilities ourselves. These things are not material; they are spiritual, mental and psychological.[1]

—Helen Gregory MacGill

In 1923, Elsie Gregory MacGill packed her belongings and left her family home in Vancouver, British Columbia. Her destination was the University of Toronto's Faculty of Engineering where she would begin her studies in electrical engineering. She was eighteen years old and caught up in the exhilaration of the 1920s. Elsie set out on her life's journey with more than the contents of her suitcases. Her parents, James and Helen MacGill, had given her a rich education and served as powerful role models of public engagement. As the west coast receded, she was confident in her abilities and in the knowledge that her family stood strongly behind her.

• • • • • • • • •

Elsie was born in 1905, the fourth child in a multigenerational family. Her two older brothers – from her mother's first marriage – were Eric Herbert Gregory (born in 1891) and Frederic Philip Gregory (born in 1894). Elsie's sister, Helen MacGill Jr., was born in 1903. The sisters developed a close bond that endured throughout their lives; their family often referred to them as HelNelsie.[2]

Elsie's mother was an unusually independent and unconventional woman. In 1886, at the age of twenty-two, Helen was the first woman in the British Empire to receive a bachelor's degree in music. She went on to complete a Bachelor of Arts and then a master's degree in 1890, the only woman in her class.[3] After completing her

Helen Emma Gregory was born in 1864 to Emma and Silas Ebenezer (Edward) Gregory. She grew up enjoying many social benefits in Hamilton, Ontario, including access to the education she sought. Her passion for music and higher learning was championed by her grandfather, Judge Miles O'Reilly.

studies, she was asked to serve as a correspondent for *The Cosmopolitan* and for the *Atlantic Monthly*, to report on the emerging political situation in Japan.[4] En route to Japan through the Canadian west from Ontario, she also wrote a series of articles on the west for the *Toronto Globe*.[5] During this journey she met and secretly married her first husband, Frederick Charles Flesher, and before she reached British Columbia she was pregnant with her first child.[6]

After Helen's return from Japan, and the reconciliation with family who had objected to her hasty marriage, the young couple moved to the Santa Clara Valley in California, where, between 1891 and 1900, they first tried their luck at farming and then Frederick trained as a physician.[7] At the same time, Helen made her first forays in feminism alongside her mother, Emma Gregory (who had moved in with Helen and Frederick after their son Eric's difficult birth and then stayed to assist with childcare). With funds inherited from Emma's father, Helen and Emma purchased two small periodicals: *Society* and *The Searchlight*,[8] and they used these publications as a forum to support the right of women to education and the vote.

In 1900, with a promise of lucrative employment in medicine for Frederick in Minnesota, the family relocated. Unfortunately, the position which had been offered never materialized. Frederick secured a new medical position in Faribault, Minnesota, and rapidly excelled. However, he soon died as a result of a violent incident with a patient,[9] and Helen suddenly found herself in need of a means to support her family. Using her knowledge of journalism she made a successful bid for employment with the *Saint Paul Globe* in St. Paul, Minnesota. Later, she become the paper's exchange editor and supplemented the income from this job with freelance work.[10]

Helen remarried in 1902 and moved to Vancouver with her new husband, James Henry MacGill (1869–1939); James had been a friend of Helen's during their undergraduate years, and they had studied together at Trinity College in Toronto.[11] Helen and James had travelled different paths after graduation in 1889, but their journeys had also had some similarities. Although James had begun his working life as a journalist, other jobs followed, and ultimately he decided to seek further education. First he took up legal studies and was successfully called to the bar. Two years later, he returned to Trinity College where, in 1897, he was ordained as a deacon of the Church of England.[12] When Elsie later assessed her father's career path she noted, "Of the three callings the Press was most nearly his vocation, the Law became his livelihood, [and] the Church continued his abiding spiritual quest."[13]

Helen Gregory MacGill was a powerful example for her two daughters. After relocating to Vancouver, Helen and her mother quickly established links with local women's rights groups, demanding much more ambitious social change than their counterparts in other parts of Canada, the continent, and, to some extent, internationally.[14] Helen identified this period between 1905 and 1910 as the height of the first wave of the women's movement in Vancouver.[15]

Among the achievements of this group was the establishment in 1909

Captain James Henry MacGill was a member of the 6th Regiment of The Duke of Connaught's Own Rifles. After his death Elsie worked to ensure that his mementos from this service were maintained for the historical record.

of the Crèche, a daycare for working mothers.[16] During this period, and having charge of four young children herself, it is not surprising that Helen sought out such reforms. She also recognized the importance of having a space where women could meet and discuss their ideas. Her advocacy led to the creation of the Vancouver Women's Building in 1911, and Helen was chosen as its president.[17]

This public engagement may also have helped Helen deal with her mother's sudden death from cancer in 1907.[18] Emma's death brought new challenges to the household, which had come to depend on the assistance that she had provided. To ease the transition and help with the needs of the family, Emma's cousin Sara

Ann Kerby arrived to live with the family, and remained until her death in 1937. Sara had previously served as a missionary with the Six Nations[19] and her strength was a much needed infusion for the family. She also became another role model for the children.

Helen Jr. and Elsie grew up in a strong feminist context that was not isolated to British Columbia. In 1916 women in the provinces of Manitoba, Alberta, and Saskatchewan celebrated the winning of the right to vote. Elsie's mother and her colleagues rejoiced in their own success in 1917.[20] A wide variety of tactics were used to call for women's access to the vote, including the theatre production of *The Women's Parliament*. This play, usually associated with Nellie McClung and her compatriots in Winnipeg in 1914,

Elsie and Helen Jr. were fortunate to be raised within a supportive family with access to their extended family, including their paternal grandmother Elizabeth Ann MacGill (seated) pictured here with their mother Helen Gregory MacGill.

was presented earlier in Vancouver, hosted by University Women's Club to which Helen belonged.[21] Helen Sr. was not the only MacGill woman to take part in this production. The two young page boys were played by Helen Jr. and Elsie MacGill. As the girls participated in their mother's work, they received on-the-job training in women's advocacy.[22]

In 1909, Helen Gregory MacGill began studying law.[23] Her studies were independent and ad hoc, but she became known and respected by her professionally trained male peers for her command of the laws concerning women and children. Some even sought her advice to better understand this branch of law.[24]

Helen's study of law enabled her to serve as a conduit of knowledge for the women's organizations she was a part of. In 1912, Helen wrote *Daughters, Wives and Mothers in British Columbia – Some Laws Affecting Them*. This was the first of several straightforward guides that spelled out options for women seeking justice within the legal system.[25] Helen's legal training did more than enable her to provide informed assistance to her feminist colleagues, it also served to prepare her to be British Columbia's first woman judge. In 1917, she was appointed to the juvenile court of Vancouver, where she championed the rights of the delinquent child. Helen's position was not created by the government of British Columbia; rather, it was achieved due to the success of the pressure exerted by women activists within the province.[26]

> She turned the Juvenile Court from a petty police court modelled on police court lines to punish bad boys and girls into a centre where all the forces of the community – church, school, industry, social service – were channelled and coordinated to help the child as an individual toward a better life. It was a revolutionary change. For the first time in any court in Canada psychological and psychiatric examinations, along with medical examinations, were included in the Court's routine. Where treatment was needed it was given promptly, regardless of the question – which municipality shall pay for it. The institutions for children were reformed and overhauled. Teachers were installed in the Detention Home (the juvenile lock-up) so that the education of the children there could continue; training programmes were

instituted in the Industrial Schools. Her greatest reform and most used tool, however, was supervised probation (returning the child to its normal life but safeguarded there by help and protection of a trained Probation Officer), rather than committal to a reformatory.[27]

Later in their lives Elsie and Helen Jr. each adopted their own brand of feminist activism, thereby becoming third-generation feminists. Reflecting on this legacy, Elsie stated, "Our direction in life is determined by something within us, our real purpose, our 'golden thread.'" Elsie identified her own golden thread as empathy toward and awareness of the oppressed in society, as well as her desire to affect social change on their behalf.[28] Helen Jr. also recognized the importance of her unique upbringing: "Local society was strongly homogeneous, but my mother's interests brought diversity right into the living room."[29] For instance, on one occasion a meeting in the MacGill's parlour featured British suffragette Mrs. Pethick-Lawrence, who "stood on a window seat in order to be seen and heard, and told about being forcibly fed with other suffragettes in prison in London."[30] Recalling the power of her mother's example in pursuing social reform, even while admitting that her actions at times were hard to cope with, Helen Jr. explained, "We were by turns embarrassed and proud of our unusual mother – on into the late teens, when it was all pride."[31]

• • • • • • • • •

It's not certain that Helen Jr. and Elsie were aware at an early age of the full importance of their mother's activism and her groundbreaking educational achievements; however, they did benefit in many ways from their parents' respect for education. Before the girls were old enough to attend regular school, their mother jump-started their education by hiring a governess to instruct them, along with a few of the neighbouring children. Together, they were taught subjects such as French and watercolour painting by a governess.[32]

Despite agreement on the importance of their daughters' education, their parents did not always see eye-to-eye regarding their children's educational path. Initially, James MacGill suggested boarding school for the girls. Helen refused to even consider this suggestion. As Elsie later explained, "My mother had been privately educated. A girls' private school was close at hand. But she learned that its graduates rarely went on to the university, and that fact decided our parents in favor of public school."[33]

By enrolling their children at Lord Roberts Public School, Helen could keep her daughters physically close to her and also influence the course of their education.[34]

Elsie and Helen Jr. loved dressing up together. Helen Jr.'s outfit testifies to the strong Asian influence of Vancouver, which was accepted by the MacGill family both publicly, through Helen Gregory MacGill and James MacGill's public work, and that of their beliefs, which they shared with their children.

The school gave the girls the fundamentals, such as reading and writing. But Helen Jr. and Elsie's learning was not limited to the school curriculum. Two women broadened the sisters' horizons: Ada Marshall and Emily Carr – the later famous artist. These women offered the girls piano and drawing lessons, respectively. Both girls also participated in Sunday school and the junior auxiliary at St. Paul's Anglican Church.[35] Education in the larger social issues also occurred at home.[36] In addition to the feminist activities in which the girls participated and witnessed, James raised social issues at home that came up in his legal practice, including the Chinese Immigration Act, which banned most new Chinese immigration to Canada. Such activities made a strong impression on Elsie and Helen Jr., who recalled that many women sought her mother's aid when they found themselves in troubling situations: "In consequence, Elsie and I had direct opportunities to learn some of the harsh facts of life at an early age."[37]

In 1911, Elsie and Helen Jr. accompanied their parents on a business trip to Europe for six months, and this was an eye-opening educational experience for them. On that trip, Helen Sr. also had a chance to enhance her connections with key feminists, such as Lady Aberdeen.[38]

Elsie was an eager high school
student with a thirst for knowledge.
Her steady gaze here would become
a trademark as she looked out boldly
and with keen observation into the
world around her.

Due to their parents' connections, the sisters also interacted to a degree with the local Asian population; however, Helen Jr. identified most of her family's relations as white, Anglo-Saxon, and Protestant.[39] Ultimately, their interactions were bound by class. According to Helen Brock, Elsie's niece, Helen Gregory MacGill considered herself superior to those around her and did not recognize faults in her children, especially her sons. From her perspective Elsie and Helen Jr. had this tendency as well, but it decreased over time.[40] Their parents also gently encouraged their daughters toward suitable friendships, which both girls accepted.[41]

Elsie's recollection that the First World War had a minimal effect on her life and that of her family indicates that at times Helen and James were protective and carefully shielded their children from real-

Helen Gregory MacGill cherished her time at the cottage. She spent many hours there with her old typewriter clacking away, as it tried to keep up with the pace of her ideas on women's rights and advancement in society.

world horrors.[42] The MacGills were geographically removed from the war. Elsie's recollection however denotes not only the degree to which Helen and James filtered the world for their daughters, but also the selectiveness of childhood memories.

The MacGills also encouraged fun. Helen Jr. recalled, "We grew up in Vancouver's West End, a magical place for children, bounded by bathing beaches and a huge natural park. Living near the water, we kept a canoe in the basement and my mother often took Elsie and me swimming before school."[43] Helen also organized summer retreats in the British Columbia interior. These occasions provided opportunities for horseback riding and other outdoor excursions.[44]

In 1920, opportunities for outdoor adventures increased when Helen purchased a retreat at Greyrocks for the family. This rustic cottage offered all who visited an escape from the demands of the city and a place to relish the bounty of nature. Elsie remembered the sanctuary and its rich environment she shared with her siblings fondly. Visitors, including many of Helen Jr. and Elsie's friends, were introduced to a place that was a fantastic backdrop for fun and celebration. To the women of the family, Greyrocks increasingly became a treasured female enclave, particularly as James MacGill was not partial to leaving urban comforts.[45]

· · · · · · · · ·

Having been raised to respect and value scholarship, Elsie and her sister were strongly encouraged to pursue higher education. Their mother's example showed that a woman could successfully pursue multiple paths during her lifetime. Elsie later wrote that her mother had demonstrated that "a woman too has a purpose and task in life beyond child-bearing and home-making; a contract to keep with life that demands her development as an individual."[46]

With their parents' support, Helen Jr. and Elsie began studies at the University of British Columbia (UBC) in 1921.[47] As with their daughters' previous studies, the MacGills were not passive observers. Rather, in addition to encouraging their further education, they both joined UBC's Convocation. Helen Jr. recalled,

> When the institution was established, a supporting public was created for it by the provision that anyone who had resided two months in British Columbia and had a degree from a British university might become a member of Convocation. The members of Convocation – my parents both belonged – voted on many matters of policy and served as an alumni association when the university was too young to have alumni. They had the effect of making broad public issues of the problems of education.[48]

The sisters took the same subjects in their first year and excelled, but their subsequent choice of disciplines in their second year could not have been more different. Helen Jr. chose to pursue a general arts degree. Elsie was drawn toward applied science.[49] She later recalled the initial spark that led her to a path in engineering: It all began with an unexpected interaction with the wonders of electricity through her early friendship with a boy who had a crystal radio set. The possibilities of this technology opened a new and intriguing avenue to her fertile mind.[50] She later elaborated, "I was always a sort of Miss Fix-it around the house…I was interested in radio work and so I started off planning to be a radio engineer."[51] The potential that this new form of communication offered the world seized Elsie's imagination and quickly eclipsed her other interests.[52]

Elsie applied to the Faculty of Applied Science; a founding faculty of UBC, which issued its first degrees in 1921.[53] She was the second woman to enter the program[54] and managed to accelerate her course of study through extensive independent work. Her grades were not extremely high, but by the end of her second year she had qualified to continue in either applied science or general arts at the third-year level.[55]

Elsie's choice of program was unusual, but it was supported by her parents. This fact is revealing, as neither Helen nor James had a scientific background. As scholars of women in higher education have noted, the backing provided by family for women undertaking scientific pursuits at this time was essential to their progress; thus, the unconditional support of Elsie's parents was an invaluable contributor to her success.[56]

Elsie did not continue her education at UBC, however. On the insistence of their father, the sisters left the west coast to continue their studies at the University of Toronto. This decision was prompted by traditions on both sides of the family.[57]

Travelling halfway across Canada was an adventure for the sisters, and the 1920s were an exciting time for young women to be setting out on their own. However, the changes were not easy. Neither Helen Jr. nor Elsie initially liked Toronto or their housing at St. Hilda's, the women's residence associated with Trinity College.[58] After her first term, Helen Jr. decided to return to Vancouver and finish her studies at UBC.[59] However, Elsie rose to the challenges of the new university, city, and province, "gleefully registered in engineering,"[60] according to her sister.

Footnotes for this chapter can be found online at:
http://secondstorypress.ca/resources and at http://feministhistories.ca/books

Chapter 2
PROFESSIONAL SCAFFOLDING

Astonished were the faces of the men of 2T7 when, as freshmen,
they realized that the sanctum of the First Year Drafting Room
had been invaded by a bold, ambitious co-ed. The architectural
"studios" had been used to the presence of ladies, and Miss Betty
Lalor found a ready welcome there. But a lady in that den of
iniquity, the first year drafting room?[1]

—Transactions and Yearbook of the
University of Toronto Engineering Society

In the fall of 1923, Elsie entered electrical engineering at the University of Toronto's School of Practical Science (SPS). The prospects looked bright for the program. Indeed, C.H. Mitchell would later note the boundless potential for the emerging fields of radio and electricity.[2] Elsie's enthusiasm was slightly tempered when she learned that her previous studies at the University of British Columbia would not be credited toward her new program, and she would have to enter as a freshman student.[3]

What was remarkable, however, was not Elsie's choice of program, but the fact that she was allowed, in 1923, to pursue that choice. The University of Toronto was ahead of its main regional competitors in accepting women into the applied sciences. In comparison, McGill University and Queen's University openly rejected and dismissed women's applications for engineering studies. McGill's program did not accept women until 1942, and Queen's denied access until 1948.[4] Given her own relative ease of access to the program, Elsie did not initially understand the difficulties other young women confronted in pursuing a similar path.

Elsie was the first woman to be accepted into electrical engineering, but she was not the first woman to study in the SPS. Earlier in the twentieth century a few women, including the first female student, Hildegarde Scott, were admitted into other disciplines such as chemistry. However, even after the First World War women's attendance at the SPS was barely noticeable, remaining locked below one percent. This did not change with Elsie's admittance; two years after Elsie's graduation from the University of Toronto, only four women were enrolled, compared to 693 of their male peers. This situation at the SPS improved only slightly in the 1930s and early 1940s, despite the fact that the overall number of women pursuing university degrees steadily increased.[5] Women were more successful in other professional schools such as medicine, dentistry, and architecture.[6] Like her mother before her, Elsie was breaking new ground on an educational path unfamiliar to women.

Entering as a freshman was frustrating for Elsie, but her previous studies were not in vain. In fact, they probably made a difference in her later success because the SPS curriculum underwent changes that greatly increased the demand on those in the program in the 1922–23 academic year. Courses that had previously been slated for second year were moved to first year, and the common first year was removed. The upper years were characterized by increased specialization. Remaining gaps were filled by new courses of a non-technical nature, including accounting, economics, and commercial law.[7]

Elsie's courses kept her busy with approximately fifteen hours of lectures and roughly twenty hours of practical lab work each week. These requirements did not include the additional hours required to study for tests and exams and prepare course assignments. The courses were arduous and Elsie struggled with some of the material.[8]

Elsie's classmates in engineering participated in various initiation antics. Here they are attempting to raid University College, ca. 1923. Actions like these may explain why Elsie opted not to participate in some of the extra curricular activities.

These were not the only obstacles she faced. In addition to adapting to a male-dominated program, she had to deal with the taxing expectations of a completely different world: St. Hilda's College. Finding lodging on campus was fortunate, and this was likely made possible by the connections Elsie's parents had to Trinity College.[9] However, the expectations placed on residents at St Hilda's were high and included both religious observance and assistance with the college administration. When her mother heard about the situation, she complained in writing to Dr. Seager, the reverend provost at Trinity University College, which oversaw St. Hilda's:

Trinity College Women's Residence on St. George Street in Toronto. Elsie stayed here during her engineering studies.

> I am extremely disappointed with the way things have turned out in connection with Helen and Elsie going to St Hilda's. Helen is home and happy but Elsie is still there and alone. Imagine then my indignation to find that she who has so heavy a course and is at the University until five o'clock is rated as a Freshman and must waste time doing fag duty and answering telephone calls.[10]

Helen elaborated on her concern about the nature of this practice by noting that it was detrimental to Elsie's ability to find a work-life balance:

> To return to the telephone I resent Elsie's time being wasted on such foolishness. She finds it hard enough to get in her studies and any exercise. Fancy then my anger to discover that certain Saturday afternoons when I am particularly anxious she should have a little relaxation and meet some of my friends she must stay to answer calls and shout them upstairs. The system seems to be inexcusably cheap and common.[11]

What Elsie thought about her mother's letter, or if she even knew of it at the time, is unknown.[12] It is also unclear whether there were further direct interventions by her parents in university-related situations; however, both parents did visit Elsie when time permitted.[13]

In addition to the pressures of the curriculum, the SPS brought other challenges. The school had a reputation for its annual fall student initiation, but the student yearbook reported that "our two freshettes [Elsie and Betty Lalor, who was enrolled in the architectural program] were not with us." No reason is given for their absence, but it is highly possible that given the "hospitality" that the sophomore students regularly arranged for the freshmen class, including "everything from tar to soft soap, not forgetting the 'staves'" provided little motivation for them to attend.[14] Moreover, Trinity College required all students to sign a declaration that they would not partake in such activities. It was understood that disregard of this promise would result in expulsion from Trinity College.[15]

Elsie is not mentioned again in the yearbook until her graduation in 1927, which suggests that she did not engage in many extracurricular activities with her fellow engineering students. This may have been due to the nature of the activities, or simply due to her rigorous course load.

• • • • • • • • •

Elsie blazed a new path in a male-dominated discipline and, in doing so, challenged the accepted gender norms just by studying

FACULTY
OF
APPLIED SCIENCE
AND
ENGINEERING
UNIVERSITY OF TORONTO

Elsie was the first woman to graduate from electrical engineering at the University of Toronto. The only other woman in her class was architectural student Betty Lalor. Betty is second from left, 4th row from top. Elsie is in the same row, sixth from left.

engineering. The context of the 1920s and the increasing presence of the Modern Woman created some room for exceptional women in aviation, including women aviators and barnstormers; however, entrenched social and gender norms were not easy to overcome.[16] Even among peers about her own age, Elsie's presence in engineering would have seemed unusual.

"Insomnia," a play produced by some of the engineers at Hart House – then a male bastion within the University of Toronto – demonstrated the attitudes of the time with respect to male and female students. As a spoof, the play anticipated university studies thirty years in the future. It portrayed the creation of two new faculties, the Faculty of Rugby for men, and the Faculty of Gold Diggers for women. The latter was portrayed as a place where "girls are no longer bored with the study of moderns, but devote their entire time to the study of cosmetics, attitudes, and others ways of attracting the male."[17]

While Elsie left few reflections about her undergraduate life, other commentaries, however, allow a partial reconstruction of her experience. Elsie was Professor John Hamilton Parkin's first female student, and her presence introduced unforeseen and embarrassing problems.[18] Prior to her arrival, engineering terminology raised few issues for Parkin, but he quickly learned that the context had significantly shifted:

> Now the terminology of engineering abounds in words used in connotations full of surprises for a professor accustomed to lecturing to males only when the class includes a female. Such terms as male and female fittings, flat bastard file, or bastard thread are examples of a less embarrassing kind. The wily male students had evidently foreseen the possibilities raised by the presence of their female classmate which, unfortunately, the professor had not. With the freedom to which he was accustomed he, in effect, called a spade a spade; from the back of the room came a raucous "Har! Har!" and the class doubled up with mirth. What the reaction of Miss McGill was the professor has no idea. He [Parkin] was covered in confusion and blushes. From that point on his lectures were censored, and any word of double entendre was replaced.[19]

Parkin's editorial work on his lectures saved him further embarrassment, and to his credit, made the classroom environment more hospitable for Elsie, and possibly even for some of her male peers.

Parkin was not the only faculty member to run into trouble because of Elsie's presence. One of his colleagues, G. Ross Workman, affectionately referred to as "Workey" by the students, also needed to modify his teaching style. As Elsie's peers recalled, the novelty of a mixed class altered his role as the Civil Section 10 demonstrator:

> Astonished were the faces of the men of 2T7 when, as freshmen, they realized that the sanctum of the First Year Drafting Room had been invaded by a bold, ambitious co-ed. The architectural "studios" had been used to the presence of ladies, and Miss Betty Lalor found a ready welcome there. But a lady in that den of iniquity, the first year drafting room? Where was Workey going to tell his stories? What new, polite exclamation of disgust were the poor freshmen to invent, for use when the ink spilled over their paper, in order not to shock the ears of so tender and unspoilt a creature? Would our "Elsie" outlive the freshman year and finally blossom forth as the only female electrical engineer of S.P.S.?[20]

Although this recollection refers to Elsie affectionately, it provides insight into how differently Elsie was perceived by her fellow male students. She was described as "bold" and "ambitious" (as well as an "unspoilt creature" and a "lady") who "invaded" the male "sanctum." The text suggests that Elsie's hard work and determination were recognized by her peers, while at the same time her presence created uncertainly and confusion within the engineering program.

Parkin further attested to the fact that Elsie gained a following with her peers: "A few of the students became quite stooped from carrying Miss MacGill's books and other impediments from lecture to lecture."[21] Whether this attention was romantic interest in their new female colleague or simply gentlemanly behaviour as it was understood at the time is unclear.[22] Elsie's only comment that might suggest a flirtation during this period of her life was made much later, in a 1978 speech accepting an honorary doctorate at the University of Windsor: "Another matter that has changed drastically is kissing. When I was a goggle eyed undergraduate, if you kissed at all, you did it privately. I was shy, as I have mentioned, so I didn't – much."[23]

Elsie was not wholly at the mercy of her environment. Her response to inappropriate behaviour or comments during one of her classes demonstrates that she knew when to stand-up for herself: "So well did she uphold her dignity that one day, in a lecture, the boys were rudely awakened from their slumber by the unmistakable sound of two feminine hands coming into very sudden contact with two masculine cheeks."[24]

Like her mother before her, Elsie was successful in her unconventional studies and graduated in her chosen field as the first woman in electrical engineering at the University of Toronto in 1927.[25] A detailed examination of her academic transcript reveals that she managed to maintain a four-year average of 70 percent, which met the requirement for graduation. While this average may seem mediocre by today's standards, Elsie had worked hard to achieve this result, even rewriting exams in her second and fourth years to enhance previous failing grades in four courses.[26]

Her grades also reflect that in her engineering-specific courses she was usually better at hands-on lab activities than with the theoretical content of lecture material. She struggled with courses such as calculus, analytic geometry, and technical English, but she excelled in descriptive geometry, statistics, and the lab sections for chemistry and thermodynamics. Elsie scored top marks in her common law and industrial management courses, which would figure significantly in her future endeavours. Considering the legal background of her parents, Elsie's success in legal studies is not surprising, and it later served her well.

Elsie also proved able to work effectively and independently. Her required summer assignment, submitted at the start of her second year and composed of construction drawings, obtained a grade in the mid-80s.[27] Like the other engineering students, she was required to complete 1600 hours of shop work to obtain practical mechanical experience prior to graduation. She met this course expectation by January of her third year.[28] In her fourth year she also undertook and successfully submitted an undergraduate thesis. As Elsie progressed through her studies she began to envision a future for herself in electrical design. This development was likely influenced by her mandatory work experience coupled with increased specialization in the field.[29]

Elsie's determination helped her to cope with the demands of her program and the challenges of her experience at St. Hilda's. This feat was acknowledged in the SPS yearbook:

> Events have shown that our worries were futile. Miss E. M. G. MacGill of Vancouver managed to look after herself in so masterful a fashion that, by the time this is published, she will be as good an engineeress as has ever worn overalls – if not better. With clever hand she steered her ship around the cliffs of annual examinations.[30]

Elsie's recognition by her peers is important and further demonstrates her success in the program. However, in calling her an "engineeress," the yearbook entry emphasizes her difference. While this new title seems benign within its setting, it was later applied in a more derogatory fashion in the United States in the context of the Second World War.[31]

Elsie's university experience was mainly positive, and she maintained a lifelong connection with her graduating class, known as "2T7." It is unlikely that she would have maintained such an attachment if her overall experience had been negative. It is possible that like many trail-blazing women engineers she simply considered herself "one of the boys" and took little notice of jibes and jokes at her expense.[32]

However, Elsie was not oblivious to the narrow-minded divisions between men and women in the university at large. Indeed, in a 1926 letter to the editor of *The Varsity*, "A Plea for Broad Mindedness", she argued that divisions based on gender are counter-productive and should be avoided:

> Must the University of Toronto retain the high school tactics by dividing the sheep from the goats in all University affairs, save those of recreation? Cannot there be more co-operation between the men and women in the University? Instead of the spirit of competition,…cannot we unite as students for the good of the University as a whole? When a man or woman enters the University, would it not be better for the University (the primary

interest) if he or she merged his or her personality as a man or woman, with that of the student, looking at university affairs from the standpoint of the student, seeking first the good of the University?

Because Elsie grew up in a household that strongly supported gender equality and excelled in a male-dominated professional school, it is not surprising she found divisions between the sexes limiting and childish.[33]

· · · · · · · · ·

Elsie's graduation in 1927 was duly recorded in the pages of the *Transactions and Year Book of the University of Toronto Engineering Society* and the *Toronto Star*, and her class photo in *Torontonesis* featured the following caption: "A smile for all, a welcome glad; a jovial, coaxing way she had."[34] Her inclusion in these publications stands out. Many of Elsie's female contemporaries in the United States were denied recognition by their male engineering colleagues. Some, such as Nora Blatch at Cornell, were deliberately overlooked and even struck from the visual record of the class photo.[35] Elsie's classmates were not the only ones who took note of her achievements. Her professors were also moved by her dedication and watched her career with interest.

Though Elsie's groundbreaking achievement was considered newsworthy, it did not guarantee her employment after graduation. This was not due simply to her gender. There were very few opportunities available for engineering graduates in Canada during this period.[36] Elsie decided to seek her fortune in the United States, and in September 1927, she found work as a junior engineer doing stress analysis at the Van Austin Company in Pontiac, Michigan.

> When I graduated I was quite clueless about what I would do. I expected to become competent in time. I think many of my fellow graduates were the same. The fact is that many of them did what I did, take a job in engineering but not in the field in which they had specialized. I had specialized in electrical engineering – (my first) job was mechanical. I think I took the first job that I heard of and applied for.[37]

Ashley & Crippen
Toronto

To Mother and Father
with much love.
Elsie Gregory MacGill
1927

Elsie graduated in 1927 from the University
of Toronto. In so doing she continued the
family tradition of attending the evolving
post-secondary institution. At 22 years of
age, she was poised to take on the world.

Not long after she started her new job, the Van Austin plant retooled to handle aeronautics, and Elsie needed to adapt her skills to rise to this challenge.[38] She was aided in this undertaking by the strong links between electrical and aeronautical engineering. Both areas depend largely on an engineer's skill in the drafting room and in problem-solving. Her training also positioned her to work on aviation instruments, as her knowledge of electrical design facilitated the precise measurements needed for flight control and aircraft integrity. Elsie's practical experience with the company was transferable because accurate stress analysis was crucial in determining whether or not an aircraft could handle the pressures encountered throughout a flight.[39] Later, Elsie affirmed the importance of keeping up with the rapid pace of change in the field of aeronautics:

> The aircraft industry and the space industry are the sources of pithy sayings such as – "if it works, it's obsolete" or "when you're through changing, you're through" – most of them joking wryly about the rapidity of change in those industries. They bring home to us the fact that scientific knowledge is now doubling itself every eight or twelve years, and that tomorrow's technical world depends upon today's products of the mind, rather than upon its products of industry and commerce.[40]

As newer sub-disciplines, electrical and aeronautical engineering may have provided a more welcoming environment for a woman engineer than the more established fields, such as civil engineering.[41] Elsie was aware, however, that she required more than a receptive mind and the willingness to shift course. She seized the opportunity to enhance her training in this new field by enrolling in advanced studies at the nearby University of Michigan.[42] This decision links her with other women professionals of the period who believed that by becoming "super-performers" they would ensure their future success.[43]

The United States had surged ahead of Canada in aeronautical engineering and also in accepting women into engineering programs. The previous fifty years had seen the establishment of a large number of land-grant agricultural and industrial colleges due to the supportive legislation of the *Land Grant Morril Act* of 1862. As historian Ruth Oldenziel notes, these institutions were also more open to women and the working class than were the "privately owned and sex-segregated universities."[44] And in the late 1920s the Guggenheim Fund provided money that supported the expansion of aeronautical engineering programs, including those at the Michigan Institute of Technology and the University of Michigan, the latter of which first started offering courses in aeronautics in 1914.[45]

Initially, Elsie started her aeronautical studies part-time; however, she was able to secure a scholarship that made full-time study possible. Her new program included theoretical courses in analytical mechanics and parameter variation in aeronautical design, as well as the application of various theories to flow problems in aerodynamics.[46]

Elsie learned how to apply her knowledge of design to the overall construction of an aircraft. She also learned how to work backwards from the complete model of an aircraft to the structure of each supporting system, which prepared her to design individual parts or, as the future would reveal, whole aircraft. Elsie applied herself to her studies, but she also made time to take photographs and participate in student groups.[47]

· · · · · · · · ·

Just before graduating from the University of Michigan, Elsie was struck down with what at first appeared to be symptoms of the flu. She experienced these symptoms for a week, and then suddenly she lost feeling in her legs. She was admitted to hospital on May 9, 1929,[48] and was subsequently diagnosed with polio.[49] Unfortunately, at the time there was much confusion about the disease, and it was not easily recognized; in fact, it was often confused with the flu. Frequently, the true diagnosis did not occur until, as in Elsie's case and that of Franklin Roosevelt, paralysis had already occurred.[50]

Given Elsie's condition, her doctors were not overly optimistic. When they cautioned she might never be able to walk again, she became very depressed.[51] There were, however, some early signs of hope. Before she left Michigan, her doctor observed a degree of recovery in her ability to use her right leg.[52] This physical sign, coupled with Elsie's determination, gave her the resources to rebound.

Just before the end of Elsie's graduate studies at the University of Michigan, she was struck by polio. She did not live this tragedy alone; her family stood by her. Helen Jr. helped care for her and get her home to Vancouver. The special relationship of the sisters radiates from this photo.

Elsie never fully accepted that she had been felled by polio. In 1933, she referred to her illness as "something akin to infantile paralysis."[53] Refusing to admit the reality may have provided her with some hope and peace of mind. Elsie was not very knowledgeable about her own medical condition, and she avoided seeking more information even when she started having other health problems later in life. Her future step-daughter later attributed Elsie's point of view to a mixture of pride and obstinacy, and an unwillingness to acknowledge weakness.[54]

Despite this serious setback, Elsie left Michigan knowing she had successfully completed her degree, which was conferred on her in hospital.[55] In the care of her sister and brother-in-law Everett Hughes, Elsie relocated to Vancouver, to continue recovering.[56] Elsie's family had always provided her with unconditional support, and it continued during this challenging period of her life.[57] Elsie did rest, but she also worked diligently through pain on her physiotherapy regime.[58] Elsie's focus impressed those around her. One long-term acquaintance said that Elsie "amazed us with her spirit. She said, 'It is not if I get along without the wheelchair but when.'"[59] Her will power paid off, and in time she was able to walk again with the support of one or two canes.[60]

This determination helped restore her to health and helped her cope with her mother's health crisis. In October 1930, Helen was admitted to hospital and diagnosed with cancer. During her illness and treatment Helen could not help very much in Elsie's recovery.

However, the family rallied around to care for and support one another.[61]

Elsie's rich and supportive background impressed upon her the importance of education and also cultivated her interest in social issues such as equality. Her family environment was crucial in helping her overcome both academic and personal challenges and laid an important foundation for the trials she later encountered.

Footnotes for this chapter can be found online at:
http://secondstorypress.ca/resources and at http://feministhistories.ca/books

Chapter 3
AN AERONAUTICAL ENGINEERING
FLIGHT PLAN

A current saying in the aviation world is that "you don't have to be crazy to be in the aircraft business, but it helps." Obviously it does help, but it is a specific craziness that is meant, a craziness that accomplishes prodigious things, a craziness that will win the war.[1]

—Elsie Gregory MacGill

While still convalescing from polio, Elsie did her best to maintain her skills and knowledge through study on her own, some design work, and writing.[2] Advances in aeronautical engineering continued in the 1930s, but the pace had slowed because of the 1929 stock market crash. Her confidence and optimism was evident in a 1931 article she wrote for the Canadian women's magazine *Chatelaine*, in which she discussed women's suitability for flight in comparison to men. From Elsie's perspective, the developments in aviation technology benefited women because airplanes were becoming easier to pilot. And though she acknowledged the challenges women would face in demonstrating they were capable pilots, Elsie believed that women's potential within aviation was boundless.[3] The popularity of women aviators during this period, combined with her own positive experiences, gave her good reason to hold this belief.[4]

Despite her effort to keep up with advances in aeronautical knowledge, Elsie knew that without continual practical application of her skills and engagement with her peers, her professional development would stagnate. Consequently, at the end of her three-year recovery she sought additional post-graduate studies. Once again her family stood firmly behind her decision, and her parents provided financial support.[5]

Elsie began a doctoral program at the Massachusetts Institute of Technology (MIT) in Boston, Massachusetts. The choice was logical as the university's reputation was built on its expertise in engineering

While it must have been a struggle to go back to school after her illness, Elsie continued to have remarkable family support. Enjoying the sun with her on June 24, 1933 are her sister (holding the umbrella) and her aunt, Jennie Williams.

and technology. MIT's graduate aeronautical engineering program had been established in 1913.[6] By the time Elsie arrived in 1932, the program provided excellent training in the latest aeronautical trends and aircraft design.[7]

Still, Elsie was one of the rare women within the engineering hallways of MIT.[8] However, as with her previous studies, this did not seem to impede her progress. While she continued to cope with the lingering effects of polio, her niece recalls that Elsie benefited from the unexpected support of the wife of MIT's president. During a visit over tea, Elsie described the challenge of climbing the steep steps to the main university building, and shortly thereafter a hand-rail was installed.[9]

Elsie's decision to return to school became a springboard for re-entry into the workforce. Unlike her sister, who completed a doctoral degree in sociology in 1936, Elsie was lured away from academia before completing her doctoral studies.[10] When an employment opportunity beckoned in Canada with Fairchild Aircraft Limited in 1934, she seized it.[11]

This choice may seem surprising, given that she had blazed a new professional trail for women by obtaining two engineering degrees and had come from a family with a history of women breaking barriers and pursuing extensive postsecondary education. However, the professional nature of Elsie's studies meant that employment outside of academia was usually the end goal. Elsie reflected on this decision in an article she wrote in 1946:

> Engineering in industry holds out the greatest promise for any engineer. Industry in the main is progressive; energy and initiative are rewarded in terms of salary and advancement, and advancement may be very rapid. Convention and public opinion exert little pressure. Management is more concerned with problems of work and costs than the social question of sex of the engineer.[12]

Elsie's employment at Fairchild Aircraft Limited offered many advantages. She was able to become self-supporting and later to contribute to her family's finances.[13] In addition to a regular salary, the job allowed her to apply her previous knowledge and new training to the rapidly advancing field of aeronautics. Moreover, the location of the company in Longueil, Québec, allowed Elsie to move closer to her beloved sister, who had moved to Montréal, Québec on account of her husband's position at McGill University.[14]

Elsie's employment in aeronautical engineering during the 1930s was unusual not only because she was a women, but also because she had paid work. Canada was just beginning to recover from the Great Depression,[15] and women were often discriminated against when competing with men for jobs. However, Elsie had a major advantage – the pool of trained aeronautical engineers was very small.[16]

Still, employment was not guaranteed. Isabel Ebel, for example, who graduated from MIT in 1932 with a degree in aeronautical engineering, did not fare as well as Elsie. Unable to find work, Isabel pursued graduate education at the Guggenheim School of Aeronautics, and was admitted to that program only because Amelia Earhart intervened on her behalf. Isabel graduated in 1934, but work remained elusive until 1939, when she found a position with Grumman Aircraft Corporation.[17] Elsie did have the advantage of more practical training and experience, and her publications during her convalescence may have raised her profile in the aeronautics community. It is also possible that she was simply in the right place at the right time.

Elsie was hired as an assistant to British chief aeronautical engineer Percival Francis Hyde Beadle.[18] During the Great Depression, Fairchild Aircraft Limited was the sole company in the fledgling Canadian aircraft industry working on new aircraft design and testing. Elsie's employment thus offered her an important advantage over colleagues in other Canadian companies.[19]

In her day-to-day work at Fairchild Aircraft, Elsie contributed to design specifications and stress testing. Among the aircraft she worked on were the Sekani and the Super 71P, a float plane.[20] One way aircraft under development were assessed was by testing them in wind tunnels at the National Research Council (NRC) in Ottawa.[21]

At the NRC, Elsie established important and enduring professional ties with other aeronautical engineers.[22] One of these was with J.H. Parkin, Elsie's former professor at the University of Toronto. He had begun working at the NRC in 1929, and had not forgotten his former student – including embarrassing instances when she was in his class – but now he oversaw the tests she conducted as a professional engineer.[23]

The required wind tunnel tests were often time consuming. J.J. Green,[24] employed at NRC at the time, recalled that the tests for the Fairchild Super 71 were especially demanding: "The tests on the Super 71 model were somewhat lengthy, because we tested the wing alone, the fuselage alone and the two in combination, with various arrangements of the pilot's cabin and wind screen."[25] He also recalled the tedious nature of the work:

> One of my precious photographs from that era is a faded shot of Elsie and me plowing through the calculations for one of her aircraft models, using a 20 inch slide-rule. Electronic calculators were unknown then and we didn't even have a good mechanical one in the aerodynamic laboratory of the NRC in those days.[26]

Tests with these rudimentary tools were laborious. As Professor Walter Vincenti explained, "In the 1940s a person using a mechanical desk calculator took three to four days to develop the ordinates of an airfoil designed to a prescribed pressure distribution."[27] Lacking a decent mechanical calculator meant longer hours, especially for a project that tested overall design, not just the airfoils. After completing the tests at the NRC, Elsie took the necessary information back to Fairchild Aircraft so it could be applied to the evolving designs.

Once a prototype had been constructed, Elsie regularly flew alongside the test pilot as an observer. She recalled that the necessary tests for models such as the Super 71P were not comfortable: "Alec Schneider [the test pilot] test flew those aircraft and I was Observer on the flights. I think they took place in the spring of 1935. There was no heat in the cockpit, of course, and the flights were bitterly cold."[28] As well as being uncomfortable, these flights were dangerous; a test that failed often resulted in the loss of an aircraft and sometimes the pilot.

To move any commercial product into full production, the initial models need to be tested many times. In addition, a receptive market for the final product is essential. This holds true for aircraft designs, especially because of the costs of development and production. At the beginning of the Second World War aviation shifted from civilian to military needs. As a result, some civilian models, including the Fairchild Sekani prototype, were abandoned before they could be perfected. Elsie recalled that the Sekani was undergoing wind-tunnel testing in the latter part of 1936 and early part of 1937:

> The Sekani [a civilian project], like other prototype aircraft developed immediately prior to the outbreak of World War II never had a chance of having "the bugs" taken out of it – and all prototypes have bugs. The urgency was turned to enlarging the plant, and getting war production underway, a more certain market than civilian aircraft development and production, and more compelling.[29]

J.J. Green described the nature of the bugs in the Sekani prototype:

> The later tests of the Sekani were not perhaps as extensive, but after the aircraft itself was flying, there was a good deal of consultation with Elsie, for it turned out, as sometimes happens that the actual speed performance and flight stability of the aircraft were significantly lower than the wind tunnel tests had predicted.[30]

When working at Fairchild Aircraft Limited, Elsie interacted with various staff members of the National Research Council of Canada (NRC) to conduct necessary wind tunnel tests. During this time she met K.F. Tupper, with whom she would work again overseas and within the Engineering Institute of Canada. Tupper was fond of Elsie as testified by his support for the Elsie Gregory MacGill Memorial Foundation.

Elsie had suspected that this might be the case, but noted that the designer and test pilot were optimistic about the potential of the aircraft to reach its projected cruising speed.[31] As Walter Vincenti observed, discrepancies between the wind tunnel tests and the resulting prototype were not uncommon: "Because of 'scale effects' associated with viscosity, results from a small model at relatively low speeds...cannot be extrapolated simply and reliably to the full-scale airplane at the speeds encountered in flight."[32] In the context of the war and having less time and resources available, the project would have had to be rushed to completion, making it more difficult to successfully market the airplane.[33]

• • • • • • • • •

The interactions Elsie had with personnel at the NRC provide insight into her professionalism and her determination to succeed. Kenneth Tupper, on staff at the time and later a vice-president of the NRC, described Elsie's resolve:

> We first became acquainted when she was working for Fairchild Aircraft in Montréal and I was one of J.H. Parkin's small staff working with the National Research Council's old seven-by-ten-foot wind tunnel at the laboratories at the corner of John and Sussex Streets in Ottawa. Elsie was one of the first customers to make use of these facilities, bringing models up to Ottawa from Montréal in her own car. She did this in the icy snowy days of mid-winter in spite of her crippling legacy from poliomyelitis. We admired her spunk. She never asked for any assistance, and as we got to know her better it was seldom offered.[34]

J.J. Green added the following comment:

Her lameness struck me as an appalling affliction for a woman with a keen and bright mind, dedicated to a professional career in the aircraft industry. But she obviously treated it as little more than a minor annoyance which was to be neither an obstacle nor a deterrent to any of her activities…I think she wanted her friends to look upon her affliction in the same way, and to some extent we did.

Green pointed out that her trips to the NRC were extremely valuable to Fairchild Aircraft; in making her way to Ottawa, she ensured the safe transportation of the fragile models.[35]

Elsie's first priority was always to meet the challenges of the engineering task at hand. She guarded her independence and did not welcome offers of assistance related either to her gender or her physical disability. She later wrote:

A woman who has passed through the long engineering training period has developed a skill and a professional pride in work, which leads her to avoid unusual assistance, and she is fully alive to the disadvantages to herself of accepting it. A woman who has spent 4 or 5 years in an engineering school has the sober, detached scientific attitude to her job that is part of an engineer's training and accepts criticism of her work as part of the job.[36]

Such a viewpoint did not mean that Elsie avoided offers of friendship. In fact her long-term contact with J.J. Green and Kenneth Tupper suggests that, professional identity aside, she sustained many valuable relationships. Moreover, although Elsie dedicated herself to her work, she did not bury herself in it. J.J. Green remembers that "she had wide-ranging interests; in those days she had an interest in music and used to practice on the piano in the ballroom of the Chateau Laurier Hotel."[37]

By 1938, Elsie had accumulated considerable hands-on experience that complemented her advanced academic training. These qualifications helped her obtain a new appointment as chief aeronautical engineer at the Canadian Car and Foundry Company (Can Car),[38] which had recently begun producing aircraft in Fort William (now Thunder Bay), Ontario.[39] This marked the first time in North America that a woman was appointed to such a position.[40] Elsie was

Elsie was accepted into the Engineering Institute of Canada in 1938 and took up the position of chief aeronautical engineer at Canadian Car and Foundry's Fort William, Ontario plant in the same year.

quick to share this news with her family through the letter network they used.[41] The salary offer was $350 per month, or $4200 per year, a high level of pay in those days for any professional.[42] Confident in the value of her skills, Elsie had already turned down another job offer:

On Friday I spent some time with the Civil Aviation Branch on Company business. While there the Dept. offered me a job! They said (this is strictly confidential and NOT TO BE REPEATED. I mean please no one say they offered me a job, because the job being in the Civil Service has to be advertised etc. and while I could probably beat any applicants, the competition is supposed to be open). They said however, that they could only offer me $2700 a year, as it would not be possible to get a more advanced classification for me. I thanked them and refused, saying that the salary did not interest me. I am on very friendly terms with the people there.[43]

Work in the civil service would have given her more job security than a position in industry, especially since the work related to the anticipated needs of the war. However, the difference in salary was too great for Elsie to consider the government job. Still, she ensured that she maintained good relations with aeronautical agencies in government.[44]

Elsie's desire to avoid offending a prospective employer and other professional contacts was likely reinforced by an earlier interaction with another section of the civil service: the Aeronautical

Engineering Division of the Department of National Defence. The department had advertised a position for a junior engineer, but Elsie's application was immediately rejected because of her sex. Later, when Fairchild Aircraft business brought her into contact with the civil service commissioner responsible for denying her this job opportunity, Elsie "backed him into a corner, and asked if he thought it was right to refuse to hire a citizen of the country, who had every qualification for the work in question, merely on the grounds of sex."[45] Gratified to hear that he agreed with her, she nevertheless found herself in an awkward situation the next time the department sought employees. The advertisement for a new job was modified to specifically include women applicants, and she was sent a personal invitation to apply. However, the position paid only $1,800 per year, and she declined.[46]

As her career developed and matured, Elsie maintained amicable relations with important figures in a variety of sectors within the Canadian aviation industry. In the meantime, her new position as chief aeronautical engineer at Can Car increased her economic security. Employment at Fairchild Aircraft had not solved her financial problems; in fact, in May 1938 she was struggling to make ends meet. Even while anticipating a change in fortune with her new appointment at Can Car, she wrote the following in a letter to her family:

> Friday afternoon, Wynne Green and I went shopping for clothes for me. I needed a coat badly, having split my old one down the back. Got quite a nice one, and a dress too. Yesterday Bonks [Helen Jr.] went with me and I bought a hat, which I needed badly. The joke is that, while in the near future I will be receiving a good salary, at present I am none too flush, and will have to skimp a bit to get my train fare etc.[47]

Elsie's specialized training, the pending war, and her increasing connections within the field of aeronautics – such as those at the NRC and the Civil Aviation Branch – likely assisted her in this significant promotion. After successfully negotiating with the company, Elsie began work in the summer of 1938, despite the fact that current chief aeronautical engineer Michael Gregor was not scheduled to leave until the autumn.[48]

The offer for her to work at Can Car substantiated her belief that industrial companies were more interested in the skills of talented individuals than in their gender. Elsie considered her age as the only unusual factor in her appointment, not her gender:

> Of course I am awfully pleased over the whole thing. It is a great chance for me. If I make good, I will be on top of the world. Probably I would get a good raise in salary within six months, and then of course there is the prestige which goes with the position. To be Chief Engineer at 33 years of age is not bad.[49]

Elsie moved rapidly up the ladder of her profession. However, her failure to acknowledge the special position she held at this point in history indicates that she did not yet recognize discrimination within engineering. There is no doubt, though, that this new appointment was a turning point in Elsie's life. She was entering industrial management, an area of study in which she had excelled in her undergraduate program at the University of Toronto.[50]

Elsie cherished her family. Here she proudly holds her niece Helen Hughes Jr. during a Christmas visit in 1939.

Upon arriving in Fort William, Elsie established herself in a comfortable residential area not far from the Can Car plant. At the same time she tried to ensure some separation between her work and her private life, requesting that engineering-related information and materials be sent to her place of work, not her home address. Her home provided a welcoming spot for visiting family members.[51]

The year 1938 saw all three MacGill women in high spirits, looking forward to new adventures and possibilities. Elsie's sister, Helen, relocated with her husband to Chicago, with a new

daughter, also named Helen.[52] Elsie's mother was awarded a Doctor of Laws degree by the University of British Columbia, an honour the whole family appreciated deeply.[53]

Helen Gregory MacGill was awarded an Honorary Doctorate by the University of British Columbia.

Though her family was far away, Elsie was not alone in her move to northern Ontario. A colleague, Bill Soulsby, took the position of general manager at Can Car, and moved to Fort William with his family about the same time that Elsie settled there.[54]

Elsie dove into her new work. Her initial duty required her to ensure the Can Car Fighter, one of the first planes produced at the Fort William plant, met acceptable stress standards.[55] The work progressed smoothly, and in December 1938 George Adye successfully tested the new aircraft in a first flight at Bishopsfield.[56] The plane drew the interest of the international community. Turkey placed an order and Can Car quickly started production. However, after the second shipment of the Can Car Fighter it became clear that these planes were destined for the fight against the fascists in Spain. The American and Canadian governments forbade further shipments.[57]

Elsie's new post provided remarkable opportunities. In her

position as a chief engineer, she designed and oversaw the successful production of the Maple Leaf II: the first aircraft designed by a woman. Can Car originally hoped to produce a training biplane, with the potential to interest the Royal Canadian Air Force (RCAF) or other potential customers. Consequently, Can Car developed the Maple Leaf Trainer or Wallace Trainer after its designer, Leland Stamford Wallace, joined the company. The company hoped to progress from prototype to production quickly. However, initial testing of the design exposed flaws that produced a very unstable prototype. [58]

In 1938, the project was turned over to Elsie. Under her supervision an entirely new design was created and given the name Maple Leaf II. She salvaged aspects of the fin and rudder of the earlier plane, but the new prototype stood completely apart from its predecessor. Elsie redesigned bracing wires to ensure the wings' integrity. To further stabilize the plane, she also redesigned the wheel apparatus and the tail construction to make sure the aircraft could pull out from a spin. The latter modification required a new feature previously untested in Canada: an anti-spin parachute. The plane was assessed as stable and reliable in acrobatic spin tests. [59]

Elsie worked with efficiency and speed. Although she started at Can Car in the summer of 1938, and had responsibility for more than one project, the Maple Leaf II prototype was ready for testing by the fall of 1939. Aviation historian Frank Ellis described this feat as a "record-breaking performance." [60]

Elsie continued participating in test flights to check the performance of the aircraft she was designing. She had faith in her designs and knew the importance of assessing their operation first-hand. Had it not been for her physical disability, there is little doubt that she would have sought her own pilot's licence. [61]

Her recounting of the Maple Leaf II's inaugural test flight testifies to the soundness of the design:

I believe the first flight was on October 30, 1939. I recall that though ground handling tests were scheduled before any take-off should be made, Wally [Oates Wallace, the pilot] forgot that the take-off speed was very low, and we were in the air and climbing almost at once – without even a decent ground run. He took a lot

of ribbing about that that evening at the customary plant celebration of the flight – at which, incidentally I followed the time-honoured practice

Elsie Gregory MacGill stands beside her plane with Canadian Car and Foundry General Manager Bill Soulsby.

and, as designer of the aircraft, paid for the party. The aircraft received its Type Certificate of Airworthiness, acrobatic category (Certificate No. 427) early in January 1940.[62]

Members of the Lakehead branch of the Engineering Institute of Canada (EIC) were onsite to celebrate the successful first flight of the Maple Leaf II.[63] A glowing description of the plane appeared in *The Engineering Journal:*

A few of the many excellent features of this aircraft from a training point of view are its excellent visibility on the ground and in the air, its stability and controllability at take-off and on landing. The take-off run is exceptionally short and the initial rate of climb is excellent. The stalling speed is low – 45 m.p.h. with a gross load of 1,865 lbs. – and the machine has no tendency to spin from the stall.[64]

Elsie completed this project despite the death of her father from cancer in January 1939, two weeks after his initial diagnosis, and the fact that her mother, Helen Gregory MacGill, became a widow without an estate to depend upon.[65] Mother and daughter coped with this loss by immersing themselves in the demands of work. Helen kept busy with her legal work and ongoing feminist activities, including presentations in the Lakehead region when she visited Elsie; Elsie sought solace in the rapidly growing demands of the Can Car plant as it responded to the international tensions of the late 1930s.[66]

Another early project Elsie undertook at Can Car was to standardize data collection during flight testing. Three categories of data were recorded: description of the aircraft and qualitative and quantitative design features. She introduced standardized forms to more easily record information for assessing an aircraft's performance and the subsequent application for the aircraft's airworthiness certificate. Elsie hoped that having systematic procedures in place would ensure efficiency, reduce production costs, and help identify problem areas that needed closer attention. Elsie later promoted the use of practical flight-testing forms in a 1940 speech to the Toronto branch of the Engineering Institute of Canada, and in an article for the *Engineering Journal*.[67]

This project was not merely a logical administrative measure; it also foreshadowed her later international work with the Provisional International Civil Aviation Organization – later the International Civil Aviation Organization – on airworthiness.[68] It further demonstrates her attention to organizational and procedural issues, an aptitude she later applied beyond the world of engineering and aeronautics. Elsie was well aware, however, that paper reviews could not provide all the answers for a designer. She valued the views and insights of the test pilot:

> The test pilot should be considered a close collaborator with the designer, not as an independent checker and debunker of the designer's plans. Familiarity of the test pilot with the type

of machine is of great advantage in the development work, but – as in every other branch of experimental science – the most important single characteristic to be desired is an open mind on the part of the experi-

Once Canadian Car and Foundry won the Hawker Hurricane contract Elsie helped direct the retooling of the plant to produce these aircraft for the Allies during the Second World War. Here she watches test flights with other onlookers (left to right) David Boyd, Brian Sheaver, Elsie MacGill and Mary Boyd.

menter. The pilot whose mind is filled with preconceived notions of how the aeroplane will behave, is more likely to misinterpret or to miss entirely the significance of certain reactions, than he who, having an open mind, looks, not for the confirmation of his own opinions, but for what there is to be found. Since the designer must lean heavily upon the test pilot and must consider his every opinion in the light of improvements to be made, this point cannot be emphasized too strongly.[69]

Elsie's respect for this partnership process demonstrates that she was at the cutting edge of her field, as attention to these key relationships was receiving increased appreciation within aeronautics.[70]

Canadian Car and Foundry (now Bombardier Incorporated) was located in Fort William, Ontario (now Thunder Bay). The plant, located not far from the shores of Lake Superior, needed to expand to include women's residences during the war.

• • • • • • • • • •

The Maple Leaf II turned out to be a casualty of the growing hostilities in Europe. In terms of aircraft production, the aviation industry gave priority to the needs of the RCAF. Since the RCAF had decided against using the new trainer, Can Car abandoned further investment in this aircraft. Elsie took the situation in stride while maintaining an interest in the plane's history after the trainer left Can Car.[71] The company subsequently retooled to produce Hawker Hurricane fighter planes for the British Royal Air Force (RAF): a major undertaking.[72] Aircraft production at the plant was relatively new, and wartime production increased the pressure for speed and efficiency.[73] Historian James R. Hansen suggests engineers need the kind of challenges presented by the Hawker Hurricane contract to demonstrate their leadership potential and move forward in their careers.[74] Elsie rose to the challenge.

The work was not a simple undertaking. Elsie reflected on the difficulties in a paper she presented to the Lakehead branch of the EIC in April 1940: [75]

> The production engineer cannot, at will, put any commodity on a mass production basis. Aeroplanes are not like baby carriages. The easy acceptance of the applicability of mass production methods to aeroplane construction arises from sad ignorance of the problems involved.[76]

Mass production of the complex parts and specific technical equipment needed for airplanes required special attention that less complicated commercial products did not. The aircraft industry, still undergoing growing pains, had not yet standardized any one model. Unlike automobile design, aircraft design was constantly evolving. In Elsie's view, the goals of aeronautical engineers clashed with the goals of mass production:

> The goal of the aeroplane designer is improved performance – particularly increased top speed. This he can achieve efficiently in two ways – by refinement of the basic pattern and by changing the basic pattern. Refinement of the basic pattern is carried out by incorporating aerodynamic improvements, employing the most improved materials, devising cunning means of saving structural weight, and streamlining the external form to reduce air resistance. Changing the basic pattern implies a fundamental change in the engineering approach. Attempts at crystallization of aeroplane design pattern are foiled by a change in the basic pattern of the aeroplane, not by refinement of this pattern.[77]

Unfortunately, the demands of wartime made mass production unavoidable.[78] Despite these inevitable challenges, the Can Car plant successfully retooled to produce the Hawker Hurricane fighter planes on order in an efficient and timely manner.[79] To accommodate the increased demand, the plant hired a large number of additional staff. As Elsie noted, expansion was the norm for aircraft companies across Canada:

> The wartime expansion of the industry provides a measure of the work accomplished. More than 9,000 employees are at work now in seven Canadian aircraft manufacturing plants, compared

Engineers and Can Car staff worked to implement the mass production of Hawker Hurricanes. Pictured here are various aircraft under construction. The teamwork and dedication lead to the successful production of hundreds of planes for the Battle of Britain as everyone gave 'That Extra Little' to get the job done.

with about 2,000 in 1936. Including the allied industries, over 17,000 Canadians are actively engaged to-day in producing aeroplanes. Many of these workers are new to industry. To introduce so great a number of inexperienced people into an industry famous for the exactitude of its requirements, and at the same time to continue to maintain the high standard of workmanship obligatory, is a crazy assignment and no task to be undertaken in cold blood. Fortunately, there is no cold blood in the aircraft industry. Also, a current saying in the aviation world is that "you don't have to be crazy to be in the aircraft business, but it helps." Obviously it does help, but it is a specific craziness that is meant, a craziness that accomplishes prodigious things, a craziness that will win the war.[80]

It took roughly two years to get the plant up to full production, at which time it was able to produce upwards of one hundred planes each month.[81] This production rate was essential because every possible plane was needed to assist the Allied cause after Germany started its blitz attacks on Britain in April of 1940.

While Elsie was in charge of overseeing the retooling and facilitating the mass production at the plant, she was also involved in the necessary design modifications for the Hawker Hurricanes. The most notable of these alterations were the ones required to winterize the fighters for cold weather, which meant incorporating additional parts. Skis replaced wheels on the undercarriage and de-icing systems were developed for the wings and propellers.[82] Elsie used the professional networks she had cultivated earlier at the NRC and elsewhere, looking for input and feedback on her designs.[83] The resulting modifications were innovative. As Frank Ellis pointed out this had never been done before with a high-speed aircraft, but under Elsie's guidance the procedure was a successful one.[84]

Elsie's success with this winterization project marked her career in a significant way. Her expertise in winter climate adaptations was later sought out commercially and nationally.[85]

· · · · · · · · ·

Despite the best efforts of the engineers and staff at Can Car, several design challenges and other problems arose in the production of the Hawker Hurricanes. In a series of memoranda to the Royal Canadian Air Force, Elsie outlined a wide range of concerns, including problems with the pipes and rivets, cables, landing gear, and engines.[86] Moreover, retooling was complex and took considerable time, which led some local residents to believe that salaries were being paid for little or no work.[87]

At times, delays caused by the slow shipment of parts from Britain did result in the undesirable suspension of work. Throughout the war, it was difficult for the company to balance the changing demands of the RAF with the availability of parts and labour.[88] During downtime in 1941 the company laid off workers, which was a very unpopular move. Therefore, when faced with a similar situation in 1942, Can Car retained its workers. From the earliest days of her contract, Elsie and the engineering department tried to find suppliers in North America capable of producing the necessary parts that could substitute for the parts produced in Britain and shipped across the battlefield of the Atlantic Ocean. However, it was not easy to find North American suppliers, as the original parts were produced according to British specifications and measurements.[89]

Despite these challenges, C.D. Howe observed that the Canadian aviation industry had undergone massive changes by 1942:

> The year before the war I think we turned out 200 aircraft. We had only a small industry working mostly on small planes for transport work, and one or two types of army planes. Today we are turning out planes at the rate of about 70 a week or 300 a month. We are independent now of outside help in furnishing planes for our great Air Training Plan, and we are also building several of the most modern types of planes that are used by fighting forces. From a small nucleus we have built up a very strong aircraft industry.[90]

When faced by rumblings in the community, Elsie rose to the defence of the company and the workers. She praised the dedication of the employees and their efforts to advance the Allied cause. One of her statements on this subject, "That Little Extra," was hung in RCAF stations across Canada:

War effort is the extra contribution of the individual. War effort is a man staying and working an extra hour or two, or five hours – without extra pay. It is a woman cutting short her noon hour to get back to finish the job. It is someone taking home his problems to solve them after dinner at night. It is someone coming back in the evening to finish an assignment. War effort is something which is as microscopic in the unit as the individual, but as mighty in the sum as an army.[91]

The workers at Can Car lived up to her tribute in many ways. For example, they volunteered their labour on Sundays to build two special Hawker Hurricanes. These aircraft were given to the Wings of Britain Fund and were dedicated to the memories of Gary Madore and Phillip Taylor, whose names they bore; both men had worked with the company and died in active service overseas.[92]

The aeronautical engineers who laboured with Elsie were also highly dedicated. It was not unusual for them to work past six o'clock at night, despite the fact that their work schedule allowed for only one day off per week.[93] Like engineers in other fields, they were essential in the pursuit of victory: the Second World War was an advanced techno-logical engagement. It required specialists to produce the needed equipment and weapons and to innovate when new challenges arose. As a result, the Second World War was sometimes labelled the "engineers' war," and Elsie had mixed feelings about this:

To the shame and the glory of the engineering profession the world over, this war is

Elsie out and about circa 1940s. By this point Elsie was coming into her own as a professional engineer and dressed the part.

described as an "engineers" war. To our shame, we engineers devote the years of peace to designing and planning for war. To our glory, we are the group to which our country turns in time of war. Heavily upon us, as individuals and as a professional unit, our national duty rests terrible and dear.[94]

One of Elsie's ways of coping was to look beyond the war to the hope for peace:

The challenge of winning the war is thrown directly to the Canadian engineer. It is our job and our duty, yet in it we can take exultant pleasure for our goal extends beyond the war into the peace to follow. We are working, not just for the satisfaction of winning the fight for our side, but for the glory of hastening peace to the world. This peace that is to come must be so com-pounded of wisdom and justice as to have intrinsic strength. It must last for longer than a generation. It must be a peace which we shall be proud to hail as the Pax Britannica, the British Peace.[95]

· · · · · · · · · ·

Although Elsie ignored her gender in her work as an engineer, it was not as easily overlooked by those around her. In assessing women's experiences during the Second World War, historians have demon-strated that the wartime context allowed many women to step out of their "normal" roles. Where most women were previously limited to domestic work, during the war some took up essential duties in industrial, agricultural, and administrative fields.[96]

Elsie was justified to some degree in dismissing her difference, and potential benefit, as a *woman* engineer during the war. Unlike the great majority of the women whose lives suddenly changed at the declaration of war, Elsie was already employed as a professional engineer. As historian Margaret Rossiter argues, women with simi-lar backgrounds to Elsie – with pre-existing scientific qualifications, training, and work experience – fared differently than those without such experience. And because the war increased demand for their skills, it was not unusual for women to secure well-positioned employment.[97]

Elsie did concede that the war years were transformative for her

Elsie became a war celebrity during the Second World War and was featured in the American *True Comics War Heroes Series* in the story "Queen of the Hurricanes: Elsie MacGill".

and the field of aeronautics: "Aeronautics, a rapidly developing field, grew up with the War, and I grew with it."[98] Her success and rapid rise within the field, however, led her to believe that the engineering profession treated both sexes equally: "While it is not a field which has attracted [women] in any considerable number, it has never been one that excluded them."[99] However, her reluctance to admit discrimination within the field of engineering changed as she advanced in her career.

That Elsie was the new chief aeronautical engineer at Can Car did not go unnoticed by the media. In fact, she became a wartime celebrity. In 1941, *Chatelaine* magazine suggested that she was "the human pivot around which turns one of the most vital operations of the Canadian war effort."[100] Beyond Canada's borders she was depicted as a heroine. The American *True Comics War Heroes Series* celebrated her career path in a story entitled "Queen of the Hurricanes Elsie MacGill."[101] Scholars Helen Smith and Pamela Wakewich note that these depictions attempted to "normalize" Elsie by highlighting her femininity whenever possible.[102] In this regard, Elsie was not so different from women who worked on the plant floor and others engaged in male-dominated war work. In both cases, the media expressed the need to report on the remarkable nature of their work, while assuring readers that this work was taking place only under unusual circumstances.[103]

For a time it may have been exciting for Elsie to see her name in newspapers and magazines. However, as she ascribed little importance to her gender within the engineering world, it must have also been difficult to be scrutinized repeatedly on account of her sex. These representations also caused tension with her co-workers, especially when the media exaggerated her role. Indeed, in some cases, Elsie was depicted as the sole person responsible for managing the Can Car plant in Fort William, which was not the case.

Some of her colleagues faulted her for the hyperbole, believing she could have done more to ensure an accurate account.[104] To what degree this may have been possible is questionable. One account in *The Globe and Mail* detailed her modesty and acknowledged that she was eager to share the credit for the work among her colleagues, which suggests that Elsie tried to correct the exaggerated depiction of her leadership.[105]

E.J. Soulsby, who played an increasingly important role in Elsie's life, took issue with the idea that she was the one who "supervised" the aircraft production at the plant:

> To say Elsie supervised the Canadian production of this aircraft is to misrepresent the engineer's function which is to determine what has to be done and to specify it quite precisely, mostly in the form of drawings. How, when and where the work is done, and how faithfully, are the responsibility of others. There is no need to overstate the engineer's job; it is of the highest importance and in a highly technical field like the aircraft industry requires a well-educated scientific and mathematical mind.[106]

Elsie would likely have agreed with this assessment, as the engineering profession strongly encourages humility in its members, despite the importance of their work. However, as Walter Vicenti notes, engineers deserve credit for their specific contributions and responsibilities related to organization and design.[107]

While Elsie had to contend with challenging media representations and celebrity, her successes had positive effects for other women. For instance, a meeting with Elsie during this period inspired Joyce Craig to begin engineering studies.[108] As well, the life of Muriel Smith, former member of the Legislative Assembly of Manitoba, was influenced by Elsie. Smith's mother had admired Elsie as a trailblazer, and Smith identified with Elsie's fascination with engineering. Smith also believed that the comic book portrayal of Elsie's life had the potential to inspire other young women.[109]

Despite the fact that Elsie's gender caught the attention of the press, she was not the only woman working at Can Car. Due to the demands of mass production and the departure of so many men to fight overseas, by 1944 women labourers comprised approximately 40 percent of the plant's employees.[110] Most of these women were nicknamed "Rosies" (after "Rosie the Riveter"), and assigned a wide range of tasks including sewing, welding, and riveting.

These women had minimal previous experience and learned on the job. By contrast, Elsie's professional training and management position put her in a unique position. Women in the plant knew Elsie, and at times she interacted with them, but she spent most of her time in the company of her male colleagues. The women

While mass production was not ideal for airplanes, the workers at Can Car found ways to make it work. Teamwork was essential and men and women worked together to ensure Britain had the supply of aircraft it required.

who remembered Elsie from those years saw her in a variety of ways, ranging from an aloof professional they found cold and uninviting to someone who was formidable and inspiring in what she had achieved in a man's world.[111]

The recollections of some of her immediate colleagues provide further glimpses into Elsie's personality and an idea of what it was like to work closely with her on a daily basis. According to aeronautical engineer Victor Stevenson,[112] she was very dedicated and meticulous when it came to specific details related to the job at hand. As a result, he noted that she did not like distractions such as idle conversation that impeded work. Another colleague described this trait in less flattering terms: "She was a crabby old bugger.... She would jump right down your throat. If you came in and said good morning, she'd say, if I wanted a weather report, I'd phone the airport. She seemed to have some kind of a deal against the world."[113] Victor Stevenson also recalled that Elsie did not always see eye-to-eye with her colleagues when determining the subsequent course of action for a task. When this happened, compromises were not always easy to achieve.[114]

Such criticisms were balanced by positive recollections. Victor Stevenson adds that Elsie had the ability to motivate those she worked with. He remembered that she had a way of recognizing the strengths of an individual, especially in relation to the serious work they were engaged in. According to Stevenson, Elsie was dedicated to ensuring a job was well done, while at the same time displaying respect and understanding for those around her. For example, his first assignment at Can Car was to design an air intake, and he felt his initial attempt had failed miserably. But when he presented his results to Elsie, she did not berate him; instead she encouraged him to keep trying. As a result, he persevered and she later praised his results.[115]

Jim Carmichael, the shop engineer, and Alex Horbrow, who worked in production and became a draftsman, described Elsie as easy to get along with. They also noted that she was supportive of the workers, taking time to get to know about their lives outside of the workplace. Jim Carmichael carpooled with Elsie to and from the plant. These regular journeys gave him a unique perspective on her personality as well as her driving abilities: "Our conversations were stimulating, as we were discussing the war news each morning; it was hair-raising to see her drive, lifting her bad leg by hand to place her foot on the clutch to shift gears!"[116]

Alex Horbow recalled that in addition to being a likeable colleague, Elsie was willing to engage with the employees at Can Car and offer them support, despite her difficulty traversing the large industrial plant:

She was a very colourful personality; she had a lot of charisma. She would walk down to the shop with her cane; she had difficulty walking. She'd come to see how the men were doing with her work. She would cheer the men up, anytime she came walking through the shop; she had a lot of respect for the workers of Can Car.[117]

Footnotes for this chapter can be found online at:
http://secondstorypress.ca/resources and at http://feministhistories.ca/books

Chapter 4
CAREER CHANGE, CONTROVERSY, AND CHALLENGE

You'll find Elsie McGill [sic] in her airy office, the huge windows framing the bright blue sky as an appropriate backdrop behind her. There is no unnecessary clutter in this office, and the glass partition between her office and the secretary's has the undulating milky glass you see at airports.[1]

—Eva-Lis Wuorio

Elsie's career at Canadian Car and Foundry ended in 1943. Until that time her work with the company and her leadership in the Lakehead branch of the Engineering Institute of Canada (EIC) appear to be exemplary.[2] Yet, in May 1943 she and plant manager E.J. (Bill) Soulsby were publicly marched out of the Fort William plant.[3] Although the reason for the dismissal was never made public, there are several possible explanations.

First of all, the production of the Curtis-Wright Helldiver bomber, built by Can Car for the U.S. Navy, encountered many problems and delays, for which Bill Soulsby and Elsie may have been blamed. Elsie was the one initially responsible for the new Helldiver contract, which required retooling the plant. The new plane had many design problems and earned the nickname "The Beast." However, these problems were not isolated to the Fort William plant, nor did they cease once Elsie and Bill left. The root of the problem appeared to be poor initial design of the aircraft, unrealistic expectations of the contracting company and the pressures of wartime production.[4] Al Norton, manager of tool and design, recalled that the sheer number of changes demanded by the American aircraft company – about 53,000 of them – made progress almost impossible:

> We had filing cabinets full of changes. Some were mandatory and we had to stop production on certain parts and put the changes

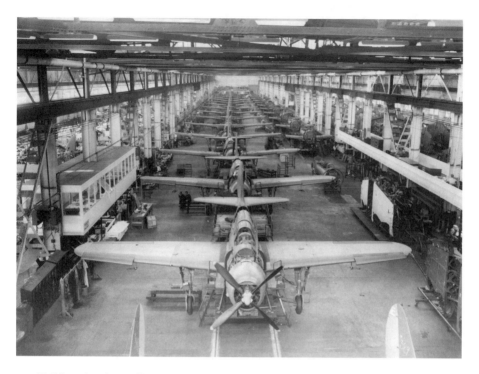

Helldiver aircraft roll off the production line. Due to the massive number of changes during production these planes came to be known by the nickname 'The Beast'.

in – even go to the airport and make the changes there. They [the Curtis-Wright Company] would find out where production was at the shop and then they'd put a hold on it at a certain point. They would introduce a change and it might take days or weeks. Mostly it was minor things – you could pick them up in your hand and carry them; but it affected so many different parts of the airplane.[5]

In fact, real progress was possible only after the new plant manager ruled that the aircraft close to completion would be exempt from any more changes and that changes could only be made on the design of the next set of planes.[6]

A second explanation for their dismissal may be the romantic relationship that had developed between Elsie and Bill Soulsby. Romantic relationships in the workplace were frowned upon, especially for professional women.[7] Historian Mary Kinnear describes the mores of the time:

The self-sufficiency of a respectable woman who could decently support herself with her own trained and tested labour was itself an affront to the notion of gendered dependence. Yet when a professional woman remained single, her supposed celibacy reinforced her image as an honorary man, whose sexuality was effectively neutered. Professional women's gender could be overlooked, so long as their numbers were small. The commonplace thinking about women's work could accommodate a few exceptional circumstances.[8]

Elsie and Bill's personal relationship did blossom romantically during their time in Fort William. Since her stint at Fairfield Aviation, Elsie had been a close friend of Bill Soulsby and his ailing wife, who died in September 1942.[9] How the relationship developed after his wife's death is not clear because the romance was not public knowledge and Elsie was not prone to discuss her personal life.

Years later several women who worked at the plant were shocked to learn that Elsie and Bill had married shortly after their dismissal. By all accounts, Bill and Elsie maintained a professional relationship in the workplace.[10] However, Elsie's colleague Jim Carmichael recalled that rumours began to circulate in some circles in the Fort William area that Elsie and Bill were spending more time together than necessary outside the workplace.[11]

Interestingly, when mentioned in the existing literature, their departure is often described as a career change.[12] This may have some validity. It is unlikely that a plant manager would have been dismissed for a romantic relationship with a female subordinate, though not at all unusual for the woman to lose her job. And so it is possible that Bill left with Elsie to look for more satisfying work.

Elsie Gregory MacGill and Bill Soulsby around the time of their marriage on June 4, 1943 with Elsie's niece Helen Hughes Jr.

Regardless of the details surrounding their leave-taking, on June 4, 1943, shortly after leaving Can Car, Elsie and Bill were married in Kankakee, Illinois.[13] *The Globe and Mail* proclaimed: "Romance has torpedoed the career of Canada's foremost woman engineer. She's going to marry her boss."[14] The paper also reported that the couple had resigned. While it is possible that a resignation pre-empted a pending dismissal, it quickly became clear that Elise had not "torpedoed" her career.

K.M. Cameron, the national president of the EIC, wrote to Elise after reading the article. He expressed disappointment that she would no longer be at the helm of the EIC's Lakehead branch, but he also congratulated her on her pending marriage and expressed the hope that she would continue her engineering work:

> I could not resist sending you the very best wishes of all your fellow members, together with our sincere congratulations to the fortunate Mr. Soulsby. If at any time he does not feel how fortunate he is, there are about 6000 of us quite ready to stand up for you.
>
> If I judge rightly, it will not mean that you will lose interest in engineering work, but that it will only mean that you are broadening out in the Managerial field.[15]

Her colleagues within the EIC seem to have encountered the challenge of determining how to address the woman they previously referred to as (Miss) Elsie Gregory MacGill. Initially, she was identified as Mrs. E.J. Soulsby in brackets after her given name, but this practice did not last long. Having established herself and her name through her extensive education, publications, and professional networks, she was determined to retain her identity as Elsie Gregory MacGill.[16]

The abrupt change of employment and location in the midst of the Second World War does not seem to have troubled Elsie and Bill. When Ann Soulsby, Elsie's step-daughter, expressed concern about the situation, the couple brushed it off. This response may be due to the fact that from the beginning of their employment neither Elsie nor Bill saw their appointments at Can Car as permanent. Both fully expected to relocate to the Toronto area at some point.[17] Elsie's adaptation to this change may also have been influenced by the experience of her mother, who had been dismissed from her position as a judge for political reasons in 1929, but was subsequently reinstated in 1934.[18]

In any case, Elsie and Bill's departure from Can Car did not damage their professional reputations. In fact, Bill Soulsby soon found employment as plant manager at Victory Aircraft Limited in Malton, Ontario, and Elsie followed a familiar engineering path by opening her own private consulting firm.[19]

During this period it was still unusual for a woman to continue a professional career after marriage. Probably the most famous example of a woman who continued her career after marriage was Amelia Earhart, who insisted on a marriage contract that assured her freedom to continue working after her marriage.[20]

Like Earhart, Elsie chose a partner who respected her ambitions and independence. Consequently, marriage did not inhibit Elsie's professional aspirations. As she had also witnessed her mother balance marriage, a family, and intense public involvement, she did not see continued work in aviation as incompatible with marriage. Indeed, she argued that professional women could balance their public and private lives:

> In Canada, most women, as most men, anticipate marrying, but this no longer means a purely domestic and social life for the women. Many women are anxious to continue their business connection after marriage. The professional woman is in the fortunate position that she can practice and manage a home concurrently.[21]

At the time Elsie was still largely blind to the discrimination she and other professional women were encountering. Later, however, she saw that her optimism did not always match reality.[22] For her part, Elsie was able to maintain a balance by compartmentalizing her life. Even though she and Bill were immersed in the aviation industry, Elsie avoided discussing work at home. As she noted, "Most of my business is my client's secret and I can't talk about it, and secondly, my husband isn't an engineer, he's got more of a financial mind."[23]

Bill Soulsby appears to have been a very loving partner to Elsie. In reflecting on their relationship after Elsie's death, he noted that "I cherish the belief that the bond of deep love that held us could hardly be matched."[24] Their mutual devotion was confirmed by friends and colleagues who remembered Elsie's commitment to her husband.[25] Bill was also very supportive and proud of Elsie and her achievements. Among other things, he transported her to and from her various engagements, a task he undertook without complaint. His daughter, Ann, confirmed his general support for Elsie's activities, while noting that his views about married women were conventional and a bit Victorian. However, Ann described her father as a "very gentle person" and expressed confidence that any conflict the couple had was resolved in open discussion.[26]

Elsie's niece Helen Brock considered the couple to be very well suited. She remembers that when she travelled with her family to visit her aunt and uncle, "they would meet us at the station with big smiles, Elsie leaning on Bill's arm. They always looked happy and at ease together."[27] She also remembers that they shared a love of Shakespeare and made annual trips to Stratford, Ontario, to attend the Stratford Festival. While Bill was the more musically inclined of the two, they both enjoyed singing together on lengthy road trips. Helen recalls, "I certainly had an early sense of two grownups who had their own fun together. That was something special about them, since most other grownups, however fond we were of them, were primarily somebody's parents."[28]

Marrying Bill Soulsby gave Elsie the opportunity to raise children, without all of the associated time-consuming demands of caring for the very young.[29] Ann and John, were eleven and thirteen, respectively, at the time of the marriage, which allowed Elsie more time to concentrate on her career and professional development, though she was not a distant step-mother. Ann recalled that Elsie fully engaged in parenting and was also influential in her education. Indeed, it was Elsie who suggested that Ann pursue a degree at McGill University, and instilled in her the importance of economic independence.[30]

● ● ● ● ● ● ● ● ●

Professional engineers often choose to become consultants at some point in their careers. For some, consulting defines their professional development, despite the greater security offered by positions in industry. In fact, sometimes engineers experience a tug-of-war between these two options. Just after setting up her consulting office, Elsie was offered a job by the de Havilland aircraft company. Although the company atmosphere might have been familiar and attractive, she declined, choosing to maintain her independence. Consulting gave her unique opportunities and challenges that employment within a company might not have: "You see, we get jobs other people don't like, or are called [in] when they get into trouble – and it's fascinating pitching in, then!"[31]

When Elsie opened her own consulting firm, she became the first woman consulting engineer in Canada, and she remained one of the extremely few women who worked in aeronautical engineering in North America.[32] Elsie was not the only woman entrepreneur in Canada, but what made her unique was that she pursued this route in the male-dominated field of engineering.[33]

As a consulting engineer, Elsie benefited by being able to determine her own pace of work, choose the kinds of work she would pursue, and the approach to take in doing it. Many of her colleagues, including C.D. Howe, saw merit in this career option:

> I have always believed, and still believe, that the life of a consulting engineer is the best that the engineering profession offers. While the consulting engineer must do without the monthly salary cheque and the social security that most of our fellow engineers can count on, ours is by far the more interesting life. We can at least choose our clients and can choose not to be associated with prospective clients unless we think that the association will be a happy one. However, we must always be alive to the fact that our association with a client is apt to be what we make it, and that failure to give satisfaction can very well damage our ability to attract new clients.
>
> Being detached from the company payroll is, I believe, an advantage. Usually we are retained because the owner has a high opinion of our reputation in the particular field that is his interest at the moment. This puts us in a preferred position in that our opinion is apt to carry more weight than the opinion from a man on the company payroll.[34]

Elsie valued being able to exercise creativity in her work. As a consulting engineer she could fully develop creative approaches to problem-solving, which she later referred to as essential not only in business, but also in the struggle for social change.[35]

Some professional women prefer to avoid situations that put them into competition with their peers. However, this was not the case for Elsie. On the contrary, because her consulting work required her to be ambitious and bid successfully for contracts, she needed to stay on the cutting edge of her field and ensure that she could offer her clients the highest level of service. Her success relied a great deal on her knowledge and reputation within the field, and on her ability to maintain her clients.

After Elsie and her husband settled in Toronto in 1943, she began the work needed to establish her consultancy. She found office space in the Physicians and Surgeons Building at 86 Bloor Street West[36] and arranged for a full-time secretary. There were no other full-time employees. When she needed additional personnel or equipment, she tapped into her existing professional network.[37] Reporter Eva-Lis Wuorio offered a glimpse into Elsie's office:

> You'll find Elsie McGill [sic] in her airy office, the huge windows framing the bright blue sky as an appropriate backdrop behind her. There is no unnecessary clutter in this office, and the glass partition between her office and the secretary's has the undulating milky glass you see at airports.[38]

Embarking on a new career path takes faith, dedication, and time. As she solidified her position, she developed a brochure to highlight her services and reputation to her clients. By the 1950s she could confidently ask her clients for $50 to $75 per day, depending on the length of the contract.[39]

To ensure her initial success, Elsie made a concerted effort to seek out clients. One of her first contacts was Ralph Bell, the director general of the Aircraft Production Branch of the Department of Munitions and Supply in Ottawa, Ontario.[40] She expressed her desire for possible employment and outlined her expertise. She argued that her skills would help the government realize its vision of post-war aviation and its desire to nurture Canadian aircraft design.[41]

Elsie's inquiries were well-placed and timely.[42] She was ready to actively engage in post-war planning. Her initial contact with Ralph Bell developed into a regular correspondence between January and May of 1944. She also initiated correspondence with fellow engineer C.D. Howe, who was the minister responsible for the department.

Elsie was not just looking for work; she was interested in proposing new design ideas. She requested guidelines for aircraft designers seeking to propose post-war aircraft and asked whether she could submit her own designs to the Post-war Committee on Manufacture of Aircraft. She used this query strategically to discuss her current projects, including a single-engine air freighter and a twin-engine, medium-weight aircraft, and to emphasize her abilities within the field of aircraft design. In her letter to C.D. Howe, Elsie highlighted her expertise and experience in engineering supervision and project management.[43]

There is no indication that C.D. Howe responded directly to Elsie, but shortly afterwards Ralph Bell informed her that firm guidelines were not yet available for designers; however, he sent her the existing rough outlines for policies and procedures. Regarding the potential need for future aircraft designs, he explained that the Department of National Defence had expressed interest in a two-engine utility trainer, and the Post-war Committee on Manufacture of Aircraft had been asked to call for design submissions.[44]

Courting the favour of the federal government was a wise move, as it held the potential of long-term, reliable employment. And, as the government was highly interested in the potential of post-war aviation, any resulting contracts would assist Elsie in staying abreast of key developments within the field, particularly as the Second World War came to an end. Although the needs of the war were still paramount, the transition from wartime to peacetime production was underway. It appears that Elsie was the only private consultant at this point to propose new design plans to the committee.[45] By opening her consulting firm during the war, she had a key advantage over other consultants and companies who were still constrained by the demands of wartime production.[46]

• • • • • • • •

Successful in her proactive pursuit of work, Elsie was included in a sub-committee of the Post-war Committee on Manufacture of Aircraft. Through this opportunity she re-established contact with her former university professor, J.H. Parkin, who served as chairman of the sub-committee.[47]

Elsie was well-positioned to engage in the latest developments in aviation. For instance, in 1943 she was sent to England by the federal government to observe the impressive British advances in aviation and, more specifically, "to investigate the suitability of war-craft for conversion to peace time use."[48] She was accompanied by Kenneth Tupper from the National Research Council (NRC) and was issued a car by the British Ministry of Aircraft Production to ensure her mobility during her stay.[49]

British engineer Frank Whittle had made major advances in engine propulsion in England during the Second World War.[50] Canadian engineers subsequently built upon Whittle's research in developing the Iroquois engine and later the propulsion system for the Avro Arrow.[51] Discussions between the NRC and the British Ministry of Aircraft Production during Elsie's visit provided the Canadians with increased knowledge of turbojet engines. Kenneth Tupper's NRC team realized that manufacturing these engines in Canada could be highly profitable and recommended exploring this possibility. Experiments with turbojet engines in the Canadian climate offered an opportunity to explore solutions to the problem of ice accumulating on aircraft in winter. Based on the recommendations of Tupper's team, a research site was established in Winnipeg.[52]

Although she was likely involved in this research, Elsie did not explicitly state that this was the case. Some records related to her engineering work at this time have disappeared, and at least some of her work required secrecy, so it is not easy to piece together all her activities.[53] However, it appears that she was engaged in the development and testing of turbojet engines in a northern climate. In addition to participating in the fact-finding mission in Britain, she had expertise in the winterization of aircraft. Moreover, Elsie's application in 1970 for distinction as a fellow of the EIC indicates that she was listed as a licenced professional engineer in the province of Manitoba during the four-year period when the Winnipeg-based research was conducted.[54] Except for this groundbreaking aeronautical engineering work, no other project in which she was involved required her to maintain a licence to practice engineering in the province of Manitoba during this time.

· · · · · · · · ·

In addition to her work with the Post-war Committee on Manufacture of Aircraft, Elsie secured various contracts for aircraft that were being considered for the commercial aviation market. Although the technology associated with the Second World War demonstrated the kind of destruction that science and engineering could produce, there were positive outcomes, such as the increased potential for civilian aviation.

In Canada during this period airline companies were a new phenomenon. Trans-Canada Airlines and Canadian Pacific Airlines had been established in 1937 and 1942, respectively. In the post-war period these airline companies were eager to revitalize and expand the fledgling trans-Atlantic service. One of the quickest means to achieve this goal was to convert aircraft and designs previously developed for the military to civilian use.[55] The bulk of Elsie's civilian contracts fell into this category.

One of Elsie's first civilian contracts concerned the Lancaster XPP monoplane.[56] The company issuing the contract was Victory Aircraft Limited in Malton where Bill Soulsby was plant manager. It is not certain if he influenced the awarding of the contract, but it is clear that Elsie was well-suited to do the work, which required winterizing the plane.[57]

Regardless of how she heard about the job, she earned the respect of those within the plant, as attested by one of the Victory Aircraft employees:

> Although Elsie preceded me at U of T by some ten years I always thought of her as a contemporary or even younger! Her many achievements and activities were – and remain – truly amazing, ever discounting the tremendous physical handicap she bore throughout her adult life.
>
> I well recall the keen interest she took and her encourage-ment for our fledgling aero engine activity at Malton. [58]

In a slightly different turn of events, Elsie was also asked by Trans-Canada Airlines to review the Avro York aircraft. Biographer Richard I. Bourgeois-Doyle notes that Victory Aircraft had been selected by the federal government to produce the plane. However, initial assessments by Trans-Canada Airlines led to the demand for an independent review, which was awarded to Elsie. The assignment required her to take into consideration design alterations based on the Lancaster aircraft. In the end, despite the repercussions for her husband's plant, she agreed with Trans-Canada Airline's concerns, and the contract was subsequently cancelled.[59]

Elsie also worked on the conversion of the Douglas DC-4.[60] The DC-4 aircraft were originally designed as transport planes for the military, but new models adapted for civilian aviation were pending. The federal government sensed the possibilities and decided to step in and assist Trans-Canada Airlines by obtaining the rights for production of the DC-4 model. The most important alteration was the installation of engines that could sustain frequent trans-Atlantic voyages.[61]

In addition to her consulting work, Elsie represented Canada at the International Civil Aviation Organization (ICAO), established to determine the rules and regulations for civil aviation in the post-war world.[62] Elsie quickly assumed a leadership role within the organization as a technical advisor on aircraft airworthiness.[63] Once again, she was the first woman to receive such an appointment.

In 1947, Elsie was appointed to chair ICAO's stress analysis committee.[64] As Canadian aviation historian Frank Ellis notes, beyond these appointments being an honour for Elsie and an important achievement for Canadian women, they also signified recognition for the nation as a whole in the aeronautical arena.[65] Elsie did not seem to attach much significance to her appointment; she pointed out that she was one of a very small group of experienced aviation personnel in Canada.[66] While her argument was correct, these developments are significant because they provided her with an opportunity to participate in shaping aviation policy. Moreover, her selection identified her as an expert in the field at the international level.[67]

· · · · · · · ·

Elsie's career appears to have been on a continual, unimpeded rise during this period. Despite some initial challenges setting up her consulting firm, she made the transition very well. However, during this time, she had to cope with a variety of family troubles.

These began in 1944 when Elsie's brother Frederick Gregory passed away suddenly due to a cerebral haemorrhage. Elsie's mother, Helen, was especially affected.[68] Shortly after this, Helen experienced two other significant losses: the Vancouver Women's Building, which she had helped to establish, was temporarily closed due to the war, and she had to accept retirement in January 1945 at 81 years of age. Ironically, her retirement coincided with the transformation of the juvenile court into a full-fledged family court complete with professionally trained justices.[69]

Helen sought solace with Elsie. In 1944, she spent the Christmas holiday with Elsie and Bill and then returned to Vancouver to settle her affairs. Her intention was to return to Toronto to live with her daughter. She planned to establish herself as a consultant in the field of family counselling, working from Elsie's Toronto office.[70] However, when she was back in Vancouver, she suffered a heart attack. It fell to Margaret Gregory, Frederick's widow, to arrange the details of Helen's move to Elsie's place in Toronto.

Helen arrived in 1945, just as Elsie was getting her consulting business off the ground. Though clearly affected by recent events, Helen tried not to unduly burden her daughter. She decided to focus on her writing in an effort to ensure that her ideas about juvenile law were not lost.

With this new goal in mind, Helen joined Elsie daily at the office, where they each worked on their respective projects. This arrangement continued until Helen's declining health made her further work impossible.[71] Knowing her mother wanted to be close to her while she continued with her engineering work, Elsie purchased a couch for her use in the office.[72] This unique situation, which lasted until 1947, allowed Elsie to balance her professional and private lives at a time when compensation for elder care was non-existent.

Helen died peacefully one morning during a visit to Helen Jr. in Chicago.[73] The loss of her mother was a major blow to Elsie, as the two women had a strong, mutually supportive relationship. Helen had played an important role in helping Elsie get back on her feet after her bout with polio in 1929. The strong bond between the two was evident in Helen's desire to be with Elsie in her final years, and also in her division of assets among the children. Elsie inherited what was left of the physical estate; her siblings each received one hundred dollars.[74] Although the full nature of Elsie's grief is unclear, her later written reflections in assessing Helen's grief at the loss of her own mother, however, suggest that it was profound.[75]

• • • • • • • • •

The post-war period saw the rapid development of the Canadian aviation industry, and Elsie received many accolades for her achievements within it. Many of her colleagues celebrated Canada's place in the aviation world and eagerly anticipated continued successes.[76]

Elsie was not as quick to applaud the changes underway. On the contrary, she was critical about the narrow focus of Canadian aviation on military projects during the Cold War period.[77] She was quite concerned about the failure to attend to civilian aviation needs.

> This lack of resource, or more accurately *loss* of resource, is perhaps directly attributable to the cumulative effects of thirteen years of concentration on military projects. The enormity of war and the immediacy of its needs stultifies civilian values and numbs civilian critical faculties. Moreover, the habit of accepting military technical aims as the only important aims closes the mind to the value and necessity of also making efforts in other directions. Long and close association with military attitudes and procedures reduces independence of thought, and channels initiative away from other fields.[78]

Her critique foreshadowed the very real problems Canadian aviation soon encountered:

> Moreover, since they [military research projects] tie up our entire aeronautical research facilities, they reduce the field of Canadian aeronautical research to their own confines and limit the sweep of Canadian aeronautical development. Every aeronautical engineer whose perspective extends back twenty years must question the wisdom of the indefinite continuation of this policy.[79]

In her 1956 submission to the Royal Commission on Canada's Economic Prospects, Elsie stood apart from the official submission of the EIC by developing her argument against continuing heavy investment in military aviation projects at the cost of a more balanced approach.[80]

The Royal Commission on Canada's Economic Prospects was tasked with developing recommendations for Canada's optimal economic development during the next twenty-five years.[81] Elsie submitted a report containing an analysis of the future aviation needs of the country: "Some Results of the Anticipated Increases in the Speed of Commercial Air Transport on Canadian Transportation Systems and Industry of the Next Quarter Century."[82] In her submission, she discussed the problems and possibilities associated with high-speed air transportation, anticipating developments up to 1980. She also assessed the nature of the Canadian industry and its needs.

She paid particular attention to the issue of access to technological knowledge. Elsie argued that military domination of the aircraft and embryonic electronics industries was detrimental to future developments because it took precedence over civilian aviation and – because the information was classified – barred public access to the information.

Elsie believed that successful industrial development hinged on reducing the "unnecessary secrecy of military-inspired research" and on facilitating open communication between the military and civilian realms of aviation.[83] She recommended that military and civilian researchers engage in effective dialogue by regularly publishing their ideas and results in journals accessible to the public. This flow of information was crucial as the aviation and electronics industries were evolving at a rapid pace in Canada, and Canadian society needed to be able to adapt alongside them. Elsie foresaw a slowing of overall societal development if the existing practices did not evolve:

> Technical advance is requisite for industrial growth and for a well-integrated, well-balanced economy, and it depends upon knowledge as well as upon materials and power. The Canadian pool of technical talent is relatively small. If industries generally, particularly the primary industries such as agriculture, forestry,

In March 1953, after a decade of living
and working in Toronto, Elsie was well-
positioned as a consulting aeronautical
engineer and was taking an active role
in the Canadian Federation of Business
and Professional Women's Clubs.

mining and fishing, are starved of trained personnel they will tend to operate in a partial vacuum, scientifically speaking. As a result their productive methods, products and market position will suffer, as well the secondary manufacturing industries they foster and [whose] expansion we look to increase employment and raise the standard of living.[84]

Those who learned of her report responded positively to her ideas, and she received requests for copies from government and university departments and libraries.[85] Her assessment of the links between technology and social change formed the backdrop to many of her future public activities.

Elsie's concerns regarding aviation were well-founded. Everything in Canadian aviation suddenly changed with the Diefenbaker government's 1959 decision to cancel the CF-105 Avro Arrow project. This decision sent the industry, and those associated with it, into a tailspin.[86] In fact, it is on account of this cancellation that Elsie's involvement with the Avro Arrow project was revealed. Although she did not provide specifics, she lost her largest contract at that time.[87] As she later stated, "After Black Friday, and in recognition of the reduction in aircraft development and production in Canada, we drastically curtailed our staff and space."[88]

During this challenging time, Elsie focused her energy on seeking other possible contracts, and she avoided any engagement that interfered with her work. Even when asked to speak at the American Society of Women Engineers' 1960 symposium, Engineering Destiny in the Decade of the 1960s, she declined:

I know I do not have to tell you about the low state of the Canadian a/c [aircraft] industry as a result of the past and continuing cancellations. You have probably heard all about it. The past year has been a grim one from the standpoint of getting work and keeping things going – and the present does not appear hopeful. This is not a year in which I can afford time or money [away] from business.[89]

Memories of the cancellation of the Avro Arrow project were on her mind again later in 1962 when she was asked to write an article for *The Business and Professional Woman* promoting her field to young women. Although pressing commitments forced her to decline the offer, Elsie suggested to the magazine's editor that if an article were to be written on the subject, it should counsel the next generation of students to focus on the fields of electronics and space engineering as those areas would hold the greatest potential at the time of their graduation. Clearly disillusioned with her own field, she noted, "[W]ith the death of the Arrow, aero engineering in Canada got a sad blow."[90]

· · · · · · · · · ·

In 1961, Elsie was asked to evaluate two models of the Fairchild Husky aircraft[91] and determine the feasibility – based on then-current airworthiness guidelines – of producing a new model: the Husky F11-3.[92] Her final report provides insight into the difficulties of the task. The existing planes had been designed to meet two previous airworthiness regulations, but the proposed new bush plane needed to meet a new set of U.S. requirements.[93] In addition, Elsie encountered difficulties when she tried to access the records of the previous models; they were scattered between Ottawa and Fort William, in poor condition, and very difficult to read.[94]

Elsie did support the production of the proposed Husky F11-3, but this aircraft never reached the prototype stage. As she had witnessed previously in the competitive aviation market, another bush plane, de Havilland's DHC-2 Beaver,[95] was already being mass-produced and was well on its way to saturating the market.

Although most of her contracts involved stress analysis and potential flaws of aircraft at the design stage, Elsie also became engaged in investigating aviation crashes. She had to work backwards when investigating the cause of a crash and decide whether or not the aircraft was to blame. In 1963, for example, she assessed an accident in which a Piper Tri-Pace Aircraft had crashed, killing all four occupants. She was asked to provide an independent review of the Department of Transport's conclusions about the crash, based on the evidence already collected. After careful study, she agreed with their conclusion that the most likely cause of the accident was wing failure, caused by excessive stressing of the plane's design during flight.[96]

In 1965, Elsie once again actively sought work with the federal government. She offered her services to a number of government departments and in July was hired to provide input on the draft "Approved Aeronautical Engineer Procedure," which later would be a part of establishing a new civil aviation policy for Canada. This opportunity was a good fit for her.

Throughout her career Elsie had worked with the evolving regulations that guided British and American airworthiness certifications. As a result of her experience with ICAO and the Association of Professional Engineers of Ontario (APEO), she was also knowledgeable about various international aviation standards. Elsie felt strongly that the time had come for Canada to create its own regulations, rather than continuing to adapt to British or American requirements.

This opportunity opened new doors for Elsie. In being asked to review this draft document, she was also being offered a chance to assess and provide comment on a future vision of Canadian civil aviation policy. She submitted detailed feedback on July 23, 1965, and as a result was kept abreast of all developments pertaining to the proposed procedure. With the release of the final report in late 1966, Elsie wasted no time in determining a place for herself within the evolving policy. She immediately applied to be design approval representative in the categories of structure and performance.[97] Her initiative was rewarded, and she was appointed to both of the positions for which she had applied. The news of her appointment came with the immediate responsibility to draft the "Operating Procedures of the Design Approval Representative Program."[98]

The appointments gave Elsie access to what was becoming the dynamic hub of Canadian aviation policy. It was also a strategic move for her consulting firm, as it allowed her to offer clients her expertise on regulatory requirements. As scholar John W. Langford notes, Elsie's appointment occurred at a time when this area was growing rapidly:

By 1968, Air Services, numbering about 11,300 officials, comprised several branches and authorities responsible for (1) the licensing of aircraft and personnel; (2) safety regulations; (3) investigations of air accidents; (4) construction, maintenance, and operation of air terminals and aerodromes throughout Canada; (5) the operation of telecommunication facilities in support of civil aviation and meteorological observation and forecasting.[99]

• • • • • • • • •

In 1967, Elsie's former classmates, C.A. Morrison and John H. Fox, were vice-presidents for Canadian General Electric and Honeywell Controls, respectively. It may be tempting to compare Elsie's career choices and position to those of her male colleagues. However, scholar Marianne Gosztonyi Ainley cautions comparing women's careers in science to that of their male colleagues is based on the assumption that the male career trajectory is the norm, which thereby reduces a woman's ability to choose her own direction and self-definition.[100]

Like her mother before her, Elsie dedicated herself to her chosen career and worked late into life. In her late sixties she was once again confronted with the challenges of obtaining work during the general slowdown and layoffs in aeronautics of the early 1970s. She continued to seek new opportunities,[101] offering to undertake work for the Civil Aviation Branch while she was in England in 1971,[102] and taking advantage of opportunities provided by her involvement in aviation, such as a flight over the Arctic Circle with Captain McGoldrick of Pacific Western Airlines in 1970.[103]

Throughout the 1970s Elsie continued working as a design approval representative, travelling to Ottawa when necessary.[104] When asked in 1978 if she would like to continue to hold the position, she said yes, explaining that she anticipated more work in the near future.[105] Indeed, it was not until June 21, 1979, at the age of 74, and after more than forty years of professional service, that she chose to relinquish her status as a consulting engineering with the APEO. Her colleagues within the organization subsequently awarded her the association's Gold Medal in recognition of all the important contributions she had made to engineering and Canadian society.[106]

Footnotes for this chapter can be found online at:
http://secondstorypress.ca/resources and at http://feministhistories.ca/books

Chapter 5
THE FULL MEANING OF
A PROFESSIONAL ENGINEER

She is just completing her year as chairman of the Lakehead branch of the Engineering Institute of Canada, first woman to be so honoured. She actually served most of two terms as chairman, for last year the chairman moved away and left her, in the position of vice-chairman, to take the responsibility. The members declare the two years the most successful in the branch's history – never were the dinners so entertaining as with Miss MacGill at the head of the table.[1]

—The Globe and Mail

Elsie understood that success as an aeronautical engineer depended on participation in professional networks as well as employment in the field. Engineering organizations linked their members and offered services such as professional development; they also helped to monitor and protect the status of the profession by means of entrance requirements and internal regulations.[2] Aware of the importance of these organizations, Elsie sought membership in the ones most pertinent to her field.[3] When she encountered barriers she was not afraid to fight for her right to participate, and the organizations that opened their doors to her obtained a valuable and hard-working member.

Elsie's first bid for membership in a professional society was a bold one. In 1936 she submitted an application to the prestigious Institute of Aeronautical Sciences (IAS) located in New York. Her request met with immediate resistance. Responding to her application, the secretary, Lester Gardner, noted that the organization was not accepting requests for full membership from women. He gave the following reason:

> Our annual dinner and other functions are held at the Columbia Faculty Club and the University Club of New York. At these dinners, owing to regulations over which we have no control, ladies cannot be present and, therefore, we have been placed in an embarrassing position regarding two or three young women who clearly rate membership in one of the grades.[4]

The IAS was not interested in discussing the matter. In fact, it stated that until at least 40 or 50 women applied, discussion of whether or not to admit women would not be worthwhile. Gardner noted that very few women had Elsie's level of education and experience, and so an open policy for women would be divisive because most of the women applicants had lower qualifications and less professional experience than she did. While charged with rejecting Elsie's application for full membership, Gardner did offer her access to partial member privileges, including a reduced rate of subscription to the *Journal of Aeronautical Sciences.*[5]

Elsie did not accept this response; instead she made a case for her reconsideration, systematically reviewing the rationale given for her rejection and offering counter-arguments.[6] She pointed out that "mixed societies all over the world overcome these difficulties as matters of everyday routine. In face of this common fact, it can hardly be a question of the Council's ability to cope with the problem." She then asked, "What do you do with men applicants whose qualifications do not meet the requirements of a full member, yet who deserve some recognition?"

As the field of aeronautics was still quite young, she challenged the IAS decision to not have women members until there were a large enough number of applicants. Elsie knew she would have to wait at least five years or more before enough women were qualified in the field. She argued that this situation was detrimental to a young professional at the dawn of her career:

> Denial of membership cuts me off from being at one with my fellow professionals and robs me of the very real support that membership in such an organization gives to the more inexperienced. I take this denial very seriously because I consider that it hinders me professionally.[7]

Gardner noted that he found Elsie's arguments logical and worthy of attention by the IAS. He promised that he would bring her case forward for reconsideration. However, he also recommended that, as a Canadian, she bolster her application to the IAS by applying to the Royal Aeronautical Society.[8]

The founders of the IAS had looked to Great Britain's Royal Aeronautical Society as a model. Established in 1866, the Royal

Aeronautical Society had a reputation of being highly exclusive.[9] In an effort to emulate this prestigious Royal Society, the IAS courted the most prominent members of the aeronautical community and carefully defined criteria for membership and a grading system for its members.[10] At this point of her career, Elsie's relative measure of prestige could have been questioned, but the arguments against her membership did not cite a specific lack of knowledge and experience; rather, they were gender-based. This is not surprising, as most of the IAS founders, in defining membership regulations, had decided that women did not warrant a place in the organization. Lester Gardner's letters to Elsie indicate that he was not unsympathetic to her desire for membership. In fact, he had challenged the original decision to exclude women. In any case, the IAS maintained its policy of excluding women until January 1939.[11]

The denial did not impede Elsie from pursuing and obtaining memberships in other professional associations. Following Lester Gardner's advice, Elsie applied to the Royal Aeronautical Society, which accepted her, and she became an associate fellow in January 1937. She was subsequently elected to the status of fellow in 1949.[12]

Ironically, her 1955 membership with the American Rocket Society led to renewed interaction with former members of the IAS. In 1963, the American Rocket Society and IAS merged into the American Institute of Aeronautics and Astronautics. Years later Elsie became a celebrated member of this organization.[13]

· · · · · · · · ·

While working at Fairchild Aircraft in Longueil, Québec, Elsie pursued membership in the Engineering Institute of Canada (EIC).[14] Her application – the first from a woman – was received by Robert William Boyle, director of the Division of Physics and Electrical Engineering at the National Research Council of Canada (NRC), and it caused some behind-the-scenes turbulence.[15] Elsie's former professor from the University of Toronto, Dr. J.H. Parkin, then director of the Division of Mechanical Engineering at NRC, recalled that Boyle did not react well to it: "He [Boyle] was shaken to the foundations, and it required considerable effort...to restore his equilibrium."[16]

During Elsie's student days at the University of Toronto, C.H. Mitchell held the position of Dean of Engineering. When she applied for membership in the Engineering Institute of Canada, he served as one of her referees.

Her experience applying for membership in the IAS helped Elsie prepare an application to the EIC. She was confident enough in her experience and abilities to apply for associate member rather than junior member status.[17] She selected referees who were familiar with her career and had clout with the EIC. In fact, although the application requested five referees, Elsie submitted six names: including former professors and the dean of engineering during her years at the University of Toronto and a government referee from the Department of Transport.[18] This was a prudent move, as one of the references did not reach the EIC until after the decision on Elsie's file had been made. Overall, her referees gave strong testimonies on her behalf. All confirmed her good character and recommended she be classed as an associate member within the EIC.[19]

As part of the process for new applicants, Elsie's name was listed in *The Engineering Journal* along with other potential applicants and members seeking advancement in April 1938. The listing included basic information pertaining to her application and the names of her referees. As well, all the existing members were expected to review her request and submit any concerns regarding her suitability to the council of the EIC.[20]

Once Elsie's application and its complement of supporting letters reached the EIC, the final review was held in May, 1938. Of the twenty-nine members who voted on her admission, twenty-seven agreed that she should be admitted as an associate member, and the remaining two split their votes between a full and a junior membership.[21] No one felt she should be barred from membership, and this decision was supported with the arrival of Elsie's sixth letter of reference. Arriving on June 4, 1938, C.H. Mitchell's letter not only "heartily" supported her application but noted that she was "One of the cleverest Electrical graduates from Toronto in recent years. She has had important posts in design of aeroplanes [and] if it were not for illness she would have gone much further by this time."[22]

While her application to EIC was in process, Elsie participated in various professional activities in her field. She likely further strengthened her case for membership when she presented her paper "Simplified Performance Calculations for Aeroplanes" to the Ottawa branch of the Royal Aeronautical Society on March 22, 1938.[23] Her presentation won high praise from *The Engineering Journal*, which noted, "We are informed that the paper reflected great credit on the author and made a definite contribution to the art of flying."[24] Successfully received by her peers, Elsie was eager to share the news with her family:

> Now to tell you about my Ottawa trip. The lecture went off very well. Had a good sized audience and a lot of interest was shown. I left a copy of my paper with some of the men, and they wrote down that they had gone over it, agreed with my method, and considered the paper a "valuable contribution". It is to be published in the Journal of the Engineering Institute. In the midst of all the present excitement I have been busy in my off time preparing the graphs and figures for publication.[25]

When she was about to leave Longueil, Québec, to take up her new position as chief aeronautical engineer at Canadian Car and Foundry (Can Car) in Fort William in 1938, Elsie received notification of her election as an associate member of the EIC.[26] This news marked the first time the organization had opened its doors to a woman.[27] However, since she was preparing to leave the region to assume her new post in Fort William, the Montréal branch of the EIC was taken by surprise. Before her departure, they hastily organized a welcome reception, which reflected the members' uncertainty as to what to expect of a woman engineer and how best to receive her. To conform to social expectations, the president's wife served tea and acted as a chaperone for the event. From Elsie's perspective, the whole experience was quite humorous:

> The amusing thing was that when I arrived – they seemed doubtful as to whether I was "Miss MacGill." They all expected someone rather hatchet-faced – you know the idea. And I arrived wearing a very giddy hat etc. It was funny. The Secretary had sent out an item to the newspaper about it…in which he spoke of me as a "Woman". He said, just before he had left – "I'd never have sent in that item that way if I had known you – you're not a woman, you're a girl."[28]

Despite initial misconceptions, Elsie made a good impression at the reception and was offered valuable assistance in extending her professional network. She was informed that the Montréal branch of the EIC would send notice of her new status to the Lakehead branch (which served engineers of the twin cities of Fort William and Port Arthur and surrounding area) and to the EIC members of her home city, Vancouver. John Challies, then president of the EIC and member of the Montréal branch, expressed regret about losing her as a local member. He also noted that Hubert Martyn Pasmore, the general manager at Fairchild Aircraft Limited, also voiced disappointment that Elsie would not be remaining in the Montréal area.[29] Elsie was obviously torn about leaving the Québec region and her colleagues, as she noted in a letter to her family: "Today is my last day at Fairchilds. I am feeling quite sad about it. However, there is so much to be done that there is little time for grieving".[30]

Despite the brief meeting with the Montréal branch of the EIC, the connections that Elsie made endured throughout her years as an EIC member.

· · · · · · · · ·

The warm reception that Elsie received from her new colleagues explains Elsie's favourable attitude to Canadian engineering organizations. After she arrived in Fort William, she joined the Association of Professional Engineers of Ontario (APEO) – the provincial licensing and regulatory body[31] – and the Lakehead branch of the EIC, where she was officially introduced on October 25, 1938. Some familiar faces were present on the occasion, including John Challies, who was visiting the branch in his role as national president. The significance of Elsie being the EIC's first and only woman member was not lost on the Lakehead branch; in fact, they drew attention to her presence in their entry to *The Engineering Journal* in December 1938.[32]

Elsie did not waste any time in becoming engaged in the EIC initiatives. Five days after her welcome to the Lakehead branch, she gave a cross-Canada address as part of six-part Canadian Broadcasting Corporation radio series on *The Engineer in War Time*. The broadcasts were aimed at helping Canadians understand the important work of engineers. Elsie's address, "Aircraft Engineering in Wartime Canada," was the third in the series and sought to clarify the goals and challenges faced by Canada's nascent aviation industry in response to wartime demands. [33]

Elsie continued to make waves in the EIC. Indeed, two years later at the EIC annual general meeting in Toronto, John Challies took pride in introducing Elsie and her presentation, "Practicable Forms for Flight Test Reporting."[34] His pleasure in Elsie's success that day is reflected in a letter and accompanying photograph of the event that he sent to Elsie's mother:

> It was my privilege, as immediate Past President, to introduce Elsie to the meeting prior to the presentation of her very able and brilliantly presented paper. Ernest Brown, Dean of Engineering at McGill University, whom you will see standing between us, was the chairman of the meeting. To say that Elsie 'stole the show' expresses the real situation very mildly. I never was so proud of a friend as I was of her on that day; indeed, all through the Institute meeting she was the centre of a practically continuous series of admiring colleagues. The best of it was that it didn't spoil her a bit. You have every reason to be proud of your daughter; as a matter of fact, she comes upon her brilliance and winsomeness naturally, for, as I explained to a group at a private dinner, Elsie very wisely chose an ideal mother.[35]

On April 18, 1940, Elsie presented another paper before her colleagues in the Lakehead EIC on the topic "Factors Affecting the Mass Production of Aeroplanes." It too was published by *The Engineering Journal*, but it also won the EIC's Gzowski Medal.[36] Elsie's contribution to the field was recognized by prominent aeronautical engineers such as J.J. Green, who recalled,

> Elsie wrote and delivered scientific papers dealing with aircraft performance analysis and I, with others, was asked to discuss some of them, and they were published in the Engineering Journal of the Engineering Institute of Canada. They all, and one in particular, I recall, represented definite advances in the science of aircraft performance testing and analysis.[37]

· · · · · · · · ·

Elsie's peers appreciated her initiative, drive, and leadership skills, and in 1942 she was elected Chairman of the Lakehead branch. Having already served as Vice-Chairman, Elsie clearly proved she was ready to take on the next level of leadership.[38] Her election added another first to her long list of groundbreaking activities; she was the first woman to serve in this capacity in any branch of the EIC.[39] Moreover, by becoming chairman she showed evidence of her willingness to assume leadership duties, such as liaising with the national body, overseeing the direction of the local branch, and chairing its meetings.[40] Over time she took on many leadership roles in both engineering and women's organizations.

Elsie's sudden departure from Fort William in May 1943 did not rupture her relationship with the EIC. On the contrary, members of the Lakehead branch recalled her leadership as both profitable to the club and enjoyable:

> She is just completing her year as chairman of the Lakehead branch of the Engineering Institute of Canada, first woman to be so honored. She actually served most of two terms as chairman, for last year the chairman moved away and left her, in the position of vice-chairman, to take the responsibility. The members declare the two years the most successful in the branch's history

– never were the dinners so entertaining as with Miss MacGill at the head of the table.[41]

Even after her leave-taking she retained the position of an ex-officio member of the Lakehead Branch.[42]

. . . .

As a young professional engineer at the end of the 1930s, Elsie understood and took advantage of the networking and professional development opportunities available to those who joined professional organizations. Initial difficulties in obtaining membership did not dissuade her. In 1946, not quite ten years after obtaining her first membership, Elsie reflected on Canadian women's access to professional organizations:

> The attitude of the professional organizations has been friendly to women. Here again it seems to be merely a question of knocking to have the door opened, but until women have applied for admittance to all the professional societies no authoritative statement can be made. Again, exclusion from one particular group is relatively unimportant, since acceptance by another is as automatic for a qualified female engineer as for a qualified male engineer.[43]

She saw the provincial associations in a similar light, and even praised them for their lack of "anti-feminism."

> Women are admitted readily to the provincial associations (Associations of Professional Engineers of the provinces), and these are probably the most important connections since provincial legislation excluding non-members from practicing is being sought and enacted. The lack of anti-feminism in these societies indicates engineers as a group to be confident, well-adjusted men who do not follow the pattern of Thurber's frustrated males.[44]

Elsie's accomplishments were also recognized internationally. She was invited to introduce speaker Dr. Lillian Gilbreth, America's "first lady of engineering," who gave the keynote address in 1949 to the First Western Hemisphere Conference of the International

Committee of Scientific Management in Québec City.[45] Reporting for the CBC, John Fisher referred to the two women as outstanding engineers. Fisher went on to lament that Lillian Gilbreth received more acclaim than Elsie, though Gilbreth was the senior of the two and had a long and distinguished career in management engineering.[46] According to Fisher, although Elsie had become well-known internationally during the Second World War, she had fallen from public view since the end of the war. This could be considered a reflection of the marginalization of women professionals in Canadian society or, as Fisher suggested, attributed to the introverted nature of the engineering community, which tended to celebrate accomplishments internally among its members.[47]

In September 1952, Elsie participated in an event in Chicago to celebrate the centennial of the American Society of Civil Engineers. She attended with a contingent of engineers from the EIC who had many ties with their counterparts south of the border. As a result, she was present to honour C.D. Howe, who was being awarded the Hoover Medal for "distinguished public service."[48] At the same time she participated in the convention of the Society of Women Engineers (SWE), an organization established in 1949 that promoted women engineers and offered a supportive environment for its membership.[49] At the SWE convention, Elsie presented her paper "The Initiative in Airliner Design," which was subsequently printed in *The Engineering Journal.*[50]

In the 1950s, Elsie's male peers increasingly acknowledged her achievements. For instance, between 1952 and 1954 she assisted the APEO in the development of their requirements for licensing aeronautical engineers.[51] In 1953, only ten years after she began consulting, her photograph was included in the exclusive Gevaert Gallery of Canadian Executives, in recognition of her influence. This group, which limited its membership to fifty, recognized significant contributions to Canada's industrial development over a fifteen-year period, and Elsie was the only woman selected.[52]

Elsie was recognized internationally by the SWE when they awarded her their annual Engineering Award in 1953. She was the second person to receive this award (Dr. Lillian Gilbreth was the first recipient honoured as SWE's "honorary member number one.") The significance of Elsie's SWE award, especially as she was Canadian, was not lost on her. The EIC had previously adopted Dr. Lillian Gilbreth as one of its twenty-six honorary members, and Elsie saw these reciprocal awards as a means to strengthen ties between these two organizations and their respective countries.[53]

Elsie received her SWE award at their national convention banquet in New York. The chairman of the award committee made the presentation.[54] In her acceptance speech Elsie celebrated the connections among women engineers and paid tribute to the engineering profession itself, identifying personal fulfillment as one of its defining features. With respect to aeronautical engineering she noted: "Some work to fly faster; some work to fly cheaper; some work to fly safer. All work primarily to fulfill themselves."[55]

Colleagues in the Association of Consulting Engineers of Canada (ACEC), which Elsie had joined in 1949, congratulated her on the award. She thanked them in writing, commenting on how she felt about being accepted by her fellow engineers:

This year I enter my 27th year of engineering practice. During that period I have had occasion to remark time and again on the open-minded and generous attitude of my male colleagues to me and to other female engineers. In this particular at least the engineering profession differs strikingly from the professions of law and medicine. I have always felt thankful for this, and very grateful to the many engineers and the several predominately-male engineering organizations that have supported and helped me so loyally in my work. I have come to believe that engineering attracts in general men who are well adjusted, who neither resent nor fear competition and whose objectivity leads them to place accomplishment and effort above personality and sex.[56]

Since many of her male colleagues supported Elsie's trajectory in engineering, it took some time before she was able to re-examine her own experiences and those of other women engineers with a critical lens. Even in the mid-1950s when some younger Canadian women began to speak about discrimination in the engineering profession, Elsie reiterated that through her twenty-six years in the profession she had never experienced any prejudice.[57]

• • • • • • • • •

Elsie maintained her professional networks such as the EIC and the ACEC while also seeking out new ones such as the Canadian Aeronautical Institute.[58] Elsie was also active in the leadership of the EIC for several decades. She served on the executive of the Toronto branch in the early 1960s, and as chair of admissions and membership at the national level between 1960 and 1963. In this position she encouraged the growth of the organization's membership, and helped establish the Oakville, Ontario branch in 1960. Elsie's peers acknowledged her dedication in January 1962, when she was accorded a place at the head table during the EIC's annual meeting. Later, from 1964 to 1967 she sat on the executive as a councillor.[59]

Membership in the ACEC offered her opportunities to advocate for high professional standards and allowed her to develop new business relationships. Again Elsie chose to become actively involved, and between 1965 and 1967 she served as a member of the executive of the ACEC's Ontario chapter.[60] Within this organization Elsie also engaged in legislative reform related to the engineering profession, including the accreditation of consulting engineers. She wrestled with problems posed by the differences in legislation across the country and between national and provincial engineering organizations. During the 1930s and 1960s attempts were made to unite the EIC and the provincial engineering organizations and to support standardized national requirements. It was not until 1964, however, that a formal agreement of understanding was reached between the Canadian Council of Professional Engineers and the Engineering Institute of Canada.[61]

Elsie seized any opportunity she had to express her opinion about the engineering profession. At a joint meeting of the ACEC and the Learned Societies in 1966, she called on her engineering colleagues to examine the application of their skills beyond the specific discipline of engineering. She reminded her peers that as members of the ACEC they were required to hold at least one other membership in a learned society. From her perspective, this requirement raised the status of a professional engineer and also increased professional competence by expanding the knowledge of the engineer.[62]

Elsie noted that just as the medical and legal professions strongly support institutions of learning, research, and learned societies, so too should engineers. She believed this would enable engineers to better meet the demands of those they served.

> More and more we find that because technology shapes social and economic change, we are required to anticipate not only the technical but also the social and economic consequences of our work, bringing subjectivity into an otherwise fairly precise profession. The extra-disciplinary contacts and additional knowledge that membership in learned societies can give, helps us to supply wise advice in public engineering matters, and to acquit ourselves of our obligation to the public.[63]

She did not view the obligation to join a learned society as something onerous: "It is not a grim business. We seek them out – we join them from choice – for love – in love affairs, the mind that begin[s] in curiosity and delight...continue[s] in satisfaction and wisdom."[64] As an expression of this view, Elsie had a membership in the Royal Society of the Arts.

Professional engineers, she believed, should contribute to educational institutions, and Elsie put this belief into practice. Starting in 1967 she served as a guide for the advisory committee on engineering technology at Seneca College and provided input to their courses in aviation.[65] She also wanted to see greater integration between science and society. In 1960, she sent a letter to the editor of the *Financial Post*, responding to an article by J.B. McGeachy, who had reviewed C.P. Snow's book *The Two Cultures and the Scientific Revolution*. Snow's book discussed the polarization of humanist and scientific cultures.[66] Elsie argued that Canadian humanists were over-represented in public affairs and national management, and this created a lack of objectivity in decision-making:

> Probably, too, it is fair to say that in Canada the scientific culture acquiesces in this, and assumes little responsibility for education, public affairs, and government (Witness the few scientists and engineers in government and public life). Perhaps a better balance would improve things.[67]

Elsie's letter described how various engineering-related developments affected the social sphere. McGeachy conceded that Elsie's ability to see the whole picture had enlightened him:

> Since the publication of my perhaps ill-advised remark that I did not know the second law of thermodynamics and considered knowledge of it useless to me in my work, I have heard from many readers anxious to explain the law and its relevance to both conduct and philosophy. Yours is the most lucid and detailed of the letters received; and I am grateful to you...I agree that a person trained in the humanist subjects, like myself, should also soak up as much science as he can hold."[68]

Elsie practised what she preached. She inserted herself in public affairs through her increasing involvement in the women's movement and its various initiatives. She continued to develop an interest in strengthening the links between scientific and non-scientific arenas. In 1973, she helped create and chair The Technology and Society Section of the Toronto branch of the EIC. The goals of the new section aligned with what Elsie viewed as important: "to promote among engineers discussions of the policies and philosophies, rather than the technicalities, or subjects of broad general interest."[69]

· · · · · · · · ·

Elsie remained connected to the University of Toronto – and to many of her former classmates through alumni activities. Although most alumni events involved social dinners and reunions, Elsie and her graduating class of 1927 – the Class of 2T7 – invested a significant amount of time in promoting engineering education. She advanced the idea of establishing a loan fund to assist engineering students in need and simultaneously create a lasting tribute to the class. The 2T7 Memorial Loan Fund was established in April 1955,[70] and Elsie retained a strong interest in it for many years, paying close attention to its management and quickly calling attention to any deficiencies she detected.[71]

In the first half of the twentieth century only minimal financial resources were available for students, and the 2T7 Memorial Loan Fund was an important one. However, when new avenues of funding became available, the fund became less relevant. Elsie championed reinvesting the funds to make a better contribution to engineering education,[72] but a decision was made in May 1967, at the 40th anniversary reunion of 2T7, for the funds to be used in an annual book donation to the library of the School of Practical Science.

Elsie had an enduring interest in her graduating class. Charlie Morrison, the class president, publicly recognized her contribution: "Elsie MacGill's abundant energy has evidenced itself in the effective needling tactics she has been exercising on your President and Secretary."[73] Morrison expressed his appreciation for her efforts by saying, "Thank you very much Elsie for keeping things alive. I don't know what we would do without you."[74]

Elsie carved out a niche for herself as an independent consulting engineer and a prominent member of numerous engineering associations. She kept very busy with many and diverse commitments in the engineering world. These experiences, crucial to her development as an engineering professional, provided a firm foundation for her subsequent feminist activism.

Footnotes for this chapter can be found online at:
http://secondstorypress.ca/resources and at http://feministhistories.ca/books

Chapter 6
TRACING FEMINIST ROOTS AND IGNITING FEMINIST CONSCIOUSNESS AND ACTION

We stand on the shoulders of our predecessors, and build on the foundations they laid. Our wider perspective and better tools of education and communication tell us that the women's movement is part of a much larger movement; that it is a facet of the world-wide democratizing process that began centuries ago; that it is an integral part of the social revolution that carries humanity forward in a great ongoing liberating wave that ebbs and flows.[1]
—Elsie Gregory MacGill

Elsie's feminist journey evolved over time. During her convalescence from polio in Vancouver between 1929 and 1932, she had extensive interaction with her mother and her mother's colleagues. As a young professional woman who had worked for more than a year as an aeronautical engineer in Pontiac, Michigan, and had completed a master's degree, this was a crucial time. Canadian women had just earned recognition as "persons" under the law as a result of the battle waged by the "Famous Five,"[2] and secured new civic rights and freedoms as a result.[3] Upon returning to Vancouver, she was able to renew her connections with the feminist movement in British Columbia.

Elsie's mother, Helen Gregory MacGill, and some of her colleagues had formed the Vancouver Business and Professional Women's Club (VBPWC) in 1923.[4] Other women across the country had formed similar clubs throughout the 1920s, and by 1930 Helen Gregory MacGill was at the forefront in creating the Canadian Federation of Business and Professional Women Clubs (Canadian Federation).[5] This organization created a supportive network of like-minded women, promoted their interests as professionals and businesswomen, and provided educational opportunities.[6]

Sometime during her convalescence, Elsie joined the VBPWC.[7] It is possible that the Canadian Federation's support of women's participation and advancement in the realms of science, engineering, and industry was an incentive for her to join.[8] In 1932, the Vancouver

The year 1929 was a pivotal year for Canadian women. On October 18, 1929 the Privy Council in England overturned the decision of Supreme Court of Canada and declared women "persons." In commemoration, these larger-than-life statues stand in testimony on Parliament Hill in Ottawa, Ontario.

and Victoria Clubs hosted the national convention of the Canadian Federation. It is not clear whether Elsie was able to participate in this convention, but her involvement in the VBPWC linked her with a supportive organization of women who worked together to improve access to training and other opportunities, and to reduce barriers to their full participation in business, the professions, and society.[9]

Elsie did not actively sustain her initial involvement in these networks, however. In the roughly twenty years between joining the VBPWC and her renewed participation in the Toronto Business and Professional Women's Club (TBPWC) in the 1950s, Elsie was busy establishing herself as a professional engineer. During most of the 1930s and 40s, she prioritized her engineering work and her activities in engineering associations over involvement in any of the Canadian clubs.

Once Elsie's consulting business was well-established and the Soulsby children were young adults, she began a new phase in her public life. Elsie's mother provided a role model for this development, effectively combining her legal work with advocacy for women. As she increasingly followed her mother's example, Elsie gradually became a prominent Canadian feminist.[10] She later acknowledged the importance of her mother's influence:

> There is deep pleasure and gratification for me in the link that this Convention has with that first Quota Convention in Banff in 1938 at which my Mother, Helen Gregory MacGill of Vancouver, B. C., was your speaker. She was a judge, I am an engineer; our occupations differ greatly. I am finding now, however, that many of her interests are becoming mine, and that in a small way I work for the objectives she sought.[11]

• • • • • • • •

Shortly after her mother's death in 1947, Elsie became aware that few Canadians knew about or understood Helen's achievements. This prompted Elsie to honour her mother by writing *My Mother the Judge: A Biography of Judge Helen Gregory MacGill*.[12] Writing of her mother's achievements and joining the vibrant TBPWC precipitated Elsie's further development as a feminist.[13]

The idea to write the book and preserve this history arose during a debate on the value of women's suffrage. While Elsie championed women's voting rights, drawing on historical and legal facts she had absorbed growing up in her mother's household, she discovered this information was far from common knowledge.

She began working on the biography in 1947. At first her efforts focused on sorting her mother's papers and determining which ones would be useful source materials. Even though by the 1950s Elsie had published a range of scientific and popular writing, she did not plan to write the biography herself. However, the unfortunate mishap of suddenly breaking her strong leg in 1953 allowed her sufficient time to write the book and bring it to completion.[14] Confined to hospital for three-and-half months and in need of something to occupy her time, she realized that she was already generating useful ideas for the structure and content of the biography. Later, when reflecting on this period she wrote:

> It was when studying and delving into the facts of her life that I became aware that her efforts seemed to follow a pattern, and were a continuation of those of the women of her family before her, and that universal manhood suffrage was comparatively recent and the women's suffrage fight, far from being the solitary struggle I had envisaged it, was simply a continuation of the general suffrage struggle. I wanted these ideas in the book.[15]

Writing the biography, published in 1955, allowed Elsie to explore her family history and better understand the forces that fuelled her mother's active public service. What she discovered, along with her participation in the Canadian Federation, influenced her own feminist development, furthering the consciousness raising that had begun in her childhood.[16] Her writing experience also established her as an amateur historian. In fact, over time she became a strong voice for the preservation of Canadian women's history.[17]

Elsie's training in science and engineering influenced how she approached the telling of her mother's life. Wanting to ensure that her account was credible, she decided to write the biography in the third person to enhance its authenticity. As well, Elsie used quotes from a speech by Justice A.M. Manson at her mother's memorial at the University of British Columbia as headings throughout the biography.[18] She gave the following reason for this decision: "It occurred to me...that use of the speech made by Mr. Justice Manson would give the statements authenticity, and take the curse off a daughter's publication."[19]

To what extent was Elsie successful in achieving her objectives? Many praised the effort, but others challenged Elsie's treatment of her mother's life. Some suggested Elsie made her mother out to be faultless and perfect.[21] Some family members even accused her of purposely avoiding discussion of events that would portray the family in a negative light, such as the extramarital affair of her brother Fred.[22] We will never know to what extent this was true. The fact that Elsie was conscientious about keeping records and preserving family history, including both positive and negative feedback about the book, tends to suggest she did her best to remain objective and factual, well aware of her personal bias on the subject.[23] Regardless of its possible flaws, the biography was important for preserving key aspects of Canadian women's history.

Publishing the biography was a major undertaking, but Elsie was determined that the work of her mother and her colleagues would not be lost or overlooked. Consequently, she was not content merely to see the book printed and move on; instead she actively promoted the first edition, and once its print run had finished, she worked hard to ensure there would be a second.[24] She dedicated a remarkable amount of time toward locating a new publisher in her lifetime; however, the second edition did not appear until after Elsie's own death in 1980.[25]

• • • • • • • • •

In 1951, Elsie joined the Toronto Business and Professional Women's Club (TBPWC). However, she did not rush into the membership.[26] Margaret Hyndman, a long-term member, recalled that Elsie first carefully observed and assessed the club.[27] Once she had made her decision, her initial reserve evaporated and was replaced by enthusiasm and active participation. As a result, she gained access to an important network of like-minded and supportive women peers.

In Margaret Hyndman's opinion, Elsie brought a "new dimension" to the TBPWC.[28] The club was particularly happy to have a professional engineer as a member. Fellow engineer Dormer Ellis, who joined after Elsie, confirmed the club's appreciation of Elsie's participation. Prior to encountering the TBPWC, Ellis had been engaged in organizations composed of male professional colleagues, so she was initially unsure of her reception in the women's club. However, Elsie's presence quickly put her at ease: "No one seemed to think I must be a weirdo because I was an engineer. They already had a member who was an engineer and everyone loved Elsie."[29]

One activity of the TBPWC that particularly engaged Elsie and

Elsie Gregory MacGill
My Mother The Judge
A biography of Helen Gregory MacGill— journalist, social reformer, suffragist, judge, and Canadian heroine.

Introduction by Naomi Black

Elsie worked hard to produce a biography of her mother, and to ensure that it would have the widest reach possible. This second edition was released after her death due to the teamwork of Bill Soulsby, Helen MacGill Hughes and Dr. Naomi Black.

also Dormer Ellis was the Occupational Information Bureau – later called Career Preview – for young women in high school.[30] Ellis knew firsthand about the importance of this work, as she had been actively discouraged by a high school teacher from pursuing engineering studies. The Career Preview demonstrated that any career was possible for young women – as attested by the accomplishments of members of the Toronto club.[31]

In addition to demonstrating that multiple career options existed for young women, the members of the TBPWC and the Canadian Federation worked to assist young women to pursue these goals.[32] In 1955, for instance, Elsie encountered an advertisement for air traffic controllers issued by the federal Department of Transport, specifying that the applicants had to be male. Elsie called on the clubs within the Canadian Federation to address this deliberate sex-typing: "As there is no reason why women should not be eligible for these jobs I suggest that the Federation protest in writing to the Transport Minister and to the Civil Service Commission."[33]

Elsie was aware of the financial difficulties that students often confronted when pursuing engineering as a career, which is why she encouraged her engineering Class of 2T7 to establish the Memorial Loan Fund in 1955.[34] She extended this kind of support to women engineers in the late 1950s when she chaired the Society of Women Engineers' Lillian Gilbreth Scholarship Fund.[35]

Elsie and her TBPWC colleagues were also concerned with the issue of financial aid for women entering the professions. In 1956, they created the Elsie Gregory MacGill Bursary, initially, intended to assist young women planning to teach science in secondary school. When they ran the first competition they realized that other factors besides financing were hindering women from entering this field of study. School principal J.B. Wylie challenged the criteria for the bursary, arguing that not enough women had the required background to merit the award and so the money should be made available to a wider range of disciplines.[36] The TBPWC held its ground, and Maie Ehasoo was selected as the first recipient. Elsie presented the award in April 1957.[37]

Over time the criteria for awarding the bursary were amended to support women interested in science and engineering and to remove the requirement of teaching in secondary school. In 1968, Elsie tried to make the bursary more lucrative by proposing an amendment that would strongly support women in science and engineering at the University of Toronto with increased funding of $750 over three years. The bursary committee reviewed the idea and determined that such revisions were unnecessary on account of women's limited enrolment numbers. The demand for the Elsie Gregory MacGill Bursary was not consistent, but it was awarded three times between 1957 and 1978.[38]

· · · · · · · · · ·

In joining the TBPWC, Elsie became allied with a very active group of Canadian women who worked diligently to advance women's status in Canadian society.[39] Initially, her participation in her local club was eclipsed by her extensive activities in the provincial and national levels of the organization; however, in the long term there were mutually beneficial and long-lasting relationships.

Shortly after joining the Toronto branch, Elsie started to serve at the provincial level in the Business and Professional Women's Clubs of Ontario (BPWCO). The provincial organization offered Elsie networking opportunities with clubs across Ontario, as well as connections with the Canadian Federation and its international parent organization.[40] Provincial conferences offered members access to interesting programs and international guest speakers. It is likely that Elsie contributed to these events from the beginning, as the 1951 provincial conference in Toronto featured Dr. Lillian Gilbreth speaking on the topic "Some problems that challenge women today."[41]

Elsie's involvement in the Canadian Federation reflected her interest in judicial reform within Canada. Her enthusiasm is not surprising given her family's legal legacy. Elsie demonstrated her own interest in the legal system when she studied common law at the University of Toronto (a course in which she excelled).[42]

As a member of the Canadian Federation, Elsie quickly assumed a number of leadership roles for which her previous activities in engineering organizations had prepared her. For example, she spent two years as chairman[43] of the jury study, tasked with educating women on their new rights as potential jurors in Canadian courtrooms.

From 1954 to 1956 she also chaired the Penal Reform for Women Joint Committee, which recommended substantial changes related to the probation, detention, and rehabilitation of women inmates. The changes advocated for women were not revolutionary. Instead, they called for the services and facilities equal to those that had been available to male prisoners since 1927. More specifically, the committee called for increases in the number of women probation officers, improvements to the reception centre, and a better means of classifying new arrivals at the Andrew Mercer Reformatory for Females.[44] The committee publicized the recommended reforms in a pamphlet for distribution to the general public.[45]

The Canadian Federation was one of eighteen women's groups within the Penal Reform for Women Joint Committee, and Elsie's involvement increased her exposure to women activists across the country. The committee included key feminists such as political trailblazer Agnes Macphail, the first woman to serve in the House of Commons and the Ontario Legislature.[46]

Elsie's additional commitments, such as chairing the Canadian Federation's Survey and Research Committee, included a study of the nation's prisons and probation and parole practice, which complemented her leadership in the Penal Reform for Women Joint Committee. She was continually learning and acquiring new information, and she felt compelled to apply it, as she explained to the Canadian Federation's executive secretary her rationale for rewriting sections of the organization's "Survey Plan of Work of Reformation Among Female Offenders in Canada."[47]

Elsie's peers acknowledged her leadership, as demonstrated by her selection as chair of the Penal Reform for Women Joint Committee.[8] Elsie's long-term involvement in penal reform gave her the satisfaction of reporting on successes as they occurred. For instance, between 1955 and 1957 she announced the creation of new juvenile and family courts and the appointment of growing numbers of women probation officers across Ontario. These triumphs also represent the ongoing living legacy of the feminism passed from mother to daughter.[49]

The Penal Reform for Women Joint Committee continued its work until 1960, when the group decided to disband, as they felt their actions had been successful in drawing attention to the need for reform. They also believed they could exert more pressure on various levels of government from within their respective organizations. To manage the dissolution and conclude the group's work, a history committee was convened, and Elsie's concern for women's history made her the natural choice for chairman of the new committee. She assumed responsibility for the final report and ensured that remaining funds and archives were properly disposed of.[50]

At this time Elsie's output was remarkable, especially considering her ongoing work as a consulting aeronautical engineer, her work on her mother's biography, and having to cope with a broken leg. The president of the BPWCO, Margery Pewtress, made special note of Elsie's contributions related to penal reform in her biannual report:

> This [C]ommittee, under the chairmanship of Elsie Gregory MacGill, did a tremendous amount of research and the final recommendations, endorsed by all the organizations represented on the Committee had considerable impact on the Government Committee. In fact, the conviction has been expressed that under Miss MacGill's guidance and enthusiastic impetus, The Archambault Report[51] [Royal Commission on Penitentiary Reform] may yet be implemented.[52]

· · · · · · · · ·

As well as her activities to reform the legal and penal systems in the 1950s, Elsie was very involved in the internal organizational concerns of the BPWCO. She served on one of its committees to revise and consolidate internal governance procedures, provincial procedural amendments and resolutions.[54] This work addressed the core functioning of the Canadian Federation at both the Ontario and the national levels, which meant that future resolutions would be better supported and less likely to be redundant. Elsie's intimate knowledge of the content and evolution of key organizational documents facilitated her rise within the Canadian Federation.

In 1955, four years after joining the TBPWC, Elsie's dedication to her local and provincial clubs was formally recognized. On September 15, 1955, she was nominated to the position of provincial president.[55] Elsie accepted the nomination, and the BPWCO subsequently elected her for a two-year term from 1956 to 1958. Elsie was ready and willing to engage in her new duties, and she chose a powerful motto for the coming two years: "The Answer is Woman Power."[56]

"Womanpower" was originally a propaganda tool employed during the First and Second World Wars to mobilize women in support of the war, both in the workforce and on the home front.[57] However, the Canadian Federation and the Women's Bureau of the federal Department of Labour reintroduced the idea and updated it to call for the full participation of women in the public and economic life of Canada in the post-war period. Elsie believed that employing women in scientific and educational professions as well as in administrative and executive posts was essential for achieving social and economic change in Canada.

In her closing address to the 1956 BPWCO conference, Elsie criticized the shortsightedness of Canadian leaders:

> The surprising thing is that this great source of talent is being blindly ignored at a time when we are being constantly warned that Canada needs ideas, needs great numbers of trained minds and skilled hands, and that our industrial development will suffer without them. Surely we can only conclude that, with a few exceptions, our officials, educators and industrialists suffer a blind spot that limits their vision to manpower.[58]

Elsie argued that women had responsibility in bringing about these changes. Women needed to demonstrate their workplace skills and abilities, and invest in the development of their own careers if they wished to become economically independent and able to contribute to the nation's development.[59] She urged her audience to have confidence in themselves and to encourage the next generation.[60]

Elsie did not take her role as provincial president lightly.[61] At this time, the Ontario organization included almost 3,500 individual members organized into seventy-four local clubs. Elsie tried to ensure that the clubs functioned as efficiently and effectively as possible, and one means to do this was by reorganizing the existing provincial structure. She worked with the Ontario clubs to establish four management districts for the province. Each district was assigned a vice-president, who also held a position on the provincial executive. The changes were designed to increase communication and delegate leadership more broadly. Elsie noted "that it was no longer possible for the Provincial President (herself a working woman) to deal personally with the organizational problems of each Club or undertake extensive Club visiting." Despite these challenges, she attended many regional meetings and kept in touch with the membership through frequent letters and memos.[62]

Elsie worked on revisions to the members' handbook, focusing on club protocol. It quickly became apparent that this work should go beyond the provincial level, and members of the committee decided to refocus the work on a national handbook. Concerned about accountability to the members, Elsie went out of her way to report on what was achieved during her years at the helm. She later used similar reporting methods in other leadership roles.[63]

In addition to provincial restructuring, Elise supervised the creation of two new committees: a Clubs Promotion Committee and a Public Relations and Publicity Committee.[64] These bodies helped to promote the goals of the organization to the wider Ontario community and to tackle membership growth, an issue Elsie championed within the Canadian Federation at all levels.[65]

As provincial president Elsie had the opportunity to associate with some international women leaders including Lisa Sergio, a prominent anti-fascist activist and commentator on international politics,[66] and Vera Brittain, a well-known British writer, public speaker, feminist, and pacifist.[67] Both of these leaders made presentations during the BPWCO International Night banquets.

After 1958, when her mandate as provincial president ended, Elsie stayed on as past-president and remained active in the provincial executive.[68] In 1960, she and Nazla Dane, the new president of the BPWCO, went with a delegation to meet with then Premier of Ontario Leslie Frost and his cabinet.[69] Their purpose was to lobby for two key resolutions passed at their provincial conference: equal pay for work of equal value (something the clubs had advocated since the mid-1950s) and representation of women on the pending provincial anti-discrimination committee.[70]

. . . .

In 1952, prior to becoming president of the BPWCO, Elsie started what would become a four-year term as Chairman of the Survey and Research Committee of the Canadian Federation. In this position she served as national historian and carried out research and other projects assigned by the national board of directors.[71] One of her tasks was to undertake a national survey to assess the treatment of women prisoners in Canada.[72] This work ran parallel to that of the Penal Reform for Women Joint Committee, benefiting both initiatives.[73]

As a chairman of a national committee, Elsie was privy to communications of the Canadian Federation's board of directors, and she was quick to offer her opinion on national decisions. Early in October 1952, she voiced her objections to proposals by the board and President Margaret Campbell to limit membership on national committees, arguing, "I believe that wide dissemination of office promotes interest and activity in organizations, and that concentration of offices in a few hands kills interest."[74] Margaret quickly came to respect Elsie's input. By December 1952, she was consulting Elsie on matters such as the Canadian Federation's response to a planned federal government bill on non-discrimination. She questioned whether the Canadian Federation should demand that the bill include specific provisions to prevent discrimination based on "sex" if discrimination against a "person" was already in the bill. Elsie responded that they should indeed pursue this route, as "'sex' includes both male and female, and its use in such a Bill would prohibit discrimination against men by women as much as the reverse; I favour such impartiality." She further pointed out that the term "person" was still not adequately interpreted as including women throughout the entire country.[75]

Elsie was involved in a wide range of women's issues and discussions that were occurring internationally. For example, during the biennial convention of the Canadian Federation held in Toronto in 1954, the members called on the federal government to ratify the United Nations Convention of the Political Rights of Women and the International Labour Organization (ILO) Convention on Equal Remuneration.[76]

At that convention Elsie had her first opportunity to address

the national membership as a whole. In an address entitled "A Blueprint for Madame Prime Minister," she envisioned the vast social changes that Canada's first woman prime minister would make possible.[77] Elsie laid out an ambitious agenda, including ratification of pertinent international conventions and the creation of comprehensive national health insurance.[78] Her prime ministerial agenda also called for improvements in the federal Department of Labour so as to avoid mass unemployment, modifications to the *Criminal Code*, a reassessment of the decision to close the women's penitentiary in Kingston, Ontario, and the establishment of a national department of education.

At the Canadian Federation of Business and Professional Women's 1954 convention in Toronto, Elsie addressed the membership with her speech "A Blueprint for Madame Prime Minister".

In her speech, Elsie noted that since the turn of the century, women's organizations had been a force for positive social change:

> Our Federation petitioned for and supported anti-discriminatory legislation. In each province, our Clubs work with other women's organizations for a great variety of causes [including] penal reform, child welfare, part-time employment for women,

employment for older workers. I mention these recent activities simply to show that the work started by the suffragists is still being carried on, and if anything, at an accelerated pace. In a single-mindedness that is awesome, this work has always [been] directed toward people, and has operated to humanize Canadian law.[79]

Elsie believed that the qualities of "humaneness, cooperation, and determination" would guide a woman prime minister; however, she acknowledged the existence of many practical barriers to achieving an ambitious national agenda, including the division of powers between the provinces and the federal government as set out by the *British North America Act*. Undaunted, Elsie recommended reforming the Act to eliminate provincial-federal conflicts in key areas such as education and healthcare.[80]

The theme of our Convention is Women – Horizons Unlimited. By analogy there are many horizons – horizons of opportunity, accomplishment, aspiration. Like the natural horizon, the limitation they place on us is only a psychological one, not a real one, and we are limited only to the extent that we recognize the limitation. If we stand still our horizon is static; if we advance it moves forward too; if we draw back it closes in on us.[81]

Elsie called on women to take up public positions as a means of expanding the horizons of individual women and to achieve social change:

A public position is a stepping stone. It gives a chance to do a job of work and to fulfill the urge to accomplish. It provides a vantage point for demonstrating capacity for greater responsibility, and for obtaining that public recognition that is so essential for advancement in public life. I think it [is] important to realize that it is the position itself, the job, that builds up the individual in the public eye and wins that national recognition upon which depends the popular acceptance of the individual as a candidate for top office. No matter how able she is, a woman cannot be king-size in a little job. The king-size jobs go by appointment! It is because few women are appointed to king-size jobs that few woman are known the length and breadth of Canada, that few women have national reputations and are recognized as leadership material.[82]

Understanding the importance of obtaining public leadership positions for women, Elsie and the Canadian Federation lobbied the government for the inclusion of women on public bodies and boards.[83]

· · · · · · · · ·

Many members of the Canadian Federation served together for decades. As a result, strong bonds formed among them. Elsie benefited from these relationships throughout the years. A glimpse of the depth and value of these ties surfaces through the letters exchanged among Elsie, Bess Forbes, editor of *The Business and Professional Woman*, Isabel MacMillan, Chairman of the Public Relations Committee, and Hazel Laycock, President of the Canadian Federation from 1954 to 1956. The women referred to one another by nicknames and initials in their frequent communications.

Together, they were heavily engaged in club affairs at the national level, including the production, under Elsie's leadership, of an authoritative list of Canadian women serving in public positions. Though their communication depended on letters sent through the post, they were in such frequent contact that Hazel Laycock was moved to comment: "Really, I've been so busy reading your interesting letters, news releases, comments, etc. as well as deciphering who was to, and who was from. I have decided to call you THE UNBEATABLE TRIUMVIRATE."[84]

These women shared joys, successes, and fears. Bess Forbes complimented Elsie's initiatives in the production of the authoritative list of Canadian women, noting, "It will be invaluable not only to our own members but [for] all women in Canada. Personally, I feel a great pride that it is one of our federation committees that has pioneered the way in this work – and done it so well."[85] Later, when Elsie expressed misgivings about the final product, Bess Forbes praised the list and Elsie's leadership:

I also agree that it is a tremendous piece of work and that it is bringing much recognition to us. All bouquets we receive re the first effort – and this next list, too, should certainly go to E.G. [Elsie] and her committee. As you say, Hazel, let's keep our fingers crossed and hope we get as good a chairman for this survey as EG has turned out to be – when she decides to relinquish the job.[86]

When Elsie gave a radio address that she thought was sub-par, she wrote, "Hope you are unable to get a radio to hear me on Matinée as I consider it very poor. I am no good off-the-cuff – if otherwise. I am trying to forget all about it just now." But instead, she received further encouragement from this group of women; Hazel Laycock noted that while she did not catch the whole program, what she did hear was excellent.[87]

While the group was generally supportive, the women also took one another to task when their opinions differed. After the first *Authoritative List of Canadian Women in Public Life* was published in 1955, Elsie started to prepare for the second. As the list would be featured at the 1956 congress of the International Federation of Business and Professional Women (International Federation), she wanted it expanded to include an international list of women in public life. Bess Forbes quickly challenged this idea, arguing that an all-Canadian publication would be more impressive: "Will you therefore take my advice for what it's worth, think the thing through sanely and logically and come up with the right answer? Please do!" She summed up her letter, noting, "Coming back at you – and with glass raised, E.G., you'll be a piker, yourself, if you don't take out all the stuff outside of Canada."[88] Elsie capitulated, and the list remained Canadian.

• • • • • • • • •

The seventh triennial congress of the International Federation was held in Montréal, Québec, in 1956: the first time the congress was hosted in North America. The event was attended by 463 Canadians, and Margaret Hyndman of the Toronto BPWC was elected as the new international president for 1956–1959.[89]

Elsie was directly involved in some of the planning for the congress, and *The Authoritative List of Canadian Women in Public Life* was released during the event.[90] The congress offered her an opportunity to attend business sessions and social and cultural events, and to engage in a wide range of networking activities. Probably the only disappointment for Elsie was the absence, on account of illness, of the International Federation's President, Dame Caroline Haslett, who like Elsie was a trail-blazing woman engineer.[91]

Among the topics discussed at the congress was the request for national federations to conduct studies on automation and how it affected both employment and standards of living.[92] Subsequently, Elsie was instrumental in responding to this request by exploring and reporting on the social benefits and challenges of technological change.[93]

The 1956 national convention of the Canadian Federation, which followed on the heels of the international congress, was Elsie's first as BPWCO president. Maudie Baylay became the new president of the Canadian Federation; therefore, the presidents at the Ontario, national, and international levels were all TBWPC members.[94] The national convention addressed the need for Canada to ratify international agreements, including the ILO Convention 100 on Equal Remuneration and the UN Convention on the Political Rights of Women, which declared the right of women to participate in government, to access public services, and to vote or hold office. The national convention also called for the increased participation of women in the public sphere and set up jury committees to help educate women who had only recently started serving on juries in Canada.[95]

By the late 1950s Elsie had gained considerable experience in the provincial and national matters of the Canadian Federation. At the national board meeting in Toronto in June 1957, she demonstrated leadership: asking questions, volunteering ideas, and moving motions. She recommended that surplus funds be reserved for establishment of a national office in Ottawa. She also moved that the theme for the 1958 convention be "Improving the Status of Women."

Elsie's subsequent appointment as chairman of the new bylaw committee in 1958 comes as little surprise. In this position she and other committee members reviewed the constitution and recommended changes to bring the document in line with the current realities of the organization.[96] Elsie's knowledge of the inner workings of the national organization was a key resource in the coming years.

In March 1959, Elsie was part of a delegation that met with then Prime Minister John Diefenbaker to promote the agenda set out by the Canadian Federation at their national convention. Among other things, the delegation asked for revisions to the *Federal Income Tax Act* and for more women to be appointed to the newly created National Parole Board. This was the first of several meetings Elsie had with Canadian prime ministers on behalf of the Canadian Federation, and it was Elsie who prepared the summary brief of resolutions for submission to the government.[97] This meeting may have been difficult for her, as it occurred shortly after the Diefenbaker administration had announced the cancellation the Avro Arrow project on February 20, 1959.[98]

Elsie took on many leadership roles in the late 1950s, but to strike a balance with her engineering work, she also turned down some appointments, including membership on the National Parole Board.[99] Still, her many activities with the Canadian Federation put her at the forefront of many social issues in Canada and honed her leadership skills. Her colleagues recognized Elsie's contributions and, in November 1957, made her a lifetime member of the Canadian Federation.[100] She was well-situated to take the next step in her feminist journey.

Footnotes for this chapter can be found online at:
http://secondstorypress.ca/resources and at http://feministhistories.ca/books

Chapter 7
A NATIONAL VISION

The common purpose of our Federation is the improvement of the economic, employment and social conditions of women, and we implement this purpose in many ways – for before a purpose can breathe the breath of life it requires specific direction.[1]

—Elsie Gregory MacGill

She's known among federation members for her great organizational ability and her quick wit.[2]

—The Telegraph Journal

In 1962, the Canadian Federation of Business and Professional Women's Clubs (Canadian Federation) held a national convention at St. Andrews-by-the-Sea, New Brunswick, preceded by a two-day board of directors meeting.[3] Going into this convention, the outgoing national president, Una MacLean Evans, urged the Canadian Federation to boost its financial and membership resources to more effectively tackle the increasingly "complex needs of Canada's working women." She also emphasized that the club needed to attract younger women into its ranks.[4] More than 450 delegates attended the event, representing clubs from coast to coast.[5] Elsie attended the board meeting and the convention as the newly appointed chairman of the international committee that linked the Canadian and International Federations and managed relations with international organizations such as the United Nations (UN).[6] However, a promotion was in store for her.

During the early 1960s the Canadian Federation worked on many issues, and this was reflected in the program, resolutions, and speakers of the 1962 convention. Workshops addressed the roles of working women in government, international affairs, club membership, and the nation as a whole.[7] Women's employment was a central concern. Marion Royce, Director of the Women's Bureau of the Canadian Department of Labour (Women's Bureau), and Esther Peterson, the U. S. Secretary of Labor and Director of their Women's Bureau – and the first woman appointed to a cabinet post in that country – were keynote speakers. The assembly passed a resolution calling for an investigation into women's part-time employment,[8] and passed other resolutions related to issues being debated nationally at the time. For example, they called on the government to establish Royal Commissions on abortion and on divorce.[9] (Abortion was illegal in Canada at that time, and the laws addressing it were ambiguous and full of contradictions; divorce was difficult to obtain.) Agreement was reached during the convention to pursue action on part-time work, equal pay for work of equal value, equality for women in minimum wages, pension benefits, and retirement age, and also to undertake studies on Canadian taxation and the effects of automation on working women.[10] There was also agreement to initiate an internal project to consolidate the Canadian Federation's records.[11] The new board of directors was charged with an ambitious total of eighty-four different objectives for the period 1962–1964.

Leading up to the convention, members of the Canadian Federation were asked to submit nominations for the new president and national board of directors. Two long-term colleagues and friends agreed to stand for the position of president: Nazla Dane and Elsie MacGill. Although both women were well qualified for the position, Elsie was elected president, and Nazla Dane became first vice-president.[12] When the results were announced during the convention, the media asked Elsie to what degree her physical limitations would influence her effectiveness, and she replied that they were not an issue: "The only thing is that I get to places on time because I know I can't run the last half mile."[13]

Despite Elsie's previous experience at the national level, she realized that she and her executive faced a major challenge, and that the majority of club members – who did not actively participate at the national level – had high expectations of the new executive.[14] Elsie got to work immediately after the election. On the train travelling home from the convention, she conducted an informal survey among her travel companions regarding their impressions of the event; this survey provided insight for planning the next convention in 1964.[15] Later, she worked with the board of directors to review and divide up the responsibility for all the resolutions passed at the 1962 convention. The board of directors delegated key issues to the provincial presidents and their respective clubs and the national club's thirty-one standing and sub-committee chairmen.[16] A few months after her election, Elsie reminded the members of the Canadian Federation that everyone had an important role to play in achieving the goals established at St. Andrews-by-the-Sea:

> We like women bosses. Ours – all 7,300 of you – are easy to please, hard to satisfy – and work us hard, too. At the 1962 Convention you issued 84 mandates for us to implement during our two-year term as Directors of Federation, in addition to the usual load of organizational and committee work. [...] 13 of these mandates are short-order items and have been dispatched. Six call for committees – PENSION PLANS, CORPORATE MEMBERSHIP, FEDERATION FUND, FEDERATION-OWNED HEADQUARTERS, MANAGEMENT TRAINING and FIVE NATIONAL REGIONS which by now have been formed. 10 need extra money, so although we can plan them now, their execution is delayed until after May 1963 when the Federation fee per Club member jumps from $3.00 to $4.50. The remaining 55 mandates involve work.
>
> Then there are the 26 mandates of the International Federation [International Federation of Business and Professional Women] from the 1962 Congress at Oslo, Norway. [...]
>
> We welcome their great program with its liveliness and vigor. We hope that you look forward with enthusiasm to replying to the questionnaires, requests for information, calls for money – that we send you to honour the projects you voted for. Good luck![17]

As national president, Elsie was process-oriented, and she applied the analytical and organizational skills she had learned in her engineering, management, and consulting work in developing detailed plans and actions for achieving the objectives of the organization. At the same time she demonstrated leadership on the specific goals of the Canadian Federation: leading delegations, writing letters and articles, and encouraging the national membership to advance working women's rights in Canada and abroad.

Elsie did not act in isolation. When she required support and information she sought assistance from key colleagues, including

Una MacLean Evans, Immediate Past President, and Nazla Dane, her friend and new First Vice-President and chairman of the International Federation Committee. Both these women supported Elsie during the early days of her presidency. For instance, Una MacLean Evans assisted with the preparation of the Canadian Federation's input to the International Federation's submission to the UN Global Study on Occupational Opportunities, and Nazla Dane reported on the status of the western clubs after a 1962 fall tour.[18]

Elsie sought advice and assistance from women such as Marion Royce, director of the Women's Bureau and a member of the Ottawa club.[19] She was happy to assist Elsie in work on employment issues and suggested that Elsie make a formal request to the government to have the Women's Bureau carry out the study of women's part-time employment.[20]

The key questions that the Canadian Federation wanted addressed included a better understanding of the demand for part-time work by both women and employers, and the overall experience of the part-time worker.[21] Royce encouraged the Canadian Federation to undertake its own studies at the level of the local clubs to provide a more complete picture of women's part-time work. After consulting with her colleagues, Elsie agreed, and a study of part-time work was added to the responsibilities of the Canadian Federation's employment conditions committee.[22]

• • • • • • • • •

Again, Elsie quickly earned the respect and admiration of the members, and as she settled into her new role she established good working relationships with the board of directors and committee members. She was quick to remind the members that she was open to new ideas, and decisions on any new course of action occurred after open discussion. As she noted in a letter to Isabel MacMillan in November 1962, "Just because I put forward an idea does not mean that I might not change my mind about it after seeing what you people say. In other words, don't count my opinion as always favouring my own idea strongly – I too can change my mind occasionally."[23] Elsie's openness to debate built respect and trust between her and her leadership team. For instance, in December 1962, Isabel wrote to Elsie, saying, "I used to be scared of you, Elsie, but since I got to know you better at Oslo [during the congress of the International Federation], I have come to appreciate that your motivation is prompted by a very real desire to raise the status of BPW."[24]

Elsie encouraged all members to write to her if they had critiques and suggestions to improve the leadership's direction. She further implored every member to do their part, first by outlining how they could help and what she as national president required from them, and then by linking their work to the larger picture of both the Canadian and International Federations:

> Obviously it is the potential that we should consider – the potential power of each Club member, no matter how new, and of each Club no matter how small, to set in motion the whole machinery of the Federation – and thereby change a situation or course of events in the community, the province, the nation – indeed, the world.[25]

As she had done during engineering assignments, Elsie produced regular progress reports and sent them to the board of directors. These reports reflected her high level of organizational ability – which she had demonstrated at the helm of the Business and Professional Women's Clubs of Ontario – and ensured transparency about her activities.[26]

Elsie's presidency was not without challenges, and sometimes she needed her executive to question her ideas. In February 1963, this task fell to Nazla Dane, who was shocked to learn that Elsie wanted to avoid formal media events during her cross-country tour to the western clubs. Nazla advised that this decision would be very unpopular with the membership: "It isn't often that I disagree with you to the extent that I feel that I must put it on the record…but I do this time and I am." She pointed out that Elsie's presence at clubs across the country would provide them with much needed publicity, and it was not something she should deny them.[27] Elsie listened to the counsel of her first vice-president and friend and altered her plans.[28]

• • • • • • • • •

The Canadian Federation was determined to increase its membership and to establish 100 new clubs across the country. Such an achievement would increase the prominence of the organization and help it achieve its goals.[29] The goal of increased membership was reflected in the theme "Reach Out and Grow," which Elsie believed all aspects of the Canadian Federation's activities should support.[30] In a presentation during Business Women's Week in 1963, Elsie reminded the membership that "we sometimes forget that many who have not joined have never been invited. Let's make sure our WELCOME mat doesn't read 'SCRAM!'"[31] Earlier Elsie had outlined her views on what the Canadian Federation's clubs were looking for in its members:

> No one can live in a vacuum – least of all the working woman.
> Our Clubs were created for women who are not content to
> be time-servers, whose interests extend beyond their own line
> of work, who want to keep informed about and participate in
> public matters, and in a broad programme to promote better job
> opportunities and conditions of work for women.

She argued that if the clubs were able to meet the needs of Canadian working women, then "[l]ike bees to a honeypot, new members" would seek out the Canadian Federation.[32] In a later address to the Toronto club members, Elsie highlighted the club's attention to the need for daycare and better opportunities for young women – issues of concern to potential new members.

One such strategy was the Career Preview initiative, seen as an effective means to increase the influence of the Canadian Federation, especially with a younger generation of Canadian women.[33] This initiative was designed to open the eyes of young women to training and careers they might otherwise not have considered due to restrictive social expectations:

> We must extend to girls and women the same degree of social
> approval to seek higher education and career training in all fields
> of endeavour that we now accord to boys and men. I do not
> say that there are fields now closed to girls – I personally do not
> know of any. I do say, however, that there is steady social pressure
> on girls to take a short-term irresponsible view of employment,

and to direct them toward "women's work" rather than opening wider fields to them, and a conscious or unconscious effort to limit women to secondary roles in business and industry, and to overlook them as candidates for training opportunities within the organization.[34]

The Canadian Federation's magazine, *The Business and Professional Woman*, supported this initiative by featuring a wide range of stories on interesting and engaging career paths held by a wide variety of women.[35] Beyond these actions, the Canadian Federation lobbied the government to increase the amount of vocational guidance available to students at all levels, as well as the available courses and facilities for technical training.[36]

The Canadian Federation wanted to become more inclusive, which required changing their letters patent. As the federation was incorporated at the federal level, such changes required the approval of the Secretary of State – which was received in September 1963.[37] The changes to the letters patent allowed for a greater focus on girls and younger women, as well as on women employed in industry and the trades.[38] Additional revisions made to the letters patent at this time reflect the organization's expanded goals:

a. To develop and train women in business, the professions, and industry

b. To work toward the improvement of economic, employment and social conditions for women

c. To work for high standards of service in business, the professions, industry, and public life

d. To stimulate interest in federal, provincial, and municipal affairs and to encourage women to participate in the business of government at all levels

e. To encourage and assist women and girls to acquire education and training[39]

These goals were similar to objectives recently updated by

the International Federation.[40] Elsie guided the clubs through the revisions, reminding them that change was an important aspect of engaging with the world around them.[41]

• • • • • • • • •

One of the ways that Elsie communicated with members and also non-members of the Canadian Federation was through their magazine *The Business and Professional Woman*. Twelve issues were produced during the period of Elsie's presidency, and each issue included the president's column. Isabel MacMillan, editor at the time, encouraged Elsie to use the magazine as a communications tool, as she believed that most members turned to the magazine rather than club mailings to keep abreast of new developments.[42]

Elsie seized this opportunity to advocate for her presidential goals and those of the Canadian Federation. For instance, she used the column to challenge all the clubs to triple the national membership to 25,000 over a five-year period. She also encouraged the publication of articles in French, which was difficult because of the associated costs. However, Elsie made sure her president's message was bilingual and that key articles – such as her speech "Deux Langues et un Point de Vue," which argued that language differences need not inhibit united action – appeared in French.[43]

Under Elsie, the magazine served as a key business tool for the Canadian Federation. Members of the board of directors, committee chairmen, and the editorial team used it to reach out to the membership and to educate and call for action on existing initiatives, such as amendments to the divorce regulations. The magazine was used to inform members on issues such as the impacts of automation in the workplace and to enlighten them about how the International Federation functioned.[44] During the 1964 convention, the May-June issue doubled as a convention issue for the first time, making it possible for members who could not attend the convention to be well-informed about the event.[45]

Time did not always permit Elsie to write for the magazine. When asked to contribute an article on engineering careers for young women, she declined.[46] Her workload made the additional commitment impossible. However, she advised Isabel MacMillan that the article should be geared toward electronics and space engineering rather than aeronautical engineering, where opportunities had diminished markedly after cancellation of the Avro Arrow project.[47]

• • • • • • • • •

Elsie continued to develop the concept of "womanpower,"[48] which had been discussed in the Canadian Federation for several years, partly in response to the federal Manpower Development Program designed to integrate unemployed and underemployed workers into a workforce that was undergoing rapid technological change. The government specified the need for vocational training, but failed to identify women as a target market, especially for the new knowledge-based positions and technology-related jobs.[49]

The public message Elsie prepared for Business Women's Week in 1962 suggested that the projected manpower deficit would be solved by womanpower, and that women's work was vital for "boosting the economy and building Canada."[50] For women to make that contribution, however, many issues affecting them inside and outside the workforce needed to be addressed. Elsie outlined these issues in a public message:

> We are concerned with the study of wage and salary rates paid to women, job levels, career opportunities, pension and retirement plans, part time employment, together with the laws and regulations, particularly affecting women, dealing with equal pay, taxation, inheritance, minimum wage, independent domicile for married women, jury service and other public matters.[51]

As she travelled across the country delivering speeches to the members of the Canadian Federation, Elsie developed the ideas she had espoused during her earlier tenure as provincial president of the Business and Professional Women's Clubs of Ontario. Advocating a belief that Canadian society was benefiting from technological change, she saw the need for women to prepare for new requirements for skilled workers. Elsie did not discount the challenges that would await women's full participation in the labour force, and she encouraged her colleagues to marshal their efforts to affect positive social change for women, especially the next generation. She said, "You cannot have drastic economic changes [due to technology] without a considerable degree of social change at the same time. Indeed, the economic change waits on the social change, not vice versa."[52]

Elsie began a cross-country tour in May 1963, beginning with a conference jointly hosted by the Alberta, British Columbia, and the Yukon clubs, and then travelling eastward, attending conferences of the provincial organizations as she went. Her schedule was demanding, but she also made time to visit members of her family en route.[53]

During her tour Elsie delivered a many speeches to club members, highlighting key topics from the 1962 convention. She paid particular attention to social changes resulting from the introduction of new technologies, especially automation,[54] which was an issue of concern for the Canadian and International Federations.[55] Even in the midst of concerns such as the loss of jobs, Elsie – as a professional engineer – was aware that the wave of technological change would bring opportunities for new employment.[56] She believed that science and technology were inherently beneficial, despite the fact that their applications were not all positive.[57] She had a nuanced view of the complexities of long-term change:

> Many of us grew up when scarcity – not abundance, and work – not leisure, were very much the rule. Down the years we have gratefully accepted the gradual increase in our standard of living, and the gradual shortening of our work-week – which result from industrialization – without giving much thought to the social changes that these produce. Few of us relate industrial and economic changes to changes in industry and commerce, government, the family – that is the changes in social institutions. We accept these institutions as relatively unchanging. Each of us probably unconsciously incorporates into our idea of the role of each, those of the new ideas that we like, – rejecting those we don't like, – we continue to call them by the same names, and so to us they seem relatively unchanged.[58]

In Elsie's opinion these technological changes had tremendous potential for improving human life:

Industrialization is based on technology, and it is the rise of technology that – for the first time in human history – is freeing humanity from want and grinding toil, and bringing closer the age-old dream of abundance and leisure for all.[59]

Her ideas were based on an optimistic belief that society could truly benefit from technological change if it was accompanied by social change. In her view, "It is only habit, custom and complacency that keep us chained to outworn ideas and outmoded institutions. Once we recognize the desirability of change we can readily find the way to accomplish it."[60]

What would these changes mean for Canadians and, specifically, for working women? Elsie argued at the TBPWC Conference on the Arts of Management that technological change would bring increasing demands on the skills and abilities of workers, and would require additional training and skill development over the course of a career.[61] She encouraged the conference participants to "take the wheel," as management training would put them in an excellent position to adapt to the changing workplace. She foresaw the shift toward a knowledge-based economy, and in this context, Elsie championed women's potential to excel:

Women will give fresh answers to these questions as the Canadian economy shifts to automation, and Canadian society undergoes the transition from a mechanized society to an automated one. Permeating the whole fabric of Canadian living, technology and automation will introduce totally new concepts of what is desirable and what is possible of achievement. The change is one to affect the whole economy, the whole social order – methods of production, distribution and utilization, techniques and procedures, types of occupations and jobs, the general structure of employment, working conditions and surroundings, hours of work, rates of pay, concepts of value, education and training, leisure pursuits, patterns of living. Our culture, which has always made it easier for men than for women to develop their capabilities may be entirely altered.[62]

However, she also cautioned against complacency, noting that ultimately the best skilled workers would reap the most benefits:

There is no turning back now even if anyone wanted to. You can't return a scrambled egg to a state of nature. Every available skilled person will be needed to man the new occupations and jobs which technology and automation create. Since women are Canada's only unutilized reservoir of talent, a greater proportion of women will be needed in employment. It will not be a question of whether to hire a man or a woman – but a question of which has the training and competence called for.[63]

To support her ideas Elsie lobbied the government to make use of the talents of women by appointing them to key public roles, such as new commissions and public boards. She also commended the government when it appointed women to these leadership roles.[64] She argued that the stereotypes and discriminatory beliefs that women were not capable of mechanical, mathematical, or managerial tasks hindered social progress:

> What may be more difficult for us as Canadians to see is that social attitudes here must change before all-out industrialization becomes possible, and that actually Canada, too, has a "caste" system of a sort. Before our nation can marshal her full resources of ability and skill, Canadian traditional attitudes toward women must change, the present waste of womanpower must cease, the reservoir of knowledge, skill and ability in the female half of our population must be brought into full usefulness.[65]

She elaborated her arguments with concrete examples:

> For working women all down the line, the unfair and unrealistic disabilities and differentials in rates of pay, wages, salaries, career opportunities, job levels, employment benefits, pension and retirement plans should be eliminated, for these discourage women from taking employment and dishearten and penalize them when they do.
>
> For married women, conditions should be such that they can seek and accept outside employment without having to overcome unnecessary obstacles and face unnecessary arguments and social disapproval. A new set of values in the marriage partnership which recognize the equality of the spouses [should] be developed and implemented.[66]

Elsie took action to effect change in this area by leading a delegation to the Royal Commission on Taxation (Carter Commission) on May 8, 1963. The Canadian Federation's brief was based on the recommendation of the 1962 convention and a detailed study involving all ten provinces and the participation of almost 200 clubs. The recommendations presented to the commissioners ranged from improvements on individual taxation to the needed changes in the *Estate Tax Act*. The proposals sought to increase women's economic independence and, at the same time, increase the stability of the Canadian economy as a whole.

From their perspective as business and professional women, the members of the delegation believed that in crafting its recommendations the Carter Commission should consider ideas such as marital income-splitting (a practice accepted at the time in the United States); a flat rate of taxation versus a graduated one; and direct tax credits. They coupled these concepts with proposed amendments to the current legislation. For instance, they argued that spouses engaged in a business partnership should not be penalized by having restrictions on their salaries because they were married. To ease the double burden of working women, they called for the introduction of housekeeping exemptions for working women. Their rationale for these changes was that "[t]ax incentives which would increase personal purchasing power would tend to stimulate a desire for a higher level of education; stimulate Canadians' savings habits, and investments in their own country's economy – and have the overall effect of increasing business and employment."[67]

Elsie also raised concerns about stereotypes that led to inequality in pay between women and men. Fundamentally, equal pay was avoided through the use of discriminatory job descriptions that favoured men over women, regardless of the actual difference between the jobs each typically held. In addition, many women found themselves blocked from job advancement or continuing education, which diminished their desire to do their best work. Elsie argued that this situation ultimately stalled national progress.[68] She called on her sisters in the Canadian Federation to alert women and girls to the changing pattern of women's employment, and to the fresh opportunities opening now to those who will accept the new knowledge. "This is the type of activity that validates the existence of the Club and makes good the Federation's claim to unique service. Our Federation is of a size and character to generate and sustain a successful chain reaction to revolutionize women's employment across Canada."[69]

Also, Elsie encouraged the clubs to consider how they could assist girls and older women in meeting their education objectives. In the case of young women she argued:

> We need a more flexible system of higher education to provide for the girl who wants to continue her formal education unbroken while marrying and raising a family. Our society approves youthful marriage and parentage for young couples, and generally considers late marriage and late parentage less desirable. Also we set an ever-increasing value on the worth of higher education and specialized training. We consider it praiseworthy when a young man persists in finishing a course of training or university work, and combines this with marriage and a job. Yet we take the view that the girl who wants to do the same thing is wrong. If she marries before completing her formal education, it is difficult, if not impossible for her to complete it. Our social attitudes and our rigid educational system force her to choose between early marriage and being well educated. This is irrational, and inconsistent and contrary to social justice. Furthermore, it is not necessary. All that is called for is that our educational system be oriented toward the needs of women as well as of men. [70]

• • • • • • • • •

In addition to her extensive tour of the Canadian Federation's clubs, Elsie led delegations to meet with two Canadian prime ministers: John Diefenbaker in 1962 and Lester Pearson in 1963.[71] The purpose of these visits was to inform the government leaders and cabinet members about the goals and recent resolutions of the Canadian Federation and lobby for the changes the organization sought.

To ensure that the Canadian Federation and its objectives were taken seriously during these brief meetings, Elsie planned the events very carefully. In advance, she asked the participating women to indicate which resolution they preferred to present – and she assigned a resolution to any delegate who did not volunteer to present one. She stressed that they needed to restrict their discussion to matters related to the resolutions from the previous convention, such as abortion, divorce, part-time work, and pensions, and to the mandate of the International Congress, including Canada's ratification of International Labour Organization (ILO) Convention 100 on equal pay. Under no circumstance were they to discuss any other matters with the prime minister. Elise's pre-planning helped her ensure the professionalism of the delegation.[72]

The meeting with Diefenbaker was an amicable affair, especially as one of their own honorary members, Ellen Fairclough, then serving as postmaster general, welcomed the delegates.[73] Elsie presented the resolutions on abortion and pensions. Even though her call for a Royal Commission on abortion had been commended by the media, the prime minister was not enthusiastic. Diefenbaker made no promises at the meeting, but he did congratulate Elsie on the quality of the brief she presented. In any case, Audrey Rider, executive secretary-treasurer of the Canadian Federation, described the results of the meeting as very positive:

> I do hope that you were not utterly exhausted after that hectic day on Wednesday. The interview and luncheon were most happy and relaxed but I did think you must have found it very wearing with those interviews by the time it was all over. You should be justifiably most proud of yourself and your briefs (memoranda, that is!). I have had occasion to telephone the P.M.'s office, the National Productivity Council and the Department of Labour today and although I have been cordially tolerated in the past, I can assure you that today the reception was rather overwhelming. So our public image is shining more brightly than ever since November 21st. Heartiest congratulations![74]

The 1963 meeting with Pearson was also positive and involved the media. The delegates revisited issues they had raised with Diefenbaker, including requests for formal inquiries into divorce and abortion. They also discussed the need for more studies on pensions and a comprehensive study on part-time work, which characterized the employment of many more women than men. Indeed, Elsie noted that a study on part-time work could potentially debunk

A delegation from The Canadian Federation of Business and Professional Women's Clubs presents a brief to Prime Minister Lester B. Pearson

SEPTEMBER · OCTOBER 1963

assumptions about women in the workforce – such as the belief that women worked part-time because they preferred it – and provide a better understanding of the demand for such work by workers and employers. In response to the need for Canada to ratify ILO Convention 100, the prime minister acknowledged its importance but explained that action had been delayed due to questions related to provincial and federal jurisdiction and other pressing national issues that had postponed its debate in parliament.[75]

The interaction with the prime minister was enhanced by Elsie's sense of humour. "The photographers and press came in at the end of the interview," she explained later, "and we had the pictures taken. He [Prime Minister Pearson] was sitting, and he asked me which side I wanted to be on, so I asked which was the Treasury side, which got a laugh." The meeting was congenial, and the prime minister strongly praised the delegation for the quality of their arguments: "This is the most impressive brief I have received since I became Prime Minister."[76]

These lobbying events put the Canadian Federation on the radar of the government's leadership, and also allowed the organization to reach out to the Canadian public through press releases and media interviews.

· · · · · · · · ·

In July 1962, Elsie led the Canadian delegation to the Ninth Congress of the International Federation in Oslo, Norway.[77] This took place less than two weeks after she was elected president of the Canadian Federation.[78] The Canadian delegation consisted of forty-three members and six directors of the Canadian Federation, with Elsie and Nazla Dane serving as the voting representatives.[79]

The delegates discussed the recent interventions that the International Federation had made at the United Nations – with input from their national federations and member clubs – on women's property rights, education, private law, and marriage. The delegates were urged to have their member clubs lobby their governments to ratify ILO

In 1963 the Canadian Federation met with Prime Minister Lester B. Pearson. He congratulated the club on the quality of their brief. The Canadian Federation made good use of this media opportunity, networking with the press and highlighting the event on the cover of its magazine *The Business and Professional Woman*.

Convention 100 on equal pay, to continue work toward women's economic rights and opportunities, to undertake studies on working women's access to childcare, and to support women in developing countries. The delegates also asked the International Federation to assist its members with strategies to attract younger generations into their clubs.[80]

The Canadian delegates took an active role in the proceedings, including participation in sessions that reaffirmed support for the United Nations, the expansion of women's education internationally, regional seminars, and the need for the International Federation's history to be compiled and recorded.[81] Nazla Dane led a session on vocation guidance and career advancement, one of four topics addressed during the workshop on the United Nations program. The other three topics included advisory services, access to education, and assistance to women in developing countries.[82] The TBPWC had been a leader in the area of young women's career development since the 1950s; by the end of the congress the International Federation passed a resolution supporting vocational guidance.

After the congress, Elsie and the delegation brought the resolutions that required national action back to Canada. One of these, "Consideration of Opportunities in Science and Engineering," was an issue close to Elsie's heart. The resolution called for each national federation to take action to support women's entry into science and engineering careers. The Canadian Federation was well on its way to meeting these objectives through its career guidance programs.[83]

During the congress the Canadian delegation committed to providing financial support for seven women training to be teachers at the United Nations Relief and Work Agency's Training Centre for Women in Ramallah, Jordan.[84] Throughout the two-year period of Elsie's presidency, members of the Canadian Federation maintained a strong interest in the Ramallah students who were featured in *The Business and Professional Woman*. Club members were also able to connect directly with the young women via site visits and letters.[85]

This new commitment aligned with the Canadian Federation's strong support for vocational training and for the United Nations Association of Canada through the UNESCO Gift Coupon Project. This fundraiser surpassed expectations during the 1960–1962 biennium, and by the time of the 1962 national convention, Canadian clubs had raised more than three thousand dollars. Elsie recommended allocating these funds via the United Nations Association of Canada to women's educational facilities in Ghana, Iran, and Nigeria.[86] The national director of the United Nations Association of Canada, Wilson Woodside, recognized the Canadian women's leadership in this area, writing, "There is, in my experience, no stauncher supporter of the ideals and works of the United Nations in Canada than your organization."[87]

By the end of the congress the members had elected a new executive for the International Federation, including two Canadian members: Ruth McGill from Regina, Saskatchewan, appointed second vice-president, and Margaret McIrvine from Ottawa, appointed finance chairman. These appointments continued the Canadian Federation's history of support for the International Federation,[88] whose president, Elisabeth Feller, expressed her appreciation of the strong and friendly Canadian involvement at the international level.[89]

In between the International Federation's congresses and board meetings, the national clubs were expected to stay in touch with international developments and respond as appropriate. For example, when the United Nation's Convention on Consent to Marriage, Minimum Age, and Registration of Marriage opened for member country signature in December 1962, Elsie, on behalf of the Canadian Federation, commended the Canadian government for voting in support of the convention and encouraged the government to become a signatory.[90]

The annual International Federation Night held by each of the Canadian clubs also introduced and connected members of the local clubs to the larger vision of the International Federation. As president of the Canadian Federation, Elsie was responsible for preparing the statement to be read by each club during its individual celebration. In her 1963 message, linked to the selected international theme "Responsibilities of Individual Freedom," she asked the clubs to reflect on the importance of public responsibility:

> To all but the faint-hearted among us, responsibilities are a welcome call on our ability and energy. Our individual responsibilities supply the zest and joy of living; our family responsibilities,

responsibilities to our friends, our work, our club, our community, nation and the world at large – life without these would be worth little to any of us.

Let us exert ourselves then, and take joy in them. Let us work for the club, the Federation and the International Federation with zest, and light-heartedness, remembering the while that our individual freedom brings us individual responsibilities, and that these are the light of our life.[91]

Her words reflected her own views on public engagement and her vision for the Canadian Federation.

In April 1964, near the end of her presidency, Elsie led a second Canadian delegation of twenty-nine members to an International Federation board of directors meeting in Canberra, Australia.[92] Much of the meeting focused on recommendations to the United Nations (UN) and its agencies. One such resolution called on the UN and other international organizations to address women's needs when planning engineering projects in developing nations; for example, water supply projects should be designed to reduce the burden on women who collected water for their households.[93] Elsie strongly supported this resolution and committed the Canadian Federation to undertake a further study on this issue if required.[94] She also moved a resolution on the expansion of UN training centres, such as the one piloted in Ramallah, and to examine post-training employment possibilities.[95]

Elsie and other Canadian delegates supported major changes in the UN's policies on women. In December 1963, the UN General Assembly had asked the UN Commission on the Status of Women (CSW) and the Economic and Social Council to prepare a draft document on the elimination of discrimination against women.[96] The CSW requested input – in the form of comments and proposals – from organizations such as the International Federation by September 1964.

The International Federation, which had held consultative status at the UN since 1947, was keen to voice the opinions of its membership. The delegates at the board meeting in Canberra prepared a series of recommendations in the form of an emergency resolution, which was subsequently forwarded to the UN. This resolution

called on the CSW to incorporate into the draft declaration existing principles that supported women's rights – principles derived from current international conventions and declarations by the UN and the ILO. The resolution also highlighted the importance of addressing marital status as a basis for discrimination, an issue that had been overlooked in other conventions. Finally, the delegates strongly supported the goal of equal educational opportunities for women in all fields.[97]

In addition to using *The Business and Professional Woman* as a tool for the 1964 national convention, it also served as a means to report on the success of the event to members. This two-page spread of the crowning event of Elsie's presidency demonstrates both the serious business and fun times engaged in by the attendees.

At the end of the CSW consultation process, a draft declaration was initiated in 1965 and completed in 1967. The resulting Draft Declaration on the Elimination of Discrimination Against Women was considered groundbreaking by scholar and activist Devaki Jain:

> The declaration made the first attempt to define discrimination against women by referring to laws, customs, regulations, practices, and prejudice as being responsible for denying and limiting women's equality of rights with men. It viewed discrimination as incompatible with human dignity and the welfare of society.[98]

At the International Federation board meeting in Canberra, members also called on the CSW to meet annually to ensure that important documents related to the status of women could be adequately discussed and debated by all interested parties.[99]

. . . .

In July 1964, Elsie presided over the biennial convention of the Canadian Federation in Ottawa. As the convention marked the end of her two-year term as national president, Elsie used the occasion to highlight the compilation of all the Canadian Federation's resolutions since 1930 and review the organization's achievements.[100] According to Elsie, the changing resolutions illustrated that "setbacks are temporary, that gains come slowly but are cumulative and lasting, [and] that the results which flow from our efforts are seldom exactly as we planned them. Yet the responsibility to plan is ours."[101]

Elsie's review highlighted the whirlwind of activities that had taken place during her tenure, including forming special committees to investigate and propose changes to Canadian laws, financial practices, and social services; encouraging the study of the emerging issues of abortion, divorce, part-time work, pensions, and automation; preparing and presenting briefs to several inquiries and commissions; writing letters to and lobbying two prime ministers; revising the Canadian Federation's internal procedures and safeguarding its history; and reaching out and encouraging the membership to take ownership of Canadian Federation's national and international goals, and to take action to achieve them.

Speakers at the 1964 national convention included Judy LaMarsh, Minister of National Health and Welfare and Minister of Amateur Sport; Claire Kirland Casgrain, the first woman to be elected to Québec's National Assembly and serve in its cabinet;[102] and Ottawa Mayor Charlotte Whitton. Judy LaMarsh offered a broad perspective on the status of women in Canada, contrasting it to the situation in the United States. She called attention to the President's Commission on the Status of Women in the United States, and argued that Canada would benefit from a similar study.[103] Her comments were prophetic: Canada did create a similar commission in 1967.

Observers and the media noted the efficient organization of Canadian Federation convention, the hard work of its members, and Elsie's leadership and ability to keep the meetings on track. At the end of the proceedings the Canadian Federation entered a new two-year period with Nazla Dane at the helm and a new slate of resolutions, ranging from continued pressure for revisions to taxes, pensions, and unemployment insurance to the establishment of forensic clinics and psychological testing of sex deviants before their release.[104]

. . . .

Elsie became the immediate past president of the Canadian Federation for a two-year period. This change in status did not much affect her participation at the national level.[105] She continued to serve in delegations at the federal level and accompanied her colleague and new national president, Nazla Dane, when she presented the 1964 convention resolutions to Prime Minister Lester Pearson and his cabinet.[106]

During this time, Elsie maintained strong links with her adopted home province of Ontario. She attended the twentieth annual conference of the BPWCO in April 1966, participating as the parliamentarian; in this role she interpreted the rules of order to maintain proper

A radiant Elsie and her sister Helen on January 16, 1965 at the Second Seminar of Occupation Perspectives hosted by the Montreal Business and Professional Women's Club.

parliamentary procedure during the meeting. She also represented the national organization, contributing comments when necessary.[107] During the meeting, she noted that the new community colleges being established across Ontario supported the BPWCO objectives for expanded vocational education. She therefore supported a resolution calling for women to be included in the management of the eighteen new applied arts and technology colleges. The resulting resolution called for the creation of a committee responsible for identifying the names of qualified women.[108] Her advocacy in this area was followed by concrete action when she served as a guide for the Advisory Committee on Engineering Technology at Seneca College in Toronto, starting in 1967.[109]

Elsie continued to be present at club events across the country.[110] On one of these occasions she had an opportunity to work alongside her sister.[111] Together, the two participated in the Second Seminar of Occupation Perspectives hosted by the Montréal club in 1965.[112] Helen's address, "Women and Authority," echoed some of Elsie's earlier speeches: "If women are to rise from low status work, there must be first an attack upon convention. And then there must be the wisest possible sort of guidance for girls from infancy and kindergarten days, to show them what work there is in the world."[113]

Elsie concluded the proceedings with a speech entitled "Woman as Boss." In her written summary of the proceedings, Phyllis Hardy, the coordinating chairman, emphasized the strength and authority of Elsie's presentation, noting that she was like a "minister in a pulpit – she was holding forth and no one could gainsay her remarks."[114]

In her detailed account of her achievements as the president of the Canadian Federation, Elsie acknowledged that she had been privileged to travel widely, including to the 1962 international congress and the 1964 board meeting of the International Federation. As a result, she recognized the importance of allowing others to have similar opportunities. Thus, when initially approached to be a delegate to the International Federation congress in Washington, D.C., in 1965, she recommended that members who had not previously had the chance be given the opportunity to attend.[115]

The engaging and supportive atmosphere of the Canadian Federation ignited Elsie's feminism in the 1950s and allowed her leadership to blossom in the early 1960s. Her involvement at the local, provincial, national, and international levels provided her with unparalleled opportunities to learn and grow as an individual, and to share her knowledge and experiences with others, notably in the areas of science, technology, engineering, and procedural planning. Elsie continued to champion the concept of womanpower that gave her a powerful platform from which to call for the full participation of women in the Canadian economy and in public life. She wholeheartedly believed that a woman, "[a]s a source of imagination, wisdom, talent and purposeful activity...[was] Canada's greatest unused potential."[116] Upon finishing her term as immediate past president of the Canadian Federation in 1966, Elsie did not have long to wait for a new adventure. In just a few months an exciting new opportunity appeared.

Footnotes for this chapter can be found online at:
http://secondstorypress.ca/resources and at http://feministhistories.ca/books

Chapter 8

ASSESSING THE STATUS
OF CANADIAN WOMEN

*It is possible that the effects of this Commission will reach further
than people think. When considering the status of women, it is
important to realize that for both men and women technology is
rapidly changing the existing Canadian patterns of employment,
full-time and part-time work – and leisure, too – and the social
and economic values upon which status is based. Insight gained
there could drastically change Canada's social philosophy.*[1]

—Elsie Gregory MacGill

Once Elsie's term as immediate past president of the Canadian
Federation of Business and Professional Women Clubs came to an
end, it was not long before she encountered a new challenge as a
commissioner on the Royal Commission on the Status of Women
(RCSW) in Canada, established in February 1967 by the Liberal government of Lester Pearson. Other countries had already established
similar commissions.[2] The relative prosperity of the 1960s, combined
with social pressures for change, including an international wave of
feminist activism, created the conditions for a public review of the
status of women in Canadian society.[3]

Canadian women's organizations, including the Canadian
Federation, had laid the foundation through several decades of
education and lobbying. In the early 1960s, newer women's groups
formed to fight for women's rights. The combination of established
organizations and the new, more radical groups created a strong
and diverse movement that advocated powerfully for changes
to the sexual status quo within Canada.[4] These conditions were
complemented by the support of at least two prominent Members
of Parliament (MP), Secretary of State Judy LaMarsh, and New
Democratic Party MP Grace MacInnis.

Canadian women's groups also lobbied for a royal commission
to study and make recommendations on the status of women.
Under the leadership of feminist activist Laura Sabia, thirty-two
English-Canadian women's organizations formed the Committee

for the Equality of Women in Canada in 1966 to demand such a commission. The members of the recently established Féderation des femmes du Québec joined their English-speaking sisters to mount effective public pressure on the federal government.[5] Laura Sabia may have provided the final impetus for establishing the commission in January 1967, when she told a reporter from *The Globe and Mail* that:

> Two million Canadian women may be asked to march on Ottawa if the federal government fails to announce by the end of the month a Royal Commission on Women's Rights...We're tired of being nice about trying to get an official inquiry into women's rights in Canada. If we don't get a royal commission by the end of this month, we'll use every tactic we can. And if we have to use violence, damn it, we will.[6]

Laura Sabia's fighting words made front-page news across the country, and by February 16, 1967, the Royal Commission on the Status of Women had been established.[7]

· · · · · · · · ·

The federal government charged the commission to "report upon the status of women in Canada, and to recommend what steps might be taken by the federal government to ensure for women equal opportunities with men in all aspects of Canadian society."[8] A rumour circulated that Laura Sabia would be chosen chairman. The federal government, however, perceived her as too radical for this role. Instead, they chose the more conservative Florence Bird, a media personality better known as Anne Francis.[9]

After the chairman was appointed, Lester Pearson and Judy LaMarsh chose the rest of the commissioners from across the country. Lola Lange, active in the 4-H Club and the Alberta Farm Wives' Union, was appointed to represent rural women.[10] Jeanne Lapointe, a professor of French literature at the Université de Laval, had previously sat on the Parent Commission (1961–1966).[11] Jacques Henripin, who headed the Department of Demography at the Université de Montréal, was included for his research on social demography. Doris Ogilvie of New Brunswick brought her extensive legal background and experience as a practising judge. The balance of the commission included Elsie Gregory MacGill and Donald Gordon. Elsie was both an engineer and a businesswoman, and Donald Gordon had a background in broadcasting and political science. This original configuration changed slightly when Gordon left the commission and was replaced by John Humphrey of New Brunswick. Humphrey brought impressive legal expertise and international experience to the commission, as he had served as secretary-general of the United Nations' Human Rights Commission and had prepared the first draft of the Universal Declaration of Human Rights.[12]

A royal commission with a majority of women commissioners, including the chairman, was a complete departure from previous practice. However, in other ways the composition of the RCSW was not so different. As scholar Cerise Morris notes:

> Its commissioners were drawn from the upper levels of society, were mainly of English-Canadian origin, and resided mainly in central Canada. The majority of the commissioners had acquired impressive social honours through their occupational accomplishments.[13]

Elsie's diverse experiences resulted in skills that contributed to the general functioning of the commission. Her experience in a male-dominated profession gave her a unique perspective on gender relations. She knew that women could and should work with men to accomplish important tasks. Elsie's history as a feminist also proved crucial in educating the other commissioners who were not so familiar with the issues.[14]

Prior to her appointment, Elsie had some knowledge about the workings of royal commissions since she had prepared an individual brief for the Royal Commission on Canada's Economic Prospects as well as a later brief on taxation for The Royal Commission on Taxation or Carter Commission.[15] She had high hopes for social change coming out of the work of the RCSW. At a speaking engagement at the University of Toronto she said:

> Review of earlier federal Royal Commissions confirms that implicit in the appoint[ment] of a Royal Commission is the idea of change. Go back to the Royal Commission on the Penal

System in Canada which reported in 1938, to that on Arts, Letters and Sciences which reported in 1951, to that on Health Services reporting in 1964, to that on Taxation which reported in 1967, and to that on Bilingualism and Biculturalism which also reported in 1967. All these Commissions considered and recommended changes and innovations. Quite properly then, the Royal Commission on the Status of Women is considering changes in the status of women – where status simply means the state or condition of a person in the eyes of the law and of other people.[16]

Elsie also looked forward to integrating into the commission's report a better understanding of the potential impacts of technological change on opportunities for women.

It is possible that the effects of this Commission will reach further than people think. When considering the status of women, it is important to realize that for both men and women technology is rapidly changing the existing Canadian patterns of employment, full-time and part-time work – and leisure, too – and the social and economic values upon which status is based. Insight gained there could drastically change Canada's social philosophy.[17]

When discussing the RCSW with members of the Canadian Federation, she argued that it had the potential to move beyond a question of women's rights or equality to consider how women were perceived in society and to assess the disadvantages women faced due to prevailing social attitudes.[18]

While Elsie was optimistic about the commission's potential for change, she was also realistic. She noted that women needed to be dedicated to achieving the needed reforms and willing to seek the support of Canadian men:

To effect any major change in the status of women in Canada, whether it be in the personal sphere of individual relationships, or at the level of social organization in government, business and the like, requires not only vigorous spokesmen and pacesetters among women, but also the firm support of men. Improvements in the status of women is simply a further extension of democracy and like all extensions of democracy, it requires the support of men. Will men help? Are they willing to share equally with women their prerogatives of major decision-making in international matters, in government and community affairs, in business and industry, in family life? I hope they will be fair minded and generous in this.[19]

In challenging both sexes to work together to improve women's status, Elsie pointed out that an examination of men's status was crucial when working toward a properly functioning society.

Elsie's sister and brother-in-law were especially supportive of her appointment to the RCSW, and both wrote to Elsie, congratulating her. Everett Hughes, a prominent sociologist who referred to himself as her "neo-feminist bro-in-law," celebrated her appointment and the opportunity it presented:

> The idea is, this job takes a new brand of research – for it is the place of women in an entirely new kind [of] labor force you have to discover – and project into the future.
>
> More power to you – you'll have to put the innovating ideas and vigor into this. [...] But you, dear sister, will have to make this the outstanding thing, the example to the rest of the world as well as to Canada, that it ought to be.[20]

• • • • • • • •

Elsie was committed to producing an objective and compelling report based on clear evidence. She assisted with structuring the commission's work to achieve this goal. As an engineer she was accustomed to identifying problems, defining goals, and determining a clear course of action. She felt that this kind of organization was essential since the commissioners had little information to work with when they began.[21] They needed first to collect the background information necessary to properly analyze Canadian women's current status.[22] Subsequent steps included calling for briefs; organizing public consultations; and compiling, analyzing, and synthesizing all the information into a final report.[23]

Conscious of the magnitude of the task, and wanting to be actively involved in all aspects of the commission's work, Elsie advocated for straightforward plans and focused work in order to complete the final report by 1968.[24] She noted the need for clear questions to guide the investigations and to lead to straightforward and well-defined, evidence-based calls for change. To ensure a positive reception from the Canadian government and from the public, the recommendations needed to be both logical and achievable, and the commissioners needed to be united.

Other aspects of Elsie's work on the RCSW reflect her engineering background. For instance, she presented a four-step plan to analyze the existing situation of Canadian women in society and what needed to be done to achieve a more equitable future. She illustrated her proposal using the example of women's representation in the Canadian Senate.[25] The first step would be to review the current representation of women, who held only 12 of 102 seats in the Senate. Using the then-existing rate of increase, Elsie determined women would obtain a total of thirty seats by 2030. The next step was to determine the desired minimum number of women – fifty for example – and calculate the "discontinuity" between the two results.[26] After applying this analysis she argued that it would be possible to clearly determine the changes needed to achieve the desired minimum, and move beyond what she called the "discontinuity step," or the difference between the two projections. In some cases these measures would require "special treatment" for women.

Elsie was aware that cases would exist where there would be no conflict between the degree of change already underway and the goals of the RCSW, but she still felt that her approach would prove valuable.[27] In her opinion, the full representation and participation of women in public life was essential to achieve women's equality within Canadian society. Her colleagues agreed, at least in part, as discussed in the principles set out in the final report:

> The fourth principle is that *in certain areas women will for an interim period require special treatment to overcome the adverse effects of discriminatory practices.* We consider such measures to be justified in a limited range of circumstances, and we anticipate that they should quickly lead to actual equality which would make their continuance unnecessary.[28]

Scholar Jane Arscott credits Elsie's firm stance regarding Recommendation 138 – increasing women's representation in the

Senate – as vital to the final result, which advocated what we now call affirmative action. Arscott states, "Had it not been for the strong and consistent line she took to have the Commission adopt an affirmative action policy, the recommendations on politics would certainly have been even milder than they were."[29]

Elsie's ideas followed on those of her mother, Helen Gregory MacGill, who called for women to have "king-sized" positions in order to demonstrate their abilities.[30] However, as the MacGill women realized, without affirmative action, qualified women would continue to be overlooked because their credentials and experience were often different, if no less valuable, than men's. Elsie's proposal for augmenting the number of women in the public sphere did not receive unanimous support in the commission. Although John Humphrey supported having more women in the Canadian Senate, he did not agree with mathematical equations based on gender, which he felt created a quota for women members at the expense of other characteristics of potential senators.[31]

As the commission's work proceeded, Elsie's views and analysis continued to reflect her training as a professional engineer, and she encouraged her fellow members not to overlook the importance of science and technology when making their recommendations. As she had done as president of the Canadian Federation, she asked her fellow commissioners the following: "In a technological society, how do technological changes affect human thought, behaviour, and society?"[32] To seek these answers she insisted on consulting specialists with expertise in areas such as computers.[33]

She was willing to defend her stance on the importance of including the insights of skilled specialists in engineering and the sciences. When a sociologist hired by the RCSW, Charles Hobart, argued that it was unnecessary to consult engineers as they were "rarely looked to for pronouncements on social issues," she openly challenged him.[34] Hobart seemed unaware of the irony of his viewpoint, given Elsie's presence on the commission.[35]

Elsie advocated the use of technology whenever appropriate in the commission's work. Early in 1967, she suggested that the commissioners consider producing a video that could be used for public education, basing her argument on films used by the American Society of Women Engineers. Although the other commissioners seriously considered her suggestion, budgetary limitations did not allow them to act on it.[36]

Elsie and Commissioner Lange experimented with using a telephone hotline at the beginning of the Victoria and Vancouver RCSW hearings to provide access for individuals who lived in remote areas of the province or who were unable to travel due to domestic responsibilities. Although this initiative fit with Elsie's desire for inclusivity in the hearings, it was discontinued because of the heavy workload it created.[37]

In a memo in November 1967, Elsie advocated the use of a "scientific process," outlining how the commissioners could use hypotheses to guide their work, and then prove or disprove them based on data collection. She noted that as within the scientific realms, this would be an ongoing process until they were satisfied with the result. In illustrating her idea she proposed three initial hypotheses:

HYPOTHESIS I – THAT in Canada the status of women is not equal to that of man....

HYPOTHESIS II – THAT in Canada women's deprivation of opportunities results from

a) cultural attitudes, and

b) the physical environments in which women find themselves placed...

HYPOTHESIS III – THAT in Canada women's deprivation of opportunities in education, employment, government, and in major decision-making can be overcome, and women be given equal opportunities with men by

a) adjustment to the environments in which women find themselves placed, and

b) by adoption of egalitarian cultural attitudes[38]

Elsie believed that women's lack of opportunities in the public realm were due to aspects of culture, accepted stereotypes, societal expectations, and the social and psychological obstacles that women encountered in the workplace.[39] Her scientific approach was a means to present these ideas in what she believed was an objective fashion, and to address them systematically. The commissioners agreed with her proposal and integrated it into their research framework and plan of work.[40]

Elsie was very concerned that the commissioners be as open-minded as possible in their work and resist biases due to their age, background, and relative status within society. She therefore challenged the commissioners to identify any personal prejudices that might hinder their objectivity. She reminded them of the goals they had set: to maximize "individual choice and freedom" for both sexes in every avenue of daily life, reduce "the range of restraints on individual choice and freedom of action," and elevate those in society who were denied privileges available to others.[41]

Aware of the difficulty of this task, Elsie created a series of questions to assist in this personal reflection:

Am I prepared to accept in principle the following:

i. Decision-making by women in no way subservient to that of men – in government, in business, in industry, in the professions, in education, in family life.

ii. Equal opportunities for women to operate in policy-making positions and in positions of high honour in government, in business, in industry, in the professions, in education and in family life.

iii. Strong public encouragement for women to enter so-called masculine pursuits – professions, trades, avocations.

iv. Equal responsibility for, and sharing in the physical care of, their children by mothers and fathers.

v. Equal tolerance for women in matters of sexual morality, including "free love," lesbianism.[42]

This list of questions makes it clear that Elsie was moving beyond the conventional calls for equality of opportunity that characterized traditional women's organizations, and that she was embracing the demand for social and sexual freedoms raised by the new women's liberation movement. She believed that multiple points of view needed to be considered during both the data collection and writing of the commission's report, and advocated that the commission seek out and consider the widest possible range of women's and men's ideas and experiences.[43]

In addition, Elsie was concerned that the provinces, which have responsibility for key services such as education and health care, should not be overlooked. She believed that limiting the report to the areas of federal jurisdiction would seriously compromise the integrity of the final report.[44] The commission's terms of reference had made room for these considerations in the wording "and such other matters in relation to the status of women in Canada as may appear to the Commissioners to be relevant."[45]

· · · · · · · · ·

The commissioners visited fourteen cities across Canada over thirty-three days to hear from Canadians on the status of women.[46] To ensure the widest input possible, the commission did not limit hearing venues to hotels, but sought out alternate venues ranging from community centres to shopping centres.[47]

Elsie noted the power of the hearings to educate and challenge both women *and* men to seriously evaluate the status quo:

> I think that the extent to which women were shown to be discriminated against in employment, in law, in education, in taxation, in immigration, in citizenship, in penal settings, and in public life shocked many people who had never before thought about it seriously.
>
> The airing given these matters at the hearings, and the wide coverage of the press, radio, and television carried the dialogue into millions of Canadian homes, and forced many women and men to reappraise and re-value our commonly-accepted, traditional ideas, customs, and practices.[48]

Elsie played a prominent role during these meetings and was able to pose precise and intelligent questions at appropriate moments. As a result, at least one media commentator referred to her as "the commissioner with the steel trap mind."[49] While acknowledging the serious nature of the commission's work, Elsie retained her ability to appreciate the lighter side of the proceedings. She called on her colleagues to maintain a cheerful disposition as, after all, it "was not a 'grouch' Commission."[50]

Florence Bird described the powerful impact that participation in the RCSW had on the commissioners:

> The public hearings did more than increase the knowledge of the commissioners. The shared experience made us aware that the wisdom and good will demanded by our mandate made it necessary for us to work together as a team. Seven strong-minded individuals from very different backgrounds became united in purpose by the power of the land; by the immense, physical power of the country itself; and also by the force of the simple human needs of the people who appeared before us.[51]

The testimonies of the women who spoke at the hearings also affected members of the media who travelled with the commission. The RCSW was widely covered by the print media, radio, and television, which relayed these testimonies to the Canadian public.[52]

Elsie was aware of the challenge these hearings created for women who were nervous about public speaking. This sensitivity helped her recognize when individuals who lacked self-confidence needed a little coaching to express their ideas and arguments, and she would encourage them to focus on their personal experiences and knowledge.[53] While she was heartened by those who came out to the hearings, Elsie acknowledged that participation was not as diverse as she had hoped. In particular, she noted the underrepresentation of men and youth in the audiences.[54]

To achieve a broader input, the commission reached out in other ways. Elsie drafted a brochure that explained the objectives of the RCSW, described how to submit a brief, and encouraged Canadians to write one. The final brochure "What do you have to say about the status of women?" was distributed through various supermarket chains, including Steinberg's, Dominion, Loblaws, and IGA. The

Canadian public responded enthusiastically, and a second printing of the brochure was needed. In the end, more than 468 briefs and 1000 letters were submitted to the commission.[55]

· · · · · · · · ·

In assessing the status of women in Canada, the RCSW was investigating questions that active Canadian feminists had struggled with for many years. Elsie embodied the knowledge and experience of three generations of feminist activists and possessed extensive experience in women's organizations. As a result, other members of the commission regarded her as a guide to Canadian women's issues. Monique Bégin, executive secretary of the RCSW, not only identified Elsie as the leading feminist on the commission, but also credited her with helping other commissioners understand and in some cases identify themselves as feminists.[56]

As is evident in her work on the commission, Elsie's broad thinking on women's rights defies easy classification. Her views do not fit into the categories that many academic feminists have used to describe second-wave feminism: *maternal* (advocating the moral authority of women based on their roles as mothers); *liberal* (advocating the need for equal rights and opportunity for women); or *radical* (advocating women's control over their bodies and liberation from the societal restraints associated with childbirth, while fighting against violence inflicted on women).[57] Rather she blended the various streams into her own unique viewpoint, which changed over time. Dormer Ellis, Toronto Business and Professional Women's Club (TBPWC) member, and engineer offers further insight into Elsie's brand of feminism:

> One of her goals was to make it not be any disadvantage to be a woman. In other words she was against any form of discrimination against them. But she also felt that women ought to take it upon themselves to improve their own status, not just wait for someone else to do it for them, so she had the idea that women should be self-supporting and independent, and that type of thing, rather than be dependent on others all the time.[58]

As demonstrated by her support for preferential treatment for women in some spheres, she incorporated aspects of what some scholars call "welfare liberal feminism," which advocated affirmative action for women while the barriers to their progress were eliminated.[59] Elsie's views on access to abortion, education and work, taxation, and other issues addressed by the RCSW further illuminate her evolving feminism.

Abortion was illegal in Canada when the RCSW started its work. However, many desperate women sought dangerous and even deadly illegal or "back alley" abortions to end their unwanted pregnancies. During the lifetime of the commission the Canadian government and organizations such as the Canadian Medical Association and the Canadian Bar Association were independently addressing the issue. In 1969, the government made changes to the *Criminal Code* that allowed for an abortion if a woman's request for the procedure was approved by a Therapeutic Abortion Committee. While this made some abortions legal, it gave control to the male-dominated medical profession. Doctors, and not women, had the final word on whether or not an abortion would be performed legally.[60] The availability of abortions therefore depended on the views of local physicians.

Elsie had what was at the time considered a radical view on abortion. From her perspective, it was an issue that should be a private matter between a woman and her doctor, and the state had no business in the decision. Elsie's views were not supported by the other commissioners. Doris Ogilvie, the New Brunswick judge, was one of her most vocal opponents, arguing in a "Separate Statement" that abortion affected two lives, and that one of those lives did not have precedence over the other.[61]

In the end, the commissioners recommended two changes to the *Criminal Code* with respect to abortion:

126. We recommend that the *Criminal Code* be amended to permit abortion by a qualified medical practitioner on the sole request of any woman who has been pregnant for 12 weeks or less.

127. We recommend that the *Criminal Code* be amended to permit abortion by a qualified practitioner at the request of a woman pregnant for more than 12 weeks if the doctor is convinced that

the continuation of the pregnancy would endanger the physical or mental health of the woman, or if there is a substantial risk that if the child were born, it would be greatly handicapped, either mentally or physically.[62]

Elsie made her own "Separate Statement" about these recommendations: "Although I support our recommendations on abortion as far as they go, I do not think that they go far enough. I think that abortion should no longer be regarded as a criminal offence but as a private medical matter between patient and doctor." She went on to predict accurately the result of maintaining the status quo: "I foresee with fear that unless the prohibitions and penalties provided in the *Criminal Code* are repealed promptly, they will linger on for a decade or two more to harass and punish women."[63] She was not alone in her views. The Canadian Federation, which in 1962 had called for a Royal Commission on abortion, submitted a brief that was in line with Elsie's thinking:

> Leaving the religious questions aside to be dealt with within the confines of the religious groups concerned, a woman should have the right to decide whether or not she wishes to carry the child which has been conceived, and if she decides not, to have skilled medical help in having a child aborted. Denial of assistance in the past has not prevented abortion but rather has resulted in many cases in exorbitant payment to those prepared to ignore the law and in painful and unnecessary deaths. The woman as a person in law should have the right to request abortion from the medical profession.[64]

Some observers have argued that the RCSW had little or no effect on the 1969 changes to the *Criminal Code* relating to abortion.[65] As the commission had not yet reported its findings, and their recommendations were not radical, this view is not surprising. However, as evidenced by the clear divide within the commission, the issue generated very strong opinions that foreshadowed the degree to which Canadians would publicly debate the question of abortion throughout the 1970s and 1980s.

Indeed, in 1970, in response to the challenges created by the 1969 amendments for women seeking abortions, a large number of

Canadian women united in a march from Vancouver to Ottawa – called the Abortion Caravan – calling for the decriminalization of abortion. Two years later the National Action Committee on the Status of Women (NAC) also adopted a pro-choice stance. Kay Macpherson, one of NAC's leaders, said that this stand was in part influenced by Elsie's "Separate Statement," though the pro-choice stance revealed a fracture within the organization.[66]

Elsie maintained her stance on abortion for the rest of her life, and she kept files on Dr. Henry Morgentaler's struggles throughout the 1970s, as well as the work of the Canadian Association for the Repeal of the Abortion Law (CARAL).[67] She was appointed an honorary director of CARAL in 1980, a fitting tribute to her dedication to this cause.[68] Unfortunately, Elsie did not have the opportunity to witness the decriminalization of abortion in 1988.[69]

. . . .

Elsie's upbringing gave her full access to education, even when she chose to pursue the male-dominated career of engineering. Acknowledging her own advantages, she desired the same opportunities for all Canadian women. One of the many obstacles that stood in the way of educational opportunities for girls was their ignorance of the range of opportunity available to them. Elsie identified sex-stereotyping in school textbooks – which depicted women mainly in domestic roles – as closing doors to future options many young women might consider.[70] She noted:

> Higher education and advanced training appear "unfeminine." Although economic conditions have changed the traditional domestic pattern of life for most women, such a girl may still anticipate a lifetime of domesticity, may cut short her education, acquire no lively interests of her own, no marketable skill, no professional competence. Her idea of what is ahead for her... scarcely extends beyond her twenty-fifth year. Our society condones this neglect of opportunities, this short-term view of life for girls, that shows them marriage as the termination of their education. Many of the hardships and dissatisfactions of women in later life can be traced to this attitude.[71]

Elsie strongly advocated the full implementation of the RCSW Recommendations 69 and 73, which addressed textbook reform and guidance programs in schools, respectively:

> 69. We recommend that the provinces and the territories adopt textbooks that portray women, as well as men, in diversified roles and occupations.

> 73. We recommend that the provinces and territories (a) provide co-educational guidance programmes in elementary and secondary schools, where they do not now exist and (b) direct the attention of guidance counsellors to the importance of encouraging both girls and boys to continue their education according to their individual aptitudes and to consider all occupational fields.[72]

She believed that these recommendations would bring about key changes that were owed to the coming generations of women: "We can do better than this for our girls. Our homes and our schools can furnish them with the nutriments that develop recognition of opportunities, aspirations to accomplishments, a long-term view of life."[73]

Elsie also continued to call for women's full and equal access to the labour market. To that end she called for the preferential treatment of women in hiring until the balance was righted:[74]

> In Canada women, to a greater or less degree, are at a disadvantage educationally, socially, economically, legally, politically and psychologically compared to men. This all-pervasive inequality is generally condoned by society, and various devices operate to make it difficult for women to overcome these disadvantages... [I]t is rational to recommend preferential treatment for women in most areas of activity, for at least a period of time, to enable them to overcome their present disadvantages quickly – the sooner to attain to equal status with men. Moreover it is simple justice to require society to promote this preferential treatment, even at some financial and other cost, in compensation for its earlier failure.[75]

As an individual, Elsie had proved more than capable as a professional engineer, and she had demonstrated the potential of women in an occupation previously considered a male domain. However, her work with the Canadian Federation of Business and Professional Women's Clubs and the RCSW made it clear that her experiences were not the norm for most Canadian women. These ideas were echoed by the brief written by her colleagues in the Canadian Federation, who pointed out that while arts degrees were becoming more commonplace for women, the "pressures of finance, marriage, and lack of job opportunities are brought to bear to discourage women from taking up professions in medicine, law, architecture, engineering and the like."[76] Elsie realized that stereotypical beliefs about women's abilities would not be easily altered. She believed that the increased presence of women in all fields was required to eradicate discriminatory attitudes.[77]

These ideas were endorsed by the RCSW, which recommended that girls be encouraged to take courses that would allow for later non-traditional career opportunities. The commission also called on the federal government to set up career information services in all local Canada Manpower Centres to advise women on "occupations, training requirements, financial help available, and labour market conditions and needs" and also to make this information available to schools in the area.[78] Recommendation 72 also called for all levels of government to review all career-related publications, and to use only those that "encourage women to consider all occupations, including those which have been traditionally restricted to men."[79]

· · · · · · · · ·

Elsie went beyond advocating equal access to the labour market; she called for the full economic independence of women.[80] She recognized this would require changes on many levels, including taxation. She had previously addressed taxation issues that she felt held women back when she had led a delegation that presented a brief from the Canadian Federation to the Carter Commission.[81]

Elsie believed that the status of married women as 'dependents' in tax legislation reinforced the social norms that inhibited women's occupational ambitions. However, on this issue she was not able to gain the full support of the other commissioners, who recommended reducing the tax exemption for wives rather than eliminating it. In addition, they recommended that the government establish a new "marriage unit" tax category:

132. We recommend that the federal *Income Tax Act* be amended in order that the husband and wife form a taxation unit and be permitted to aggregate their incomes, under a special tax rate schedule, in a joint return signed by both spouses with the option to file separately if they so desire.[82]

In Elsie's opinion, the idea of a "marriage unit" contradicted the commission's overall aim of encouraging the full development of women as strong, independent individuals:

The current "individual" basis of taxation accords more nearly with this view than does the "marriage unit" basis. It is a facet of the independence of the individual, and also of tax equity between individuals. For these reasons, I am against the introduction of the "marriage unit" basis. As our Report shows, there are ways other than that of eliminating taxation policies that discriminate against married women.[83]

She argued that encouraging the continued dependence of women was problematic for the marriage and family as it limited the woman, burdened the husband, and set a negative example for any children within the family. While she acknowledged that some tax exemptions or credits were necessary for dependent children or elders, she advocated individual taxation for spouses.[84]

• • • • • • • • •

Elsie's hope that work on the RCSW report would be completed by 1968 quickly proved unrealistic, but it did not lessen her drive for efficiency. In fact, during that year she advocated that the commissioners meet during the summer to discuss the final report. She worked steadily on the report, undertaking tasks such as editing chapter drafts. One of her objectives was to ensure that the final revisions by the editors did not substantially change the ideas intended by the commissioners.[85] To assist this overall process she asked that tentative deadlines be set for the completion of each chapter.[86] She also argued that commissioners needed to pour all their energy into the final report and avoid the distraction and temptation of trying to galvanize immediate change themselves.[87]

While it is fully expected that commissioners take an active role in writing the final report, Elsie went further than most. She wanted to be kept abreast of all the internal workings of the RCSW, not just those materials provided to the commissioners. She asked to be included in the commission's mailing list for its critical path and network, which tracked the day-to-day progress of the commission's staff on all the work being done for the final report, overseen by Monique Bégin.[88] Bégin later commented on Elsie's dedication:

> The amount of work she could do always astonished me. I noticed every time the Commission met, that she had read every page of every document we sent her.
>
> It was a great challenge to work for her since she would always respond, and the most fascinating aspect was that so-called revolutionary ideas just seemed ordinary to her. Her mind was always open.[89]

Elsie also undertook various speaking engagements to promote the commission's work.[90] For example, in 1968 she addressed the annual International Women's Day luncheon of the Pioneer Women's Organization of Montréal, where she argued that until social change occurred women would not be fully equal within Canada. She also believed that this change could occur rapidly. To illustrate her point she referred to examples from science and technology:

> Let us not fall into easy thinking that social improvements can only be introduced gradually. There is no rule about this. The pattern of the past need not be repeated. Speed of implementation depends probably on the degree of effort expended. Let us realise also that recommendations will not come in of their own volition – with time. Something more than time is required. A unique start must be made. The space engineers did not put satellites into orbit by repeating their flight failures so many hundred times. Improving the status of women in Canada need not be a long-drawn out operation but could be done quickly if Canadians decided they wanted it that way.[91]

Elsie retained a strong feminist identity throughout the work of the RCSW. She was not willing to compromise her principle beliefs, preferring to stand alone on subjects such as abortion and taxation. Her scientific rigour and procedures brought order to the deliberations, while her feminist point of view, which made women's equality the bottom line, strengthened the analysis and recommendations of the commission. At the same time, she also invested heavily in the success of the RCSW, leading Florence Bird to refer to Elsie as her "right hand" and "the moving force behind the RCSW."[92] Later Florence recalled, "Elsie had more guts than anyone I have ever known. She also had a fine mind, a warm and generous heart and a stern conscience to which she listened. And she had a wonderful sense of humour and of the ridiculous that enabled her to laugh instead of weep."[93]

While acknowledging its limitations, Elsie embraced the report, and advocated that it was a significant beginning, as the report itself acknowledged: "Action that is appropriate today may become obsolete; new approaches may be needed. Moreover there is a need to keep a continuing watch in order that women's rights and freedoms are respected."[94]

Footnotes for this chapter can be found online at:
http://secondstorypress.ca/resources and at http://feministhistories.ca/books

Chapter 9
KEEPING THE PRESSURE
ON AND MOVING FORWARD

The Report has been called a radical document, a revolutionary document – but only, I think, by people who have never looked at it. Not only is the Report far from radical, but its Recommendations are very conservative. They had to keep within the Commission's mandate.[1] This is why I say that the Recommendations ask for very little. This is why they are only a first step. Asking for "equal opportunities" is only asking that, that which most people believe should be available to everyone, be made available to women. In simple justice, this should be delayed no longer.[2]

—Elsie Gregory MacGill

The *Report of the Royal Commission on the Status of Women in Canada* (RCSW Report) was submitted to the federal government on September 28, 1970. It received widespread media attention. *Toronto Star* journalist Anthony Westell described it as "explosive:"

At 2:11 p.m. in the House of Commons Monday, the Prime Minister rose, bowed politely to the Speaker, and tabled a bomb, already primed and ticking. The bomb is called the Report of the RCSW in Canada, and it is packed with more explosive potential than any device manufactured by terrorists. As a call to revolution, hopefully a quiet one, it is more persuasive than any FLQ manifesto. And as a political blockbuster, it is more powerful than that famous report of the controversial commission on bilingualism and biculturalism.

This 488-page book, in its discreet green, white and blue cover, demands radical change not just in Québec, but in every community across Canada. It is concerned not merely with relations between French and English, but between man and woman. The history of the problem it describes and seeks to solve is not 100 years of Confederation but the story of mankind.[3]

Elsie was determined that the report would not collect dust after the initial publicity ended. Together with the other commissioners she waged a vigorous public education campaign in support of the

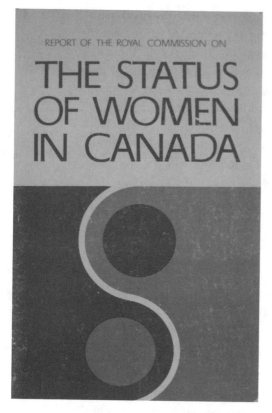

REPORT OF THE ROYAL COMMISSION ON

THE STATUS OF WOMEN IN CANADA

The Report of the Royal Commission on the Status of Women in Canada was tabled in the House of Commons in 1970. Elsie and others endeavoured to ensure that it had the widest distribution possible and that it had no opportunity to gather dust.

report and its 167 recommendations. As a result, the publication of the document did not reduce Elsie's workload. Instead the report provided a springboard from which to launch a new stage in the struggle to raise the status of women in Canada.[4]

She worked passionately to educate the public about the report, its contents, and the means by which it could be implemented. Not only did she respond to many direct requests to speak about the report, but she also helped Florence Bird with the numerous invitations she received as chairman of the commission, by serving in Florence's stead. Even after the RCSW was officially dissolved, the commissioners and executive secretary Monique Bégin maintained the ties they had forged during the intense three-and-a-half years.[5] This communication helped them adjust to their post-commission lives and work together in the absence of official support. As Lola Lange complained in a letter to Elsie, "[N]ow when we need advice, and moral support, from the other commissioners, we are left out on a limb." Commissioners Lange and Ogilvie both looked to Elsie for help with their public speaking engagements.[6]

Elsie addressed many organizations and used each opportunity to actively promote the ways in which the RCSW Report and its 167 recommendations could be used to affect social change in Canada. For instance, she reached out to organized labour, attending the Ontario Federation of Labour's Human Rights conference on Sex Discrimination in March 1971 where she distributed copies of the report. The event gave Elsie an opportunity to network with other women's advocates, including MP Grace MacInnis; artist Maryon Kantaroff; Lita-Rose Betcherman, director of the Province of Ontario's Women's Bureau; and Sylva Gelber, director of the Women's Bureau of the federal Department of Labour (Women's Bureau). In November 1970, Elsie addressed the special conference on women's rights organized by the British Columbia Federation of Labour, where she challenged unions to assume a leadership role in addressing the report's recommendations:

> The local unions, the provincial Federations of Labour, the Congress of Labour each have a part to play in creating a more equitable climate for women in Canada to work in. When we look back at the 1970s will we see that it was the labour unions that led in the establishing of equal opportunities for women in Canada?[7]

Although she was committed to bringing the contents of the RCSW Report to the wider public, Elsie admitted that her schedule drained her:

> I too have been doing quite a [lot] of speeches. Fortunately, they have been mostly to groups without much publicity, so I have been able to repeat myself. Even so, a couple or three evenings a week is a lot of time to spend on this – particularly when it is for free.[8]

An occasional benefit came when Elsie was able to combine a speaking engagement with a family visit.[9]

Elsie and her fellow commissioners distributed their complimentary copies of the report widely and encouraged people across Canada to buy and read it.[10] However, initially, there was limited public access to the report. In December 1970, Lola Lange told Elsie that it was next to impossible to obtain a copy in Alberta and the other western provinces:

> I thought I'd let you know that as of Friday no copies of the Report were available in Alberta, and that no govt. outlet is going to handle them. It's to be handled thru [sic] Information Canada offices – of which Alta and Sask. [Alberta and Saskatchewan] do

not have any. How's that for being in the boondocks! I personally went to 2 independent bookstores in Calgary – one had ordered a supply 2 weeks ago, and didn't have them yet – the other promised to order some. In Edmonton I turned the problem over to the Women's Bureau.[11]

Lange's frustration was echoed and reinforced by Jeanne Lapointe in Québec:

Two months ago – Feb 1st – the printing bureau decided to make a reprint of 5000 copies. The contract, signed last week, went to a private firm. Jessie Armstrong was told just now that the reprints will not be available until April 20th. It makes me spit. I sent three copies to the Liberal Party Task force since they had none & could not find any. How can people study a report which is not available?

Lola tells me the library at Calgary has one copy – in French. Isn't that a fine example of government efficiency?[12]

The efforts of the commissioners and the demand for the report eventually forced the government to sort out printing and distribution. Four-and-a-half years after the RCSW Report was issued 16,471 English-language copies had been sold and 3,285 copies of the French version.[13]

• • • • • • • • •

Elsie was a strong advocate of the RCSW Report within the Canadian Federation of Business and Professional Women's Clubs (Canadian Federation). She wanted to ensure that the report and its recommendations – which the clubs had called for and supported – were fully understood,[14] so she argued against the adoption of "What's in It?" a study guide prepared by the National Council of Women. Her rationale was that reading only the guide would lead to a superficial knowledge of the report and its highlights; instead she felt a comprehensive understanding of the whole document was needed. The Canadian Federation accepted her arguments and advocated for their members to become familiar with the entire report.[15]

To make the lengthy and – for some – daunting report more

approachable, Elsie wrote an article, "Status of Women Report Reading Hint: Tackle the Report in Six Easy Steps," which was featured in *The Business and Professional Woman* in March 1971.[16] She acknowledged the limitations of the report's format, but reminded readers that the ultimate goal was to make it "a best seller." Rather than recommending a cover-to-cover reading of the whole document, she suggested starting with the table of contents, terms of reference, and criteria and principles. To stimulate interest in specific chapters, she then advised a thorough reading of the final recommendations.

Elsie continued to promote the report in forums organized by the Business and Professional Women's Clubs.[17] Her address in Medicine Hat, Alberta, on April 2, 1971, was open to the public and prefaced a full-day seminar on the RCSW Report. Attended by other women's groups in the region and by the mayor of Medicine Hat, the event ignited action in support of the report and its implementation.[18]

During the 1971 congress of the International Federation of Business and Professional Women Clubs, the president drew attention to the RCSW and its final report:

> The report of the Royal Commission on the Status of Women in Canada should be read and studied by all Federations and Associate Clubs. The recommendations can serve as guidelines or starting points for discussions and research in each country. We have in this report a ready-made basis for comparison. Let us all use it to benefit the Status of Women in our own countries.[19]

· · · · · · · · ·

Determined to see concrete results from the work of the commission, Elsie lost patience with the federal government, which was not as responsive as she hoped. Her frustration was tangible during her address to the twenty-third biennial convention of the Canadian Federation, where she lamented, "We (the commissioners) are expected to THINK BIG – but CHEAP!" Her exasperation was compounded by the fact that the Canadian government seemed to spare no expense when it came to the development of natural resources, such as the proposed Mackenzie Valley Pipeline. Elsie argued, "The skills and talents of women are one of Canada's great under-utilized national resources. Our governments and institutions should think BIG about developing them and thereby benefit our whole Canadian society."[20] She called on the government to implement all the recommendations of the RCSW.[21] She argued that actions to enhance equal opportunity for women would dovetail with other key government priorities, such as employment, and she encouraged the government to prioritize the recommendations.

In January 1972, Elsie took part in a panel organized by the Toronto Business and Professional Women's Club (TBPWC). She and Jan Steel, who represented the Liberal Party Task Force on the Status of Women, discussed the progress made in the two years since the report was released. This was especially timely since the federal government was beginning to consider the interdepartmental committee's December 1971 analysis of the report.[22]

Elsie was concerned that the increasing speed of technological change made concrete action to improve the status of women all the more urgent. She expressed this concern at the University of Manitoba in 1972:

> But is the need for change generally accepted? Well, it had better be – for rapid change is all about us. Atomic energy, antibiotics, electronic controls, television, computers, jet flight, moon landings, space explorations, satellite communications have all become commonplace within the last thirty years. These new technologies bring new solutions to problems, and bring new problems, and these can produce further social changes. Because of this the Commission stressed the point that its Report and its Recommendations were only a beginning....[23]

The challenge of monitoring all the developments related to the report kept Elsie extremely busy, and she admitted that it was difficult to keep abreast of all them. However, she remained determined. As she said in a letter to Doris Ogilvie in 1973, "Of course the important thing, I think, is to keep moving forward."[24] This conviction helped her maintain momentum in advocating for the recommendations of the RCSW. To that end, she encouraged and supported the TBPWC to advance new resolutions based on the recommendations.[25]

Elsie ensured that she remained up-to-date and informed by keeping in touch with like-minded women such as Monique Bégin, who was elected as a Liberal member of parliament for the first of several times in 1972.[26] She also stayed engaged with other members of the federal government. In 1972, for example, after reviewing *Status of Women in Canada 1972*, a report by the federal government's interdepartmental committee, she contacted her MP, Donald MacDonald, to discuss what still needed to be done.[27] The following year she wrote to John Munro, then Minister of Labour, to thank him for sending her a copy of *Status of Women in Canada 1973* and to congratulate the government on some of its initiatives, including the creation of the Canadian Advisory Council on the Status of Women (CACSW), which was to advise the government on an ongoing basis.[28] However, she was also quick to outline the areas that needed improvement.[29] In particular, she questioned why the federal Human Rights Commission had not yet been created. Elsie took the opportunity to remind Munro of the need for women in high-ranking positions:

> A woman who is truly honoured in authority raises the aspirations of other women, and strengthens their confidence in their own ability to achieve. Seeing men in public office has always provided boys with incentives to achievement; the lack of women there has withheld this stimulation from girls.[30]

She argued that implementing the RCSW Report's recommendations would not be costly or detract from other government programs, but could in fact benefit them:

> Mr. Munro, implementation of the Recommendations need not wait upon other projects that the Government contemplates. It is not a question of the Recommendations OR reducing inflation; OR increasing employment; OR expanding the manufacturing sector – or indeed any other aims or goals. It can be argued that implementation of the Recommendations would have the effect of advancing these. Furthermore, the costs of implementing the Recommendations are modest – extremely modest when compared with some of the much-discussed projects.[31]

In addition to celebrating the creation of the CACSW Elsie kept a close eye on its activities and opened dialogue with its members.[32] After reviewing its 1974 publication *What's been done? A Report by The Advisory Council on the Status of Women*,[33] she wrote to Katie Cooke, president of the advisory council, to congratulate her and her team. She acknowledged the importance of tracking the progress on implementing the RCSW recommendations, but she advised the advisory council to go further: "I am also happy to see that the Advisory Council – and the government, too, I hope – recognizes that the three and one-half years gap, and changing times call for further action, and consider the Recommendations of the Royal Commission on the Status of Women as only 'a beginning.'"[34]

Elsie maintained communication with the CACSW as it evolved. In addition to reading and commenting on their publications, she sent new information to the members. When necessary, she was not afraid to call them to account; in 1978, for instance, she reminded Yvette Rousseau, the new president of the advisory council, to continue citing the RCSW Report in advisory council publications. Elsie acted on her belief that every Canadian woman had a responsibility to support the work of the CACSW; otherwise there was the risk of jeopardizing the achievements to date and the attainment of the remaining goals.[35]

· · · · · · · · ·

Elsie's drive to ensure that the RCSW Report was not overlooked came with a price.[36] When the editor of *Chatelaine*, Doris Anderson, asked if Elsie would let her name stand in the magazine as a potential candidate for federal election, Elsie declined. Although grateful for the vote of confidence, she explained that she had neither the time nor the financial resources for such an undertaking:

> My time on the Commission showed me that it is well-nigh impossible to operate a business which is built on confidence in the principal, with any degree of success, and expend most of my time, energy and money elsewhere. Although the Commission lapsed months ago, I still have many calls on my time to speak about the Report and Recommendations. I consider I have an

obligation to do this. I am of course very desirous of seeing the Recommendations implemented.[37]

At times, Elsie's feminist and professional commitments also compromised her ability to attend to family matters. She did not see her brother Eric Gregory during a lengthy illness before his death in 1972; although soon after she did visit with her brother's widow.[38] Despite sacrificing personal time to advance her feminist goals, Elsie had a deep commitment to her family, as attested by several of her colleagues. While at times she needed to be creative in how she maintained contact with her far-flung family, she did so willingly.[39]

Elsie sometimes found herself out in front of some of her feminist colleagues. For example, she was eager to support developments in the black women's movement for change in the Toronto area. She proposed a motion at the Soroptimist Club of Toronto to support the participation of the Canadian Negro Women's Association in the first National Congress of Black Women scheduled for April 1973 in Toronto.[40] Elsie outlined the history of the Canadian Negro Women's Association and its international links, including those at the United Nations, but her enthusiasm was not enough to carry the motion. In fact, she opted to withdraw the motion in its entirety, rather than see it tabled while its value was assessed by a committee.[41] She expressed further disappointment when some of her friends regarded the event in a negative light instead of seeing its importance for the women's movement: "I am sad to find that some of my friends suspect the Congress is [a] front for Communist activity. I think that they are overly suspicious, and wrong, and that the suggestion is simply a put-down."[42]

The experience during the RCSW had opened Elsie's eyes to considering all women's needs. Thus, even when she lacked wide support for her ideas, she did not give up. In this case, although she was unsuccessful in getting support for the Canadian Negro Women's Association, she asked to attend the congress as an observer. This initiative was rewarded, and she attended the keynote address by Rosemary Brown, then member of the legislative assembly for Vancouver-Burrard, and the first black woman to be elected to a provincial legislature in Canada.[43] In attending this event Elsie was able to network and expand her contacts among black women.

In addition, Elsie monitored the concerns of First Nations women. When the Supreme Court of Canada was ready to examine the status differences between Aboriginal men and women in the Jeannette Lavell and Yvonne Bédard case in February 1973, she worked to build support for the women among her colleagues, explaining in a letter to her family:

> I am trying to alert women in Ottawa so that there will be non-Indian women present in the courtroom giving support to the Indian women, and their Associations. It is a tremendously important case – for if the federal government can discriminate against one group in one federal Act (the Indian Act here) then it can legislate against some group in any other federal act.[44]

· · · · · · · · ·

Elsie was also keen to see the creation of the Canadian Human Rights Commission, one of the recommendations of the RCSW.[45] She joined a delegation of the Canadian Federation that met with a number of cabinet ministers in February 1977 to encourage them to take immediate action and pass Bill C-25/1977 to create the commission as soon as possible; this would prevent the bill from lapsing at the end of the parliamentary session, as had occurred with the previous bill, Bill C-72/1975.[46]

After the Human Rights Commission was established later that year, Elsie and members of the Canadian Federation were eager to use it to advance the equality of women. The Public Affairs Committee of the TBPWC strongly supported a resolution urging the Human Rights Commission to act on the long-standing, nation-wide goal of the Canadian Federation: equal pay for work of equal value. The successful resolution read as follows:

> THAT CFBPWC urge the Canadian Human Rights Commission to issue just and equitable guidelines indicating the extent to which, and the manner in which differences in remuneration between male and female employees shall be permitted and to include these provisions in Regulations to the Act within six months of the Act coming into force.[47]

The resolution was based on the RCSW's call for a better legislative definition of equal pay, now often referred to as pay equity.[48] The addition of a time limit was an important element of this resolution. A Canadian Federation member suggested a friendly amendment to replace the six-month time limit to "as soon as possible." However, Elsie spoke strongly against this amendment: "If we say "as soon as possible" we are letting them off the hook. The [federal Human Rights] Act actually came into being in 1977 and why should we let them off the hook. It is due now. It is July and they are late."[49] Elsie understood that constant pressure was required to achieve substantial social change.

The efforts of the Canadian Federation and other groups achieved success when, in 1978, the Human Rights Commission finally defined the language pertaining to equal pay for work of equal value.[50] Elsie's interest in the Human Rights Commission and its ongoing work continued throughout the rest of her life.[51]

• • • • • • • • •

At the same time as the RCSW commissioners and established women's organizations pressed for implementation of the RCSW's recommendations, new organizations were forming to unite women's groups in the demand for change. Joint action by women's groups had been effective previously. The Committee for Equality of Women in Canada, which included more than two dozen women's groups, and la Fédération des femmes du Québec, both founded in 1966, had successfully lobbied for the creation of the RCSW. In 1971, after the RCSW Report was complete, Laura Sabia once again called on women's organizations to unite. This time the goal was to see the RCSW's recommendations fully implemented. As Sabia had declared earlier, "Only in joint action can we make sure that the Report will not gather dust on some Parliamentary shelf."[52]

Thirty women's organizations responded to the call. They united in 1971 to create the National Ad Hoc Action Committee on the Status of Women, and the new organization held its first convention in April 1972.[53] The convention hosted a variety of workshops, meetings, and plenary sessions in which to debate the issues and form a concrete plan for future action. The Liberal government had hoped that the participants would decide during this meeting to support its proposed advisory council.[54] Instead, the convention created an independent organization: the National Action Committee on the Status of Women (NAC). Although the federal government had gone ahead and established the Canadian Advisory Council on the Status of Women, the organizations participating in the convention demonstrated that they would forge their own path.[55] The resulting organization demonstrated that Canadian women were willing to stand behind the RCSW Report and fight for ongoing social reform.[56]

Elsie strongly supported this action, and she played a significant role during the founding conference. As a keynote speaker alongside Florence Bird, she called attention to the inadequate response of the federal and provincial governments to the RCSW: "In the year and a half since the Commission's Report was made public, only a few of the Recommendations have been implemented. About twenty-five of the one hundred and four Recommendations directed toward the federal government have been promised, or have been implemented in principle, in whole or in part." This, Elsie said, was "strictly 'slow motion.'"[57]

Elsie challenged the women at the conference to examine their commitment to social change: "But how deeply converted are we? How profound is our conviction that the implementation of the Recommendations is of tremendous public importance? Will we take positive steps to bring about change?"[58] Using a series of very specific questions, she went on to outline the range of actions that she thought were necessary to galvanize government action on the status of women:

> Do we see a need to build much greater public support for the Recommendations as a step toward convincing those in decision-making positions that their particular public is set on having the Recommendations fulfilled? Will we go out into our communities and enlist the support of local groups? Will we set up a roster of knowledgeable speakers on the subject to provide wide coverage? Will we engage in dialogues on the Recommendations with the heads of our public institutions, the managers of our local banks, department stores, supermarkets and businesses

and industries employing many women? Will we talk over the Recommendations with editors and writers in our local newspapers? About sex exploitation and sex-typing with public relations firms? Will we enlist support for the Recommendations among the local officials in our law courts, jails and reformatories? In the political arena, will we impress on the local big-wigs of our political parties the importance of implementing the Recommendations? Will we nominate candidates, especially women candidates pledged to support them? Will we ask elected candidates for their views? Will we put our vote on the line? Will we keep alive committees such as the National [Ad Hoc Action] Committee on the Status of Women, and its counterparts in the provinces, and continue to hold policy meetings like this Conference?[59]

Speaking from years of experience, Elsie wanted to open the eyes of those assembled to the work ahead. She sensed that the time was right for substantial social change:

During its cross-country hearings the Royal Commission was well received by the public, but it met some hostility, too. Some women saw its existence as a criticism of their life style. Some men saw it as an attack on themselves. They saw it as a "zero-sum" game where gains made for women meant losses for men. Today the attitudes are less fearful and more generous. Instead of concentrating on "what the change will do to me" women and men are considering how the change will help "my niece, my daughter when she grows up."[60]

Elsie's passionate appeal did find receptive listeners at the conference, including Laurell Ritchie, a young union activist who identified with her arguments: "The keynote speaker on the Saturday morning was Elsie McGill [sic], who represented the Business and Professional Women. She was radical, far ahead of some of the union women. She had a lot of stature, and she quietly supported the insurrection."[61]

Elsie's subsequent commitment to NAC was significant. Consistent with her administrative activities in the Engineering Institute of Canada and the Canadian Federation, she helped ensure the functioning of the new organization by drafting its first constitution. She also developed an Index of NAC Policy Recommendations for the years 1972 to 1978.[62] NAC member Brigid O'Reilly describes these actions as fundamental to ensuring the strength of the organizational structure, while at the same time facilitating the flow of information among the various committees and the overall organization. Elsie also introduced "archival thinking" to NAC, a contribution that ensured the preservation of NAC's legacy.[63]

Kay Macpherson, a prominent member of the Voice of Women and future NAC president, saw Elsie as the "continuing architect of NAC's organization."[64] She also applauded Elsie's ability to define clear aims and objectives, and also the power of her feminist convictions. Not surprisingly, many of NAC's priorities coincided with Elsie's, including investment in day care and family planning, as well as equal pay for work of equal value.[65]

Elsie continued to contribute to NAC over time, providing advice and guidance to new leaders as they took office. Dr. Lorna Marsden, NAC chairperson between 1975 and 1977, considered Elsie's knowledge and assistance indispensable.[66] Marsden recalled that Elsie "honed in like a mosquito" on the crux of an issue and identified the best and most effective course of action. Kay Macpherson, who succeeded Marsden as chairperson from 1977 to 1979, remembered that both of them received daily calls from Elsie, in which she outlined actions required by NAC to ensure progress.[67]

At NAC meetings, Elsie was heavily involved in moving resolutions, as well as preparing briefs and presentations to support them. She served on committees such as the Nomination Committee, which she chaired, the Constitution Committee and, in 1979, the Person's Year committee. She willingly assisted in routine tasks such as taking minutes,[68] and seized every opportunity to attend key events, especially the NAC annual general meeting in Ottawa. As Kay Macpherson recalls, Elsie made new friends on her way to the annual general meetings, travelling via bus, wheelchair in tow, and was present at each business session.[69]

Lorna Marsden considered Elsie's advice and support fundamental to ensuring NAC's success. Kay Macpherson agreed: "She had a great sense of humour and a keen eye for political timing and promotion of equal rights for women."[70]

Fellow engineer and feminist, Ursula Franklin, described how Elsie's engineering background and her experience on the RCSW contributed to her work in NAC:

> You see in her life those two streams, one is a sense of justice that must have come from her mother's work, and the other is her real ability in design to focus on the task and those two things came together when after the RCSW...it became apparent that substantial actions from the women themselves were required to make the recommendations...into genuine change...[W]hen NAC was created it was a good deal of Elsie's experience that went into NAC's constitution and into how it functioned, and that sense of functionality that the engineer brought [to] the task to be accomplished [identifying] the [goals], how we best get this done, that together with her considerable mental capacity. And the RCSW had given her an enormous exposure to what women in the world...were facing...[and] gave her an understanding of what was [needed] to design an organization that would translate the recommendations into some kind of reality.[71]

NAC was a venue where like-minded women could advocate for the implementation of the RCSW's Report at the national level; however, some of the recommendations were specific to the provinces. Although the existing women's organizations could tackle some of the issues, new organizations were needed. Elsie joined one of the new organizations, the Ontario Committee on the Status of Women (OCSW), established in 1972.[72]

Through the OCSW, she continued to advance many of her long-term objectives, including equal pay for work of equal value, human rights, and pensions. She was involved in preparing OCSW briefs for presentation to the Ontario Human Rights Commission and the Royal Commission on the State of Pensions in Ontario in 1976 and 1977, respectively.[73]

Wendy Lawrence remembered working with Elsie in the OCSW. She recalled that during the meetings Elsie "was attentive, not attention-seeking. She would speak usually if prompted by others seeking her expertise. She was also witty and cheerful, though could also be ironical and satirical." Despite the duration of Elsie's activism, and her retirement from engineering, Wendy

Lawrence noted, she supported the OCSW because of its advocacy for women's rights in the province. Elsie was an important role model in the OCSW, an "achieving woman of the previous generation – but also a feminist and activist and link to earlier feminism," who played an important role as a bridge between the first and second waves of Canadian feminism, while at the same time mentoring the next generation of Canadian feminists.[74] She recalled that Elsie endeavoured to ensure new recruits were aware of the importance of Canadian women's history by recalling tales about the work her mother and her colleagues had done during the early part of the twentieth century.[75]

Elsie was a vital member of the feminist movement in the 1970s. She convinced, cajoled, and challenged women to use the RCSW Report as a potent tool to advance the status of women in Canada. She worked tirelessly to support women's organizations as they evolved during that decade, actively engaging in feminist institution building, offering support to individuals, and serving as a role model. She contributed an ambitious and optimistic vision of the future.[76] She took her work very seriously, but, as her feminist colleagues remember well, always with a sense of humour and *joie de vivre*.

Footnotes for this chapter can be found online at:
http://secondstorypress.ca/resources and at http://feministhistories.ca/books

Chapter 10
SPEAKING OUT ON BEHALF
OF WOMEN ENGINEERS

*[Women] do meet handicaps in their professional development
that male engineers do not. These hinder them in their career,
prevent them from making their full contribution to their profession and damage, not only them, but the whole profession by
diluting its quality and its worth and value to Canada.*[1]

—Elsie Gregory MacGill

Prejudice against women choosing a career in engineering has a long
history. This perspective was not limited to men but even included
some women who identified with women's advancement. As historian Carroll Pursell demonstrates in his study of British women
engineers, certain women thought engineering was a poor choice
for a woman:

> [Caroline] Haslett [an electrical engineer] related a telling anec-
> dote concerning Emmeline Pankhurst. Finding herself next to
> her at a dinner party, the leader of the suffragettes asked her what
> she did for a living. Pankhurst met the requested information
> with an exclamation: "But surely, that's a very unsuitable occu-
> pation for a lady, isn't it?" Although the story appears to render
> Haslett more solidly feminist than her companion, Pankhurst
> went on to inquire whether she ever met with discrimination –
> which Haslett flatly denied! The territory indeed appeared as yet
> to be unmapped.[2]

Like Caroline Haslett, Elsie felt that she had not been discriminated against in engineering. During the 1940s and 1950s Elsie's
successful progression in the field and good fortune in finding many
supportive male colleagues largely blinded her to discrimination
within engineering. She claimed that engineering lacked rigid barriers that barred women from entering the profession:

In Canada there has never been a battle of the sexes over the question of women entering engineering and unless a sudden fascism overwhelms our country, there probably will never be one. Regulations that are hangover of the purely masculine era in this profession will be eliminated when the demand is made. For...there is plenty of room in Canada for another good engineer, male or female.[3]

Elsie resisted being singled out as a *woman* engineer. She wanted to be identified first and foremost as an engineer. She also had difficulty accepting that there might be systemic discrimination against women in the engineering profession. While she had fought for her own rights early in her professional career and denounced sexism both in the public service and in the Institute of Aeronautical Sciences, it took some time before she could see barriers to women in engineering as more than personal hurdles to be overcome. Even in 1946, when considering the lack of women in engineering education, she placed more weight on the lack of women's demand for entrance than on university policies or existing social attitudes:

These exclusions, however – which will probably vanish with time and the present governing bodies – signify little, since they are not general. In the past 20 or 30 years, at least, these regulations would have prevented no woman from obtaining the engineering course she wanted. If the door was closed in one place it was open in another. That it did not open sooner was probably because there was no demand. That it does not stand open everywhere is, no doubt, due to lack of demand.[4]

In the 1950s Elsie worked with the Society of Women Engineers (SWE), the Toronto Business and Professional Women's Club (TBPWC), and the Engineering Institute of Canada (EIC) to support women interested in pursuing careers in science and engineering. She continued to believe that with proper encouragement, financial support, and mentoring, more and more women would enter the profession.[5] As Ursula Franklin and others later argued, this belief was based on the premise that simply by helping the next generation of women get the appropriate training, they would have all the tools necessary to pursue any career, including employment in engineering.

After her role on the executive of the Canadian Federation of Business and Professional Women's Clubs (CFBPWC) was over in 1967, Elsie started to publicly challenge the dearth of women in science and engineering. In the summer edition of *The Business and Professional Woman*, she argued: "What is needed to stabilize the position of women in science and engineering in Canada, is numbers – many, many more women to fill up the ranks of scientists and engineers." Elsie's belief was supported by the *Engineering Journal*'s records, which showed that in 1966 only 116 members of the 43,066 professional engineers across Canada were women.[6]

In addition to calling for a greater number of women in science and engineering, Elsie supported young women who took up the challenge. As a member of the EIC's Toronto branch, for example, she met with the two young female engineering students who had been invited to the organization's annual meeting and dinner in February 1967.[7] Some of Elsie's male colleagues also encouraged women to enter and stay in engineering.

As early as 1957, the *Engineering Journal* provided information about engineering as a vocational prospect for women. In 1966, the editor noted that while women engineers might require some accommodation when they had young children, they could make unique contributions to the profession: "Perhaps women engineers and scientists might even contribute a unique creativity and vision in the application of science to the needs of society. So far, men alone haven't done too grand a job of this in some important areas."[8] A year later, Elsie praised the EIC for taking concrete actions to recruit both women and men to the field in its vocational guidance publication *Engineering Careers*.[9] However more was needed to ensure that women would enter engineering education and continue in the profession.[10]

Elsie's belief that the number of women pursuing scientific professions would increase with the right support quickly eroded in the 1970s. The catalyst for her change of mind was an article in the *Canadian Aeronautics and Space Journal*. Its author, Dr. F. P.J. Rimrott, a mechanical engineering professor at the University of Toronto, called for a new education program to train women as "engineering aides." He argued:

A serious lack of adequately trained women in engineering offices on one hand and a surfeit of gifted young women in search of acceptable professional careers on the other call for the introduction of a degree course for Engineering Aides at universities, a step which would benefit young women, the engineering profession and the national economy in general.[11]

He supported this call for a new, subordinate women's role in the profession as follows:

If women are to participate more actively in the shaping of our future, those areas within the wide spectrum of engineering must be found and singled out which appeal to women and where they stand a good chance of competing successfully with men. Engineering means primarily design and synthesis, areas which are presumably the realm of men. Let us not argue this point here. But there are other aspects of engineering, such as analysis, experimentation, communication and documentation, phases of work where women are known to find appealing assignments.

Women favour jobs that do not involve certain duties of which some are, unfortunately, characteristic of engineering, such as design, risk projects, travel, field or shop work, physically and mentally demanding tasks, supervisory functions and major responsibilities.[12]

Elsie not only was taken aback when she first read the article, but also assumed it was not meant to be taken seriously.[13] When she realized this was not the case, she wrote a letter to the editor of the journal, in which she condemned Rimrott's overt sex-typing:

I agree that in the "team" concept of today's activities there is ample room for talents other than the creative ones...of the professional engineer – but don't let's single out women as special candidates for the supportive role of engineering aide. To subject a new occupation to traditional sex-typing would, in my mind, be a retrograde step indeed.

As she advanced her argument, she explained the danger of basing ideas on conventional beliefs and expectations of the sexes:

We are aware that differences in the educational motivation of girls and boys are more likely to be rooted in our culture and in their upbringing than in their nature or biological characteristics. In the past our society typed certain occupations as being more appropriate to one sex than the other, and in many fields this tradition lingers on despite economic and technological changes. Consequently, the selection of an occupation today often continues to be more a matter of what that individual has learned to consider appropriate than of what that individual would really prefer to do. This may explain why fewer men than women enter nursing, and why fewer women than men enter engineering.[14]

Elsie argued that engineers needed to eradicate stereotypes within the profession, not further entrench them: "To my mind we in the engineering profession would serve Canada better by bending our energies toward reducing rather than augmenting sex-typing in our field."[15] Elsie's response was not an overreaction, as during the Second World War American women had been trained as engineering aides. As the concept of aide implies, these positions were subordinate, temporary, and offered few possibilities of advancement. Once the war ended, the aides for the most part were terminated when men, with full qualifications, returned to their former positions.[16]

Rimrott's article provoked an intense debate, and the managing editor arranged to publish the responses in a subsequent issue of the journal.[17] Of the four respondents, three, including Elsie, challenged the ideas outlined in the article. Dr. B. Tabarrok, a West German, initially conceded that new curriculum to attract women would be useful, and a degree for women worth considering. However, he challenged the method outlined, which placed women at a disadvantage within engineering: "In the present days of "equal rights for women"…it would be a sad mistake to tailor such a programme for functions of an assistant or an aide to an engineer." Dr. H.F. Muensterer, also a West German, felt that a secondary role for women in engineering was problematic: "As long as men cannot affirmatively reply to the question 'If I were a woman, would I elect to become an Engineering Aide,' the attempt of attracting women to engineering is doomed to fail." He called into question whether it was best to change the curriculum to attract women into engineering or to reduce the social stigma surrounding women in non-traditional careers. The high participation of women in engineering in the Soviet Union seemed to suggest the latter.[18]

The final commentator, Dr. R.G. Fenton of Toronto, wondered what kept the number of Canadian women in engineering so low. Recognizing women's absence as an unfortunate loss to engineering, he suggested Rimrott's ideas might help rectify the gender imbalance. However, his support did not extend to the chosen program name, which he stressed was problematic.[19]

Rimrott, given the opportunity to respond in writing to his critics in the December 1970 issue of the journal, stated that his proposal was not intended to create "second-rank engineers" but a "*different* kind of graduate." He concluded that women, not engineering programs or the profession at large, were responsible for prejudice against the discipline and that his proposal would serve as a means to reduce sex-typing, as it would bring more women into the male-dominated field of engineering.[20]

The debate moved beyond the printed page to an open discussion hosted by the Ontario section of the American Society of Mechanical Engineers (ASME). Ironically, the debate on women in engineering took place during the society's dinner meeting and ladies night.[21] Moderated by Richard Needham of *The Globe and Mail*, the event featured Dr. Rimrott and included a panel of experts: Elsie; Beryl Lake, head of guidance for William Lyon Mackenzie Collegiate Institute; and Dr. P.A. Lapp, author of *Ring of Iron: A Study of Engineering Education in Ontario*.[22]

To prepare for the debate Elsie had made extensive notes on her ideas and arguments. She passionately opposed Rimrott's proposal, but she was tactful: "I cannot look at this occasion as a confrontation, or a chance to win a black belt for women in engineering." She exposed how the article reflected problematic attitudes toward women and limited their prospects: "Traditional attitudes about the kind of work that women should do, or can do, restricts their occupational alternatives. These attitudes affect not only the expectations of girls and hence their training…but also the kind of employment that is open to women." She further argued that as a result society still "persists in regarding the role of women as secondary and supportive to that of men," a view that encourages men and not women to pursue a career in engineering.[23]

Elsie called on universities, colleges, and the Department of Manpower to tackle the problem by revising all job descriptions to ensure that they favoured neither women nor men. She also urged her fellow engineers to support women within the profession, especially when family and professional responsibilities conflicted.[24] Following the debate, J.N. Turnbull, chairman of the Ontario section of the ASME, wrote a letter in which he praised Elsie's performance:

> It takes courage to voice comments in public, especially on this subject which now has considerable emotional content. Judging by the response from the floor, I am certain that the panel stimulated those attending to think more deeply about the subject. Hopefully, this increased awareness will benefit both women and engineering.[25]

While Elsie was in the heat of the debate over Rimrott's article, she was not oblivious to efforts on behalf of women in other branches of the profession. For instance, she commended J.B. Carruthers of the Association of Professional Engineers of Ontario for taking up the case of women engineers who were seeking equal access to employment in the field.[26]

· · · · · · · · ·

By her seventieth year Elsie had been a practising engineer for almost half a century and she began to reflect more deeply on the engineering profession's relationship with women. Overall, while Elsie had faced her share of challenges, her status as a trailblazer did not greatly impede her progress. This was especially true during the war, when the knowledge and skills she possessed were in short supply. As one of a few specialists in her field, she did not need to continually prove herself.[27] However, she began to see that her experience was exceptional.

As she became more aware of the challenges women engineers faced, Elsie became increasingly vocal about the situation and determined to make a difference. She began to write and speak publically about these difficulties. During International Women's Year in 1975, the *Engineering Journal* published a special section on women in engineering. It highlighted women's achievements in the profession and featured an article by Elsie, entitled "Women Engineers Meet a 'Corset of Victorian Prejudice.'"[28] She wrote:

> We hear the phrase "Exceptional women who have made it in a man's world." Well, there are no exceptional women and no exceptional men either. The person referred to is a normal woman or man with more degrees of freedom than most normal people have. Boil down all the discussions and I think this is the essence of the matter. It can be taken as the answer not only to "what do women want?", but to "what do women need?" In all aspects of life, they need greater degrees of freedom of choice, and greater degrees of freedom of action.

She continued:

> [Women] do meet handicaps in their professional development that male engineers do not. These hinder them in their career, prevent them from making their full contribution to their profession and damage, not only them, but the whole profession by diluting its quality and its worth and value to Canada.[29]

In the article and at a later speaking engagement, Elsie admitted that she too had experienced prejudice during her engineering career. One example she cited centred on concerns expressed for her personal safety when she insisted on participating in test flights in the aircraft she designed. As she explained, a dangerous assignment offered the same risks to men or women.[30] In her *Engineering Journal* article she referred to these situations as "managerial misconceptions and hang-ups that the men don't [have to deal with] – a corset of Victorian prejudice into which the women, but not the men, are squeezed."[31]

Elsie described some additional obstacles faced by women engineers, including the belief that women were unable to deal with extreme working conditions such as high or low temperatures. She lamented that often women were moved sideways in an organization instead of receiving promotions they deserved, thereby being blocked from career advancement. She described how frustrating it was for a woman applying for an engineering position to be asked, incredulously, "You're a what?"

If you consider a woman engineer an oddball, even though you hire her, you are apt not to take her employment seriously, and you're not very likely to give much thought to her need for professional development. Yet, when a woman engineer applies for engineering work, she is not just looking for a job; she is building a career.[32]

Elsie believed these problems could be solved if her colleagues truly believed in the full participation of women engineers in the profession.[33] Overall, as her understanding of women's status within engineering was changing and maturing, she discovered that the integration of large numbers of women into engineering required institutional and administrative changes supported by the profession as a whole.[34]

Elsie's call for the equal treatment of women within the engineering profession foreshadowed subsequent developments. Multiple voices, including those of Ursula Franklin, Claudette Lassonde, and Monique Frize, later called for social and institutional changes that required "more than just numbers."[35]

The special Women in Engineering section of the *Engineering Journal,* and Elsie's article within it, provided a refreshing glimpse of women within the profession and offered a degree of promise for further advancement of women.[36] However, it also exposed some of the internal tensions Elsie was struggling with. For example, she took issue with the biographical note that accompanied her article. It did not stick to the facts about her professional engineering career alone; it also called attention to her age, physical ability, and extra-curricular activities:

> Elsie Gregory MacGill is one of the pioneers of women's entry into the engineering profession. Though she is now *70* years old *and uses a wheel chair* she runs her own consulting practice in Toronto, and speaks to many groups about women's rights, women engineers' rights in particular.[37]

Elsie believed that she was not being accorded the same respect as her male colleagues who would have been acknowledged for their professional achievements alone,[38] a reaction that exposes some of the conflicts between Elsie's professional and feminist identities.

Although her public testimony about discrimination toward women in the engineering profession and her desire to help women in engineering complemented one another, she did not want to call too much attention to her status as a woman engineer or a feminist activist within the world of professional engineering. After all, viewing herself as an engineer and not a *woman* engineer had served her well throughout her career.

Scholar Linda Christiansen-Ruffman suggests that other women pioneers also experienced difficulty with their identity as professionals and women. She argues that one of their coping mechanisms was to reject references to their female identities and thus become "invisible as women" within their professions.[39] This appears to be have often been the case for Elsie when she had her engineering hat on.[40]

Elsie's advocacy for women in engineering and other women's growing consciousness within the profession led to new initiatives for change. Acknowledging how few women there were in the profession, some engineers at Ontario Hydro decided in the late 1970s to form a supportive national organization, Women in Science and Engineering (WISE). The goals of this action were to create networking opportunities and at the same time encourage more women to engage in science and engineering.[41]

The founders of the organization sought assistance from Elsie in February 1979. As founding president, Claudette Lassonde wrote to Elsie:

> We believe that such an organization can encourage young women to go into these fields and also increase our self-confidence in trying to achieve both at the educational level and in the industry. We also hope that we will be able to raise the awareness of the Canadian private industry to the presence of very qualified engineers who happen to be women. But we are a very small group, having only approximately 45 members. We need a lot of moral support and some role models to look up to.[42]

Claudette Lassonde told Elsie she was "the Number One Canadian woman engineer to look up to," and she hoped that Elsie would do WISE the honour of speaking to them about her own experiences as a woman in the profession, while offering any advice she could. Elsie agreed to the request and arranged to speak to the group on April 23, 1979.[43] During her speech she acknowledged that women face unique challenges in engineering and so need to remain self-confident and not doubt or question the importance of their presence in the workplace.[44] Elsie was well-received by the membership, and left a lasting impression on the organization, which later recognized her as its first honorary member.[45]

Elsie also made a point of celebrating the achievements of other women engineers. When Danielle Zaikoff was elected as the first woman president of the Canadian Council of Professional Engineers (CCPE) in 1978, Elsie wrote to congratulate her:

> Please accept my warmest congratulations on your elevation to the presidency of CCPE. It is, I am sure, a recognition of your professional ability and of your good work for the Order of Engineers of Québec.[46]

Footnotes for this chapter can be found online at:
http://secondstorypress.ca/resources and at http://feministhistories.ca/books

Chapter 11
SEIZING THE POTENTIAL OF
INTERNATIONAL WOMEN'S YEAR

*I.W.Y. [International Women's Year] has opened the door but
that does not guarantee that anyone will pass through it. Inertia
breeds isolation. We need to push that door wide open and let all
women pass through it and in so doing make a better society, but
you have to do your part.*

In the end it's all up to you.[1]

—Elsie Gregory MacGill

After several years on the Royal Commission on the Status of
Women, followed by actively promoting the commission's recommendations, Elsie did not seem to know how to slow down. At a
time in life when most people tend to reduce their activities and
retire, she became involved in new feminist projects.

Pressed by the International Federation of Business and
Professional Women (International Federation) among others, the
United Nations declared that 1975 would be International Women's
Year (IWY).[2] Elsie believed that activities in celebration of IWY
could be catalysts for further change. Asked to join the federal gov-
ernment's speakers' bureau, Elsie made speeches that year about the
status of women at a number of venues, including the Action '75
IWY conference in Ottawa, the IWY celebration at the Canadian
National Exhibition in Toronto, the Tuesday Luncheon Club of
St. Lawrence College, and to the nursing administration at the
University of Toronto. She also provided the Federation of Women
Teachers Association of Ontario with background information for
their IWY film *Visible Women.*[3]

Despite the year's focus on women, Elsie reinforced the need
for the participation of men:

And give the men a break. Don't keep them on the outside. Let
them join us in our projects to help other women. They too are
confused by changes in the social structure, because, like us, they

were conditioned as children to the stereotype expectations – Mother in one role, Father in another. Show them that a fairer deal for women means a fairer deal for men.[4]

With this in mind, she advocated that women's groups identify initiatives and programs for IWY that they would work toward achieving by the year's end.

Elsie viewed IWY as a key opportunity for the Canadian Federation of Business and Professional Women's Clubs (Canadian Federation) to advance their agenda, so she called on her sisters there to engage in new projects for IWY. She wanted the organization to be able to look back on the year with pride: "My push for IWY is aimed at trying to get each Club, organization association, group, etc., focusing its attention on some one (or more) aspects toward accomplishing some specific object – of which it can be said in years to come – "THIS WE OBTAINED in 1975, I.W.YEAR."[5]

Members of the national executive responded positively, and asked Elsie to serve on the Canadian Federation's ad hoc committee for IWY. However, she declined this role as she was more interested in other projects implemented under the IWY umbrella.[6] She was particularly interested in two projects on issues that deeply concerned her: the elimination of violence against women, and the recognition of women's history and their contributions to society.

· · · · · · · · ·

In the 1970s, women activists throughout North America began to address the issue of rape and domestic violence.[7] The RCSW Report had avoided dealing directly with violence against women, except for recommendations related to allowable testimony in rape trials.[8] While not initially seeking to lead Toronto-based IWY activities, Elsie was drawn into a project of the Toronto Business and Professional Women's Club (TBPWC) to support the Toronto Rape Crisis Centre, and became co-convenor, with fellow club member Shirley Griffin, of an ad hoc committee to oversee this work.[9]

The project had two aspects: providing financial support to the Toronto Rape Crisis Centre, which had only recently opened its doors; and encouraging a review of the existing legal responses to rape. The TBPWC met its financial commitment with a donation to the centre in February 1975. After assessing the existing reports on violence against women and debating how best to expand public discussion of the issue, the ad hoc committee decided to organize a public meeting on rape. The committee hoped that the project would increase "the general public's awareness regarding the serious psychological, physical and cultural implications of the widespread crime against women, Rape – the only crime in which the victim is doubly violated, first by the attacker and then by society."[10] The event was also designed to raise critical awareness of the laws related to rape, as well as to publicize the services offered by the Toronto Rape Crisis Centre.[11]

The meeting, "Rape – myths and realities," took place on October 1, 1975, at Toronto's St. Lawrence Centre. The event started with a short film on rape prevention, followed by an expert panel moderated by Judy LaMarsh. The panellists included a psychologist, criminologists, and a crown attorney.[12] The meeting was packed; an overflow crowd of more than 500 people attended, and many had to be seated in the lobby. The event provided key information on a serious matter and at the same time increased the visibility of the TBPWC in current affairs.[13]

These activities were timely. In 1975 and the years that followed, key reforms were made to the *Criminal Code* due to demands by women's groups.[14] The Canadian Federation as a whole campaigned on the issue of rape. One of the organization's 1978 resolutions demanded that these crimes be defined in the *Criminal Code* as gender-neutral assaults rather than sexual offences. They also asked for changes to the *Canada Evidence Act*, in order to make the complainant's previous sexual history inadmissible in court.[15] Although written in 1978, this resolution foreshadowed the creation of "rape shield" laws between 1982 and 1991.[16]

· · · · · · · · ·

As well being involved in IWY projects at the local club level, Elsie lobbied for the creation of federal and provincial resource centres on women's historical and contemporary achievements. At its twenty-fourth biennial convention in 1974, the Canadian Federation called for the creation of a Canadian Women Resource Centre and encouraged the provincial organizations to lobby for similar centres in each province.[17] Except for the case of Ontario, there is very little information available about efforts to establish a national centre or multiple provincial centres. In Ontario, Elsie's enthusiasm and tenacity led the Business and Professional Women's Clubs of Ontario (BPWCO) to support development of the Ontario Women's Resource Centre.

Elsie's dedication to establishing this Ontario centre echoes her mother's determination to found the Vancouver Women's Building, which was established in 1910.[18] Like her mother, Elsie envisioned the centre as a place where women and organizations could meet and work. She also wanted it to be a place where women's histories and achievements would be honoured and preserved.[19] The project was approved at the annual BPWCO conference in May 1974.[20] The resolution clearly specified the two main aspects of the proposed centre: first, "to collect, cross-reference and house archival material on women of Ontario and their activities in the Province"; and second, "to provide space and facilities for individuals and groups to organize exhibits and view films related to women's activities."[21]

The work evolved into a province-wide campaign that lasted until 1979.[22] Elsie prepared a detailed message to all BPWCO members to ensure support from all parts of the province, not just Toronto, the proposed location for the centre.[23] The project was supported by 52 local clubs and the provincial organization.[24] Ontario club members lobbied at Toronto city hall and the Ontario legislature. The project was supported by Margaret Campbell, a Member of Provincial Parliament (MPP) from Sudbury, and organizations ranging from the YWCA to the Canadian Advisory Council on the Status of Women.[25] When she approached former minister of revenue A.K. Meen in 1976, Elsie proposed using the recently vacated Metropolitan Toronto Central Library for the Ontario Women's Resource Centre (OWRC), arguing, "It would be a very positive action that would emphasize the fact that the Government of Ontario has a real interest in and desire to improve the status of women throughout the province."[26]

Elsie was the driving force in this project, but she was also strongly supported by two successive BPWCO presidents, each of whom approached the Women's Program Division of the Ontario Ministry of Labour, the Ontario Heritage Foundation, the Premier of Ontario, and the Minister of Culture and Recreation for Support. None of these efforts bore fruit.[27] Undaunted, Margaret Jackson, provincial president of the BPWCO, made another attempt in 1976, seeking the assistance of then Minister of Culture and Recreation, Robert Welch. After outlining how the various sectors of the provincial government could come together in a united effort to make the centre a reality, Margaret Jackson reiterated Elsie's arguments:

> We see the Ontario Women's Resource Centre as an institution which the women of Ontario will find invaluable, and which will stand as a noble and generous recognition on the part of the Government of Ontario of the exploits and achievements of women down the years in developing the cultural life and values of the province. Moreover, establishing the Ontario Women's Resource Centre in the Metro Toronto Central Library Building will continue unbroken the long history of cultural public service for which this building was planned and built some 66 years ago".[28]

Elsie was concerned that a failure to create the OWRC could be damaging to the BPWCO as this project was the biggest the Ontario clubs had ever undertaken.[29] As she wrote to fellow member Helen Verdin in 1976, "We are in so deep...that we must proceed or BPWC's reputation will suffer badly."[30]

Despite Elsie's standing in the Canadian Federation, the proposal met with internal challenges. Her request for financial support from the Canadian Federation's Centenary Year Fund was not granted. She was told that the proposed resource centre did not fit the fund's revised mandate.[31] As this fund had been established during her tenure as national president, with the original goal of supporting "extraordinary educational and other projec[ts] for the women of Canada," this restriction must have deeply frustrated Elsie.[32]

As the campaign for the OWRC entered the year 1977, Elsie continued to press for its creation.[33] Early in January, she renewed communications with the Minister of Culture and Recreation in the hopes of convincing him of the value of the proposal. Strongly emphasizing the need for comprehensive versus piecemeal provincial funding, she refused to accept available Wintario lottery funds for the project.[34]

The challenges confronted in securing funding were compounded by competition for the chosen site: the Metropolitan Toronto Central Library building.[35] The competitor for the site was none other than Elsie's own alma mater, the Faculty of Applied Sciences and Engineering at the University of Toronto! The engineering faculty wanted the property for its own library, and was already negotiating with the Metropolitan Toronto Council.[36] Upon learning of this plan, Elsie wrote to the Vice-president of Planning at the University of Toronto to propose sharing the building. However, the university had plans for the whole space and was not open to Elsie's proposal.[37]

This defeat did not derail the campaign. The committee on behalf of establishing the OWRC encouraged the Ontario club members to keep promoting the initiative after the Faculty of Applied Science and Engineering was awarded the location for a limited period of four years.[38] Elsie proposed that the BPWCO allocate $20,000 over a two-year period to support individual clubs in collecting and managing materials for the eventual creation of the centre. However, the Ontario clubs, while supportive of the ongoing campaign, had no more financial resources for the project. They did, however, agree to approach Ontario community colleges about the possibility of assisting in the cataloguing of the archival materials that had been collected.[39]

Perhaps the key barrier to the creation of the resource centre was a rival campaign for a Women's Cultural Centre in Toronto. Successfully incorporated in July 1975, the Women's Cultural Centre sought funding through a combination of private fundraising and grants. It was also able to acquire a building for the centre in September 1976: Toronto's former city morgue.[40]

While planning for the Women's Cultural Centre progressed, Elsie continued the fight for an OWRC funded by the province. In a letter to then Premier William Davis, she noted that while the Women's Cultural Centre provided an excellent venue for the local Toronto area, its scope was not province-wide and not as comprehensive as that of the proposed OWRC. She called on the province to support the provincial centre in the same way it funded the Royal Ontario Museum and the Archives of Ontario, arguing that it would serve all the women of Ontario and ensure the legacy of women's important contributions to Ontario's history.[41]

While Elsie was determined to illustrate the differences between the two projects, the TBPWC invited the Helen Notzl, president of the Toronto Women's Cultural Centre, to speak at one of their meetings. She outlined plans for the Women's Cultural Centre, including a library space, an area for art displays, and a restaurant. These objectives were very close to those of the OWRC.[42] Indeed, the largest difference between the two ventures seemed to be that the BPWCO proposal for the OWRC called for full public funding, and there was little to show for its efforts; by contrast, the Women's Cultural Centre had funds from multiple sources and was only months away from opening its doors.

Elsie nevertheless stubbornly persisted in arguing for the OWRC, even when it became necessary to defend the project within the ranks of the BPWCO.[43] Her tenacity may have stemmed in part from her knowledge of the long gestation of the World Center of Women's Archives in the United States, a project that took more than ten years to realize.[44]

It is not clear how Elsie reconciled her vision of an OWRC with her support for other projects to collect and preserve historical records of women and their organizations. During her mandate as president of the Canadian Federation, she had arranged a transfer of the organization's records to the National Archives.[45] Not only were these records accepted, but the archivists contacted Elsie in 1974 to ask for her own records. In response to this request she wrote:

> I am very pleased to learn of the Archives activities in seeking out material on the contributions of Canadian women to Canadian life, and records of organizations etc. For the past decade I have been urging individuals and associations to file such records with the appropriate archives." However, Elsie said she had few personal papers to contribute and anticipated donating the materials she did have to the British Columbia Archives.[46]

The gathering and archiving of women's records had another competitor. Early in 1975, an archivist at the Archives of Ontario observed that they were currently storing documents from the BPWCO and that the provincial facility was best suited to the professional care and management of documents requiring preservation.[47] This letter was an early warning sign that the OWRC would be fighting an uphill battle to convince the provincial government of the necessity for a separate facility.

This situation was compounded by the changing economic realities in the latter 1970s and the 1980s that reduced government support for new programs. Securing a large investment of public money to support the OWRC proved impossible. However, the proponents of the Women's Cultural Centre – which opened in 1979 – succeeded with support from prominent women such as sculptor Maryon Kantaroff, author Margaret Atwood, and politician Judy LaMarsh.[48]

Elsie conceded defeat, at least temporarily. Along with Joan Wilson, co-chair of the OWRC's Committee, Elsie recommended to the 1980 BPWCO conference that the centre's committee be disbanded until the Toronto Metropolitan Library building became available again in 1982. Then, if the BPWCO board of directors deemed the venture viable, the committee could be reconstituted to continue its work toward establishing the centre.[49]

Elsie's feminist dedication and determination were recognized provincially when she was named "an outstanding woman of the Province of Ontario for International Women's Year, 1975" by Premier William Davis.[50]

Footnotes for this chapter can be found online at:
http://secondstorypress.ca/resources and at http://feministhistories.ca/books

Chapter 12

RECOGNITION AND CELEBRATION

Your career has assuredly generated both honour and distinction
well deserved and this has, in turn, reflected with great favour on
Canada's engineering fraternity.[1]

—Paul B. Dilworth

Elsie's lifelong dedication to the engineering profession and the improvement of women's status did not go unnoticed. Her peers voiced their appreciation for her unique ability to serve both the engineering and feminist communities.

While she had achieved early accolades from the Engineering Institute of Canada, The Society of Women Engineers, and the Gaevert Gallery of Canadian Executives, the full recognition of Elsie's contribution at the national level began in the late 1960s and continued into the 1970s. The first of these honours was the Canada Centennial Medal awarded by the Governor General of Canada in 1967.[2] Four years later she received the Medal of Service. In 1973, she was recognized with the greatest national honour, the Order of Canada. In 1977, she received the Queen Elizabeth II Silver Jubilee Medal, awarded to individuals who have made a significant contribution to their community or to Canada.[3]

Elsie was keen to ensure that others were recognized for their achievements nationally. Between 1967 and 1979, for example, she nominated thirty-seven people (women and men) for the Order of Canada. Thirteen of these were awarded the honour, including her friend and colleague Ursula Franklin.[4]

• • • • • • • • •

The vibrant nature of Elsie's character is tangible in this photo from her October 1971 investiture ceremony for the Order of Canada.

Elsie was honoured by several universities, and especially by the Faculty of Applied Science and Engineering at the University of Toronto. In 1973, the centenary year of that faculty, the university awarded her an honorary Doctor of Laws degree.[5] Elsie excitedly wrote her family to share the news, reminding them of a similar award made to her mother in 1938, and saying, "After long (one minute) serious consideration, I have decided to accept."[6]

The university chose Dr. Margaret Bassett, of the Department of Electrical Engineering to prepare and read Elsie's citation.[7] Like Elsie, Margaret Bassett had begun her studies in electrical engineering and went on to graduate studies.[8] Elsie later wrote to her, saying, "I was very pleased and proud to be presented by a female member of the Faculty, and one in the Department in which I first graduated."[9] Elsie's award was only part of a very full day that she shared with engineering colleagues and her family. She wrote:

The Engineering Convocation on June 1st was a wonderful day for me. Helen and Everett were here from Cambridge, Mass, and

they and Bill and I were luncheon guests of the Chancellor
that day – as were the two other
engineers receiving LL.Ds.
Both of the latter were long-
time friends of mine – so it was
a very joyful occasion. That
evening we were guests of the
Engineering Alumni Society...
Wonderful fun![10]

Many of Elsie's feminist col-
leagues sent their congratulations.
As long-time colleague Isabel
MacMillan wrote to Elsie:

It's good to know that recognition has been accorded to
one who has given so much
of herself to improving not
only the status of women but
of all people in Canada and
elsewhere who need help and
encouragement as they seek to

Elsie MacGill and Bill Soulsby in their garden on
Bennington Heights Drive after the ceremony
where Elsie received her honorary doctorate at the
University of Toronto.

abolish discriminatory practises. And all the while "making it" in
a male-dominated field![11]

The honorary doctorate from her alma mater was the first of
four that Elsie received. The University of Windsor awarded her
this honour in 1976, and Queen's University and York University
followed suit in 1978.[12]

In June 1977, on the fiftieth anniversary of her graduation, Elsie
was further honoured by the University of Toronto as "a worthy
member of the engineering profession, a good school man, and an
alumnus in whom the University takes great pride." In June 1980,
she was inducted into University of Toronto's Hall of Distinction.[13]
Nor was Elsie forgotten by the first university she attended, the
University of British Columbia, which singled her out with an
award of distinction in 1975.[14]

Elsie posed in her convocation regalia
for her honorary doctorate from the
University of Toronto.

• • • • • • • • •

Elsie's colleagues within the various professional organizations to which she belonged also recognized and celebrated her achievements.[15] The Engineering Institute of Canada (EIC) made her a fellow in 1972, recognizing excellence in engineering and services to the profession and society.[16] Although individuals could apply for a fellowship within the EIC if they met the eligibility requirements, Elsie's situation was unique. Her colleagues within the Toronto branch of the EIC met and agreed that she should be nominated as a fellow and that her application should be sponsored by the branch.[17] The general manager of the EIC, Byron Kerr, noted that Elsie had distinguished herself as an engineer and made significant contributions to the country as a whole.[18] The February 1973 edition of the *Engineering Journal* featured Elsie and six other new fellows on the cover.[19]

A year later, Elsie received the EIC's Julian C. Smith Award "for achievement and development in Canada."[20] William Leslie Hutchinson was responsible for submitting Elsie's nomination, and he gave the tribute during the awards ceremony, noting:

> During her career, she has been active in many organizations, both professional and social, not only in Canada but abroad as well. And being active to Dr. MacGill means contributing to the utmost as those of you who have worked with her in the E.I.C. will know where her efforts on the Branch, Regional and National levels have reacted greatly to the benefit of this Institute and the Profession in Canada.[21]

At the provincial level, Elsie's talents were recognized with her appointment to the Ontario Building and Material Evaluation Committee (BMEC) in 1975. This was not just a token appointment during International Women's Year. She brought a wealth of knowledge and experience to this position, as well as important networking connections in the National Research Council, industry, and the universities, which was very useful to the work of BMEC.[22] In addition, she brought experience in public inquiries that allowed her to guide procedures and encourage efficiency. As a result of her contribution of expertise, in 1980 she was made chairman of the BMEC.[23]

Elsie's colleagues within the Association of Consulting Engineers of Canada (ACEC) recognized her contributions to the world of consulting engineering. By unanimous decision in 1976, they made her an honorary member of the board of directors at the international congress and annual meeting of the International Federation of Consulting Engineers and ACEC.[24]

Colleagues in the Association of Professional Engineers of Ontario (APEO) acknowledged Elsie's important contributions when in 1979 they awarded her the APEO Gold Medal. This award is made to an engineer who is recognized as giving "outstanding service to the country" and "is recognized by a section of the public as a dedicated and successful servant who is making or has made large sacrifices of time and effort for the public weal."[25]

The public presentation of the award was made by APEO president Tim Benson. Elsie subsequently gave an acceptance speech, entitled "Cracks in Aircraft," in which she discussed the issue of aviation safety. She kept the tone light and emphasized the importance of looking to the future, where she envisioned everyone having access to a means of air transportation for their daily needs.[26]

Elsie noted that the award sent her "soaring into the wild blue yonder, especially when I consider the long line of twenty distinguished engineers who have preceded me in this honour."[27] Elsie's well-known sense of humour further lightened the mood when she described how times had changed economically since the first award was bestowed on C.D. Howe:

> It is ironic that though my service is much less than Mr Howe's, the intrinsic value of my medal is about eleven times greater than that of his – when the price of gold was fixed at $35 an ounce with fluctuations either way limited to 20 cents.
>
> Perhaps Bill [Soulsby] and I should ask for a police escort going home tonight.[28]

• • • • • • • • •

Early in her feminist career Elsie received support and recognition from her sisters in the Canadian Federation of Business and Professional Women's Clubs (Canadian Federation). Through a lifetime membership and in her nominations for provincial and national leadership, she was recognized for her guidance and influence within the organization. Colleagues took pride in her wide range of accomplishments, celebrating them alongside her.[29]

Liz Neville, president of the Toronto Business and Professional Women's Club (TBPWC) in 1979, benefited from Elsie's support and insights; she remembered that Elsie "made me work really hard, but she was there beside me all the time, and brought herself to bear...when we made presentations...I just wouldn't have had the insight and the nerve...if I hadn't known that there were people like Elsie."[30] Dormer Ellis recalled that with Elsie, obstacles in the path were never seen as a reason for abandoning a cause:

> What I noticed particularly about her, was that she always thought that you should find a way around obstacles. You can't just say 'Well, I can't do that'. She'd say 'Of course you can, you just find another way around it.' And that was very useful in many aspects of life.[31]

Elsie earned respect from her women colleagues not just for her knowledge and expertise, but also for the nature of her leadership.[32] Indeed, as Canadian Federation member Charlotte VanDine reminded Elsie, "Anyone serving on a board of which you were the President or chairman, was never given the impression that she worked "under" you, or "for" you, but she always worked "with" you."[33] And Ruth Jesshope noted,

> To me and to many other members Elsie continued to be BPW itself through her constant efforts, support, and commitment throughout the years, indeed right up to the time of her death. Provincial Conferences and National Conventions lost a lot of their spark the few times that Elsie was not able to attend. It was her quick mind and her dedication to the highest goals for BPW, as well as her tireless faith in women, that brought orderliness out of the chaos during business sessions when discussions on resolutions or reports strayed from the issue, or lost their objectivity".[34]

Her Canadian Federation colleagues were not the only women who noted Elsie's important contributions as a professional and as a feminist. In 1975 she received the Amelia Earhart Medal from the International Association of Women Pilots.[35] In 1979 the Zonta Toronto I Club awarded her its Outstanding Adventurer award;[36] this included a medallion and $400 for the charity of her choice, which she donated to the University of British Columbia in memory of her mother, and to the Zonta Club's Amelia Earhart Scholarship Fund.[37]

Elsie remained active in the TBPWC and the Canadian Federation, even in her final years of life. She attended the seventieth anniversary of the Toronto club at the Royal York Hotel in 1980 and the subsequent BPWCO Conference in Windsor. In July 1980, Elsie travelled to Montréal, Québec, for the Canadian Federation's national convention and fiftieth anniversary celebration; once again she addressed the membership.[38]

· · · · · · · · ·

Elsie never wanted to draw attention to the physical challenges she was forced to deal with since contracting polio in 1929. Those around her quickly learned that they needed to look beyond them, as she did.[39] Elsie demonstrated throughout her life that obstacles, including physical limitations, were something to face and work around. Indeed, she argued that her disability actually allowed her life to be "more interesting." She said, "Frankly, my feeling for the whole business is that I enjoy living and there's no sense in letting anything spoil life for you."[40] Dormer Ellis noted that Elsie saw her increased need for a wheelchair later in life as a tool to achieve her objectives, and rather than being "wheelchair bound," Elsie was "wheelchair liberated."[41]

Elsie was appointed to the Canadian organizing committee for the International Year of Disabled Persons (IYDP) scheduled for 1981, and served as a member of the Community Liaison Program Sub-Committee.[42] In this role she put her networking skills to use drawing attention to events and projects that promoted IYDP objectives, encouraging, for instance, the Ontario's Building Code Commission and the Building Materials Evaluation Committee (BMEC) to consider incorporating persons with disabilities into their membership.[43]

Elsie did not see herself as a modern-day heroine. In fact, as more recognition was given to her achievements and to her collection of awards, she sometimes felt overwhelmed by the pressure of media attention and the demand for details regarding her personal life. As she said to one reporter:

> I'm vastly over-exposed. There's nothing special about me. Anyway, people don't want to know what I've done. All they want is personal bilge – do I have a cat, do I cook? Well, I won't tell you any of that stuff. I can't stand being asked the same old questions. Sorry to be such a curmudgeon, but that's what I am.[44]

Elsie's close friends and colleagues knew better. Fellow Canadian Federation member Charlotte Van Dine challenged Elsie's comments: "You may be many things to many people, but one thing you are not, and that is a 'curmudgeon', even when it comes to interviews. You couldn't be a curmudgeon even if you tried – but I have to admit it is a lovely word!"[45]

Elsie celebrated the distinctions she received, but wanted to ensure that others just as deserving were not overlooked. In her busy life she still made time for her colleagues, friends, and family and increasingly sought solace in quiet pleasures, including her gardens at home in Toronto.[46]

Footnotes for this chapter can be found online at:
http://secondstorypress.ca/resources and at http://feministhistories.ca/books

Chapter 13

A SUDDEN LOSS...

[An] unexpected illness, has robbed the [Canadian Aeronautical and Space] Institute of one of its most distinguished Fellows.[1]

—J.J. Green

I loved and admired Elsie deeply, her ideals, her intelligence and courage, her attention to others, her sensitivity hidden under this beautiful smile, this wonder wit of hers.[2]

—Jeanne Lapointe

You know how profoundly I have always respected Elsie, for her combination of compassion and competence, for her integrity, her sense of justice and her sense of humour, her ability to keep cheerful has often been an example to me.[3]

—Ursula Franklin

Throughout the summer and early fall of 1980, Elsie was active in committee meetings and events organized around the repatriation of the Constitution and what became the Canadian Charter of Rights and Freedoms.[4] Elsie's death on November 4, 1980, came without warning and left her family, friends, and colleagues at a complete loss.

Elsie had travelled to Cambridge, Massachusetts, to visit her sister and brother-in-law. She arrived suffering from a cough, but refused to see a doctor. During the visit, her condition worsened and she was forced to enter hospital. Shortly afterward she passed away.[5]

On November 26, 1980 a "Service of Gratitude and Reminiscence" was held in Elsie's honour at the University of Toronto's Knox College Chapel. The list of attendees and speakers reflected Elsie's diverse connections in the worlds of engineering and women's activism, and included fellow engineers John Fox, J.J. Green, Jack Dyment, William Leslie Hutchison and feminists Margaret Hyndman, Florence Bird, and Lorna Marsden, who spoke of "a friendly, warm human being with a keen mind, brave spirit and a waggish sense of humour."[6] Elizabeth Hughes Schneewind, Elsie's niece, spoke on behalf of Elsie's sister Helen, and Bill Soulsby spoke in remembrance of his life partner.[7]

Elsie's life touched many people. Though she received countless awards, she may not have realized the full extent of her influence. In the months after her death, her husband received numerous letters of condolence that provided touching accounts of her life and spoke to her dynamic personality. As one of her engineering colleagues testified:

> I have known Elsie since I became a member of the Branch [of the Engineering Institute] almost 30 years ago and I can truly state that she was the most dynamic member the Branch ever had. She set an example which many members followed, but no one was able to accomplish as much as she did. I might add that Elsie was also a source of inspiration for my wife, Dr. Rose Sheinin; we both mourn her passing.[8]

Elsie's leadership was also acknowledged by organizations and initiatives that continued the work to which she had dedicated herself. The official report from the Second Convention of Women Engineers in Canada, for example, was dedicated to her memory.[9]

Elsie's colleagues in the Canadian Federation responded in multiple ways to her loss. The Toronto Business and Professional Women's Club, which remembered her fondly as "Our Elsie," created an Elsie Gregory MacGill Commemorative Fund.[10] At the national level, her contributions were honoured in both official languages in the pages of *The Business and Professional Woman*. Geraldine Farmer, president of the Canadian Federation wrote the following tribute:

> Elsie has touched and enriched not only our personal lives but also the lives of all Canadian women, all Canadians. Her incisive mind, her courage, her indomitable spirit, her lively humour, her love of humanity, her hope and persistence in making our world a better place in which to live, have permeated her lifelong humanitarian activities.
>
> Let us hope that the spirit of Elsie Gregory MacGill will live on in the Federation. She has provided us with a great legacy – a working and successful model for serving humanity, a model

that may be emulated by young and old. She has thrown the torch to us – a torch of extraordinary brilliance, direction, warmth and encouragement. Let us ensure that we keep it alive.[11]

• • • • • • • • •

The Elsie Gregory MacGill Memorial Foundation created in 1984,[12] was a joint project of Elsie's engineering and feminist colleagues; it exemplified the degree to which she had forged connections between these two areas of her life.[13] The annual award, consisting of five thousand dollars and a sculpture by Canadian artist Maryon Kantaroff, was to be bestowed upon "a person of exceptional achievement, who may direct it toward improving the physical environment and/or equality of opportunity for

Maryon Kantaroff produced statues to accompany the monetary awards for the recipients of the Elsie Gregory MacGill Memorial Fund. The statue pictured here was awarded to Dr. Ursula Franklin in 1987.

women, men and disabled persons in legal, educational, social or economic spheres."[14]

The award was intended for research in areas that Elsie embraced, such as engineering and applied science, or women's studies.[15] The sculpture comprised two distinct sections that merged to reflect the "flowing creativity and logical structured thought and action" of Elsie's life, while at the same time "representing the ancient female relationship of wise grandmother, mother and daughter."[16] The first recipients, who clearly embodied the spirit of the award, were Jeanne Lapointe, Laval University (1986), Ursula Franklin, University of Toronto (1987), and Dormer Ellis, Ontario Institute for Studies in Education (1988).[17]

• • • • • • • • •

ELIZABETH (ELSIE) GREGORY MACGILL, O.C.
1905 – 1980

ELSIE MACGILL WAS THE FIRST WOMAN GRADUATE IN ENGINEERING
FROM THE UNIVERSITY OF TORONTO IN 1927 AND THE FIRST FEMALE
MEMBER OF THE ASSOCIATION OF PROFESSIONAL ENGINEERS OF ONTARIO.
ALTHOUGH CRIPPLED BY POLIO, SHE CONTRIBUTED SIGNIFICANTLY TO THE
DEVELOPMENT OF THE CANADIAN AIRCRAFT INDUSTRY 1934-43, DESIGNING
THE MAPLE LEAF II TRAINER AND OVERSEEING PRODUCTION OF HURRICANE
AND HELLDIVER FIGHTER PLANES. AFTER THE WAR SHE SERVED AS TECHNICAL
ADVISOR TO THE UNITED NATIONS CIVIL AVIATION ORGANIZATION SHE
WAS PRESIDENT OF THE CANADIAN FEDERATION OF BUSINESS AND PRO-
FESSIONAL WOMEN'S CLUBS 1962-64 AND LATER A MEMBER OF THE ROYAL
COMMISSION ON THE STATUS OF WOMEN IN CANADA SHE WAS
APPOINTED TO THE ORDER OF CANADA IN 1971 AND RECEIVED
THE PROFESSIONAL ENGINEERS GOLD MEDAL IN 1979

TORONTO HISTORICAL BOARD
1987

This plaque, unveiled by the Toronto Historical Board, stands outside the Sir Sandford Fleming building at the University of Toronto.

Elsie continues to be remembered by those who knew her in life and those who came to know her through the recollections of others. In her adopted hometown of Toronto her memory has been kept alive. The University of Toronto featured her in its 1985 exhibition "100 Years: Women at the University of Toronto."[18] Later, the Toronto Historical Board unveiled a plaque in her memory at the University of Toronto, a joint effort by the Association of Professional Engineers of Ontario and the Elsie Gregory MacGill Memorial Foundation.[19]

In 1992, the Canadian Science and Engineering Hall of Fame officially opened in Ottawa at the Canadian Museum of Science and Technology. Elsie was featured alongside other prominent individuals who had made significant contributions to Canadian science and technology such as Maude Abbott, Sir Frederick Banting, and Wallace Turnbull. The twin goals of the Hall of Fame were to honour selected individuals and portray them as potential role models for young scientists and engineers.[20]

Remembrances and recognition of Elsie have continued into the twenty-first century. In April 2000, the Canadian Engineering Memorial Foundation – an organization established to remember the fourteen young women killed during the Montréal Massacre on December 6, 1989 – renamed an award previously known as the Women Friendly Schools/Faculties Award as the Elsie MacGill Award.[21] In 2009, the first Elsie MacGill Northern Lights Award was created to honour "Canadian women who have demonstrated determination, enthusiasm, courage, and personal accomplishment in the aviation or aerospace industry," and who had also made significant contributions over a full and active career, or who show extreme promise for their future career in aviation or aerospace, and are recognized as role models for other women.[22] In March and June 2012, two separate awards were made: first, Elsie was commemorated at the twenty-third International Women in Aviation Conference in Dallas, Texas when she was inducted into the Pioneer Hall of Fame; secondly, Parks Canada unveiled twin plaques in Thunder Bay, Ontario, in honour of the former Canadian Car and Foundry plant (now Bombardier) and Elsie's contributions to aviation during the Second World War and to the advancement of women's equality.[23]

A variety of authors have also kept Elsie's memory alive. Richard Bourgeois-Doyle wrote the first book-length biography of Elsie's life, *Her Daughter the Engineer*, and Jeanette Lynes' novel, *The*

These stunning glass pieces are given to each recipient of the Elsie Gregory MacGill Northern Lights Award.

In June 2012, Parks Canada officially unveiled plaques commemorating Elsie Gregory MacGill and Can Car outside the main office of the Bombardier Inc. plant in Thunder Bay, Ontario.

Factory Voice, portrays a fictional character based on Elsie's life.[24] The spring 2011 edition of *SWE: Magazine of the Society of Women Engineers* featured Elsie's story, introduced as "a rich, powerful story that deserves to be better known."[25] Consequently, Elsie's determination to preserve women's history has continued with her own story.

• • • • • • • • •

Elsie Gregory MacGill rode the waves of technological and social change that rocked the twentieth century. She believed that anything was possible even though relentless pressure might be needed to counteract the forces that threatened to stall positive progress. In the latter part of her life Elsie sought to convince the next generation to commit themselves to continue this work. In an address to the graduates at the St. Lawrence College of Arts and Applied Science in Kingston, Ontario, on May 31, 1975, she said:

I take for granted that you will advance your particular discipline, and I hope that you see it as more than something that gains you a livelihood. I think that with your training you are well placed to promote social goals, to open opportunities for everyone and to free people from the stultifying attitudes and practices that hamper their development.

All of us, be we nine years old or fifty-five, have stake in the future because we live in it. You who are young have the greatest stake for you have the longest time there. HOW WILL YOU USE YOUR EXTRA TIME?[26]

Her vision of the possibilities included women's full participation in society, especially in relation to policy and decision-making, and she was "hopeful that the young people growing up today will view 'equal opportunity' as the natural order of life."[27]

Elsie's life was packed with achievements as a woman, an engineer, and a feminist. Her family provided her with a strong foundation and support throughout her lifetime. Many of her male colleagues openly admired her exceptional talent, and the engineering associations to which she belonged accorded her full rights and benefited from her dedicated service. As a result, she did not initially understand the barriers that made progress difficult for other women in her field. However, once she became aware of this difficulty, she advocated for change on behalf of women – even though she never fully resolved her own discomfort with the label "woman engineer."

Although she was slow to start feminist activism, she became a force to be reckoned with when she joined forces with others who fought to improve the status of women in Canada. Her meticulous attention to detail and strong commitment to action served her well within the Canadian Federation of Business and Professional Women's Clubs and as a commissioner on the Royal Commission on the Status of Women in Canada. Her feminism evolved from early efforts in support of equal treatment and opportunities for professional women to the more radical gamut of rights demanded for women in the 1960s and 1970s, including women's control over their bodies, respect for different sexual orientations, and openness to all women's participation within the women's movement.

A feminist biographical study of Elsie's life helps trace the evolution of the engineering profession and the feminist movements of the twentieth century. At the same time, it acknowledges her humanity and limitations. Elsie was physically challenged throughout her life due to her battle with polio as a young woman. For a large part of her life she was also bound by the limitations of her class within society, which was reinforced by her participation in associations composed mainly of professional men and women. However, she was willing to learn and quick to adapt as she demonstrated by acknowledging mistakes, failures, and changes of heart.

Ultimately, Elsie was a determined and persistent professional engineer and feminist, who was not only driven to achieve multiple goals, but who also took time to enjoy life. Her engineering colleague and close friend J.J. Green described her perhaps as well as anyone could when he wrote:

> Elsie was gifted with a number of superb human qualities. She had enormous courage and spirit, a great sense of humour (her laugh was warm and spontaneous) and an intense dedication and persistence in everything to which she set her hand. She was never a believer in half measures and neither time nor distance was ever a deterrent to her full participation.... The quality of her support and her contributions was always of the highest rank, be it judged professionally or by any other standards. She was always cheerful and steadfast, viewing the future with a calm optimism. Above all else, she was a great inspiration to her friends and colleagues who drew strength and confidence from her courage, wisdom and tenacity. It was a great privilege to have known her.[28]

Footnotes for this chapter can be found online at:
http://secondstorypress.ca/resources and at http://feministhistories.ca/books

AFTERWORD
MEETING ELSIE GREGORY MACGILL

It's clear that, deep down, MacGill is convinced there's nothing special about her knowledge or her strength. That certainty (and the unconscious generosity of spirit that assumes we're all equal) is no doubt at the heart of her success. Yet if she's so ordinary, how has she managed to lead such an extraordinary life?[1]

—Judy Steed

Elsie's story has fascinated me for the better part of a decade. I first encountered her while student teaching at Sir Winston Churchill Collegiate and Vocational Institute in Thunder Bay, Ontario. During my placement, I helped teach a course on Canadian history. In discussing the Second World War we took a minute to focus on Elsie and her achievements. At first she really did not make a big impression on the students, who were in the process of piecing together the events of the war as whole; she was just another name. That changed when they found out that this historical figure had actually lived and worked nearby. The industrial plant a few blocks away, now owned by Bombardier, was then Canadian Car and Foundry and produced airplanes for the Allies during the war. From 1938 to 1943 Elsie was its chief aeronautical engineer.

As my year at Lakehead University's Faculty of Education came to an end, and I anticipated the next step of my academic journey as a graduate student in history at the University of Ottawa, Elsie once again entered my life. A phone call from the professor who would become my graduate supervisor led to a discussion of Elsie. Dr. Ruby Heap asked if, as a resident of Thunder Bay, I was familiar with Elsie. Ruby was in the process of cataloguing all of Elsie's files at the Library and Archives of Canada and asked if I would be interested in taking up this work. Though I knew little about Elsie at the time, I agreed to learn more. A few months later, with a copy of Pamela Wakewich's *The Queen of the Hurricanes* in hand, I began what would become an extended relationship with Elsie.[2]

Following Elsie's trajectory raised my own feminist consciousness and I too joined the Canadian Federation of Business and Professional Women's Clubs of Canada. This organization has openly supported my work and offered me multiple opportunities to learn about the dynamic Canadian women's movement.

To better understand Elsie's fascination with engineering, I have also tapped into several outstanding networks of women scientists and engineers, including l'Association de la francophonie à propos des femmes en science, technologies, ingénierie et mathématiques,[3] the Natural Science and Engineering Research Council of Canada's Chairs for Women in Science and Engineering,[4] the International Network of Women Engineers and Scientists[5], and Women in Science and Engineering. On the aviation front I have explored aviation museums, spoken with pilots and aeronautical engineers, both past and present, and even spent some time in a flight simulator.

In a letter to Lakehead University President W.G. Tamblyn about Elsie's biography of her mother's life *My Mother the Judge: A Biography of Helen Gregory MacGill*,[6] she wrote: "My Mother [Helen Gregory MacGill] visited the Lakehead periodically when I was there, and addressed various groups. Perhaps the story of her life will encourage more Lakehead students, particularly girls, to interest themselves in the public affairs and service of their community and nation."[7] It is my hope that Elsie's story, as well as her mother's and those of their colleagues, will encourage many other women and men to be bold in pursuit of their lifework and their ideals.

Footnotes for this chapter can be found online at:
http://secondstorypress.ca/resources and at http://feministhistories.ca/books

A NOTE ABOUT SOURCES

This account of Elsie's life would not have been possible without a vast collection of rich resources made available to me in various locations and mediums. Scholars of women in science and engineering often are challenged by a scarcity of detailed records and materials, due to the failure to recognize the historical importance of individual women prior to the loss of their personal and professional papers.[1]

This was not the case with Elsie Gregory MacGill. While Elsie's records have their own gaps, their existence is largely due to her own respect for women's history, which was nurtured when she realized that the story of her mother's achievements was being forgotten. Writing *My Mother the Judge: A Biography of Helen Gregory MacGill*[2] was the start of her dedicated work to preserve women's history.

Elsie's concern with documenting women's history dovetailed with the growth of the second wave of the women's movement and the rise of Canadian women's studies in academia.[3] These developments found support in the acquisition policies of the Public Archives of Canada (now Library and Archives Canada). In fact, Elsie was contacted directly in 1974 by Dominion Archivist W.I. Smith regarding the possibility of obtaining her personal records to enhance the holdings of Canada's national archival repository.[4]

Elsie responded positively to this request and supported the initiative.[5] In addition to revealing a wealth of information on multiple aspects of Elsie's public life, these records also provided a rich trove of resources regarding her private life.

A surprising aspect of her records is their range. Elsie's practice of extensive correspondence continued throughout her life. Her typed letters, easily identifiable as they are riddled with grammatical and spelling errors and corrections, were often referenced or referred to by other members of the organizations to which she belonged. Elsie elected to keep all her feminist resource materials, including those pertaining to the internal workings of the Royal Commission on the Status of Women, even though she had been the one to call for their destruction upon the completion of the commission's work.[6] It is not clear why she kept these materials, but I am grateful for the insights they provide.[7]

While there is a much information pertaining to Elsie's involvement in various engineering societies and her related work in these areas, not as many materials are available to flesh out her educational and early work experience between the 1920s and late 1940s. Reasons for this situation include university regulations regarding the retention of school notes, confidential work, and Elsie's own admission that she lost some of her materials. Indeed, even after Elsie opened her own consulting business a lot of her work remained highly confidential, which frustrated hopes of detailed analysis in this area.[8]

In addition to the wide array of materials available at the Library and Archives of Canada, I have further utilized materials from the Archives of Ontario, Canadian Broadcasting Corporation's Digital Archives, and the University of Toronto Archives to fill in gaps in Elsie's own personal records. These resources are complemented by a wide range of personal interviews and written correspondence with her colleagues and family.

The quotations within this book that had spelling mistakes have been corrected to ease the readability of the text. Please also note that full footnotes are available online at: http://secondstorypress.ca/resources or at http://feministhistories.ca/books.

BIBLIOGRAPHY

LIBRARY AND ARCHIVES OF CANADA

Association of Consulting Engineers of Canada Fonds

Canadian Federation of Business and Professional Women's Fonds

Engineering Institute of Canada Fonds

Elsie Gregory MacGill Fonds

Records of the Post War Committee on the Manufacture of Aircraft

J.J. Green Fonds

Marion Royce Fonds

Royal Commission on the Status of Women in Canada Fonds

Senator Lorna Marsden Fonds

ARCHIVES OF ONTARIO

Elsie Gregory MacGill Fonds F4526

Ontario Business and Professional Women's Clubs Fonds F207

Toronto Business and Professional Women's Club Fonds F2085

ARCHIVES OF THE UNIVERSITY OF TORONTO

File Number A-73-0026/269(48) – Elsie MacGill's University of Toronto Application – 1923.

Course Calendars 1923–1927

The University of Toronto Engineering Society Transactions and Year Book.

CANADIAN BROADCASTING CORPORATION (CBC) ARCHIVES

CBC Digital Archives, "Equality First: Call for Call for the Bird Commission", http://www.cbc.ca/archives/categories/politics/rights-freedoms/equality-first-the-royal-commission-on-the-status-of-women/call-for-the-bird-commission.html, Medium: Television, Program: CBC Television News, Broadcast Date: February 3, 1967, Guest(s): Florence Bird, Lester B. Pearson, Duration: 2:10, (Accessed November 14, 2012).

CBC Digital Archives, "Equality First: Canadian Feminists Fight for Change", http://www.cbc.ca/archives/categories/politics/rights-freedoms/equality-first-the-royal-commission-on-the-status-of-women/canadian-feminists-fight-for-change.html, Medium: Television, Program: CBC Newsmagazine, Broadcast Date: March 28, 1967, Guest(s): Laura Sabia, Announcer: George McLean, Host: Gordon Donaldson, Duration: 5:03, (Accessed November 13, 2012).

CBC Digital Archives, "Equality First: Women in the Labour Force" http://www.cbc.ca/archives/categories/politics/rights-freedoms/equality-first-the-royal-commission-on-the-status-of-women/women-in-the-labour-force.html, Medium: Radio, Program: Agenda, Broadcast Date, March 9, 1968, Guest(s): Phyllis Poland, Reporter: Marion McCormick, Duration: 4: 42, (Accessed November 14, 2012).
"Students scrutinize Lady Godiva Ride", Original broadcast date: February 4, 1990,The CBC Digital Archives Website, Canadian Broadcasting Corporation, http://archives.cbc.ca/society/crime_justice/clips/2239 (Accessed April 11, 2011).

Canadian Business and Profession Women of Canada Clubs – Index of Resolutions (1950s-1990s):

"BPW Canada- Index of Resolutions" available from http://www. bpwcanada.com/Resolutions/Index-Resolution.pdf (Accessed December 9, 2007).

INTERVIEWS

Interview with Monique Bégin, May 24, 2006.

Phone Interview with Naomi Black, July 6, 2006.

Phone Interview with Elizabeth Hughes Schneewind, July 2006.

Interview with Dr. Ursula Franklin, July 13, 2006.

Interview with Dormer Ellis, July 15, 2006.

Interview with Liz Neville, July 15, 2006.

Interview with Ann Soulsby, August 7, 2006.

Interview with Lorna Marsden, August 8, 2006.

Phone Interview with Brigid O'Reilly September 2006.

Emailed Response to Interview Cathleen Morrison, November 15, 2006.

Interview with Victor Stevenson, December 22, 2006.

Interview with Wendy Lawrence, April 19, 2007.

WRITTEN COMMUNICATION

Email correspondence with Mr. B.L. Riddle, Librarian, National Aerospace Library, Farnborough, England, July 6, 2010.

Email correspondence with Muriel Smith, December 17, 2008.

Written correspondence with Helen Brock, September 2013.

Correspondence between Helen Brock and Richard Bourgeoise-Doyle, October 2007, provided by Helen Brock, September 2013.

PRINTED MATERIAL - NEWSPAPERS / PRINT MEDIA

The Business and Professional Woman
Chatelaine
The Chicago Daily Tribune
The Chronicle Journal
The Daily Gleaner
Le Devoir
The Globe and Mail
The Engineering Digest
The Montréal Star
The New York Times
Oakville Telegram
The Ottawa Citizen
Ottawa Journal
Saturday Night
The Toronto Sun
Today
Toronto Star
SWE: Magazine of the Society of Women Engineers
Thunder Bay Business
Vancouver News-Harold
Vancouver Province
Vancouver Sun
Vanity Fair
The Varsity
Winnipeg Free Press

JOURNALS

The Engineering Journal
The Canadian Aeronautical and Space Journal
The Canadian Consulting Engineer

REPORTS

Brodie, Janine and Isabella Bakker. *Canada's Social Regime and Women: An Assessment of the Last Decade*. Ottawa: Status of Women Canada, March 2007.

Canada. *Women at Work in Canada: A fact book on the female labour force of Canada*. Women's Bureau. Ottawa: Queen's Printer, 1957.

Canadian Advisory Council on the Status of Women. *10 Years Later: An assessment of the Federal Government's implementation of the recommendations made by the Royal Commission on the Status of Women*. Ottawa: CACSWM, 1979.

Ellis, Dormer. "These Women are Engineers." Questionnaire survey prepared for the 2nd Convention of Women Engineers of Canada. Toronto: Ontario Institute for Studies in Education, 1983.

EXPO 67 Information Manual – Universal and International Exhibition of 1967, Montréal, April 28–October 27. Information Services – EXPO 67.

EXPO 67 Official Guide. Toronto: Maclean-Hunter Publishing Company Limited, 1967.

The Expert Panel on Accountability Mechanisms for Gender Equality. *Equality for Women: Beyond the Illusion*. Ottawa: Status of Women Canada, 2005.

Government du Québec, *Rapport Parent: Rapport de la Commission royale d'enquête sur l'enseignement dans la province de Québec*, Québec: Ronalds-Federated Limited, 1966.

Munro, John C. *Status of Women in Canada, 1973*. Ottawa: Office of the Co-ordinator of Status of Women Canada, 1972.
Paltiel, Freda L. *Status of Women in Canada, 1972: Report*. Ottawa: Office of the Co-ordinator, Status of Women, 1972.

Proceedings of a Conference on A Science Policy for Canada. Canadian Institute on Public Affairs and the Canadian Broadcasting Corporation, Toronto, February 28 to March 2, 1969.

Report of the Committee on the Operation of the Abortion Law. Ottawa: Minister of Supply and Services Canada 1977.

The Report of the Royal Commission on the Status of Women in Canada. Ottawa: Crown Copyrights, 1970.

Royal Commission on Canada's Economic Prospects. Ottawa: Queen's Printer, 1956.

Royal Commission on Government Organization. Ottawa: Queen's Printer, 1963.

Royal Commission on Taxation. Ottawa: Royal Commission on Taxation, 1967.

United States. *President's Commission on the Status of Women, 1963*.

Women's Bureau. *Fields of Work for Women: Physical Sciences, Earth Sciences, Mathematics*. Ottawa: Department of Labour, Canada, 1964.

BOOKS

Adams, Annemarie and Peta Tancred. *"Designing Women" Gender and the Architecture Profession,* Toronto: University of Toronto Press, 2000.

Adamson, Nancy, et. al. *Feminists Organizing for Change: The Contemporary Women's Movement in Canada*. Toronto: Oxford University Press, 1988.

Ainley, Marianne Gosztonyi. *Creating Complicated Lives: Women and Science at English-Canadian Universities, 1880–1980*. Marelene Rayner-Canham and Geoff Rayner-Canham eds. Montréal and Kingston: McGill-Queen's University Press, 2012.

Ainley, Marianne Gosztonyi eds. *Essays on Canadian Women in Science*. Montréal: Véhicle Press, 1990.

Aitken, Sally, Helen D'Orazio and Stewart Valin, eds. *Walking Fingers: The Story of Polio and Those Who Lived With It*. Montréal: Véhicle Press, 2004.

Allen, Richard. *The Social Passion: Religion and Social Reform in Canada, 1914–1928.* Toronto: University of Toronto Press, 1971.

Ambrose, Susan A. et. al. in *Journeys of Women in Science and Engineering: No Universal Constants.* Philadelphia: Temple University Press, 1997.

Antrobus, Peggy. *The Global Women's Movement: Origins, Issues and Strategies,* New York: Zed Books, 2004.

Anderson, Doris. *Rebel Daughter: An Autobiography.* Toronto: Key Porter Books, 1996.

Andrew, Caroline and Sandra Rodgers, eds. *Women and the Canadian State/Les femmes et l'Etat canadien.* Montréal: McGill-Queen's University Press, 1997.

Atomic Energy of Canada Limited. *Canada Enters the Nuclear Age: A Technical History of Atomic Energy of Canada Limited.* Montréal & Kingston: McGill-Queen's University Press, 1997.

Ball, Norman R. *"Mind, Hearth, and Vision": Professional Engineering in Canada 1887 to 1987.* Ottawa: National Museum of Science and Technology/National Museums of Canada, 1987.

Backhouse, Constance. *Carnal Crimes: Sexual Assault Law in Canada, 1900–1975.* Toronto: The Osgood Society for Canadian Legal History, 2008.

_____. *Petticoats and Prejudice: Women and Law in Nineteenth Century Canada.* Toronto: Women's Press, 1991.

Backhouse, Constance and David H. Flaherty eds. *Challenging Times: The Women's Movement in Canada and the United States.* Montréal: McGill-Queen's University Press, 1992.

Bannerman, Jean. *Leading Ladies: Canada – 1939–1967.* Don Mills: T.H. Best Printing Company Limited, 1967.

Bird, Florence. *Anne Francis: An Autobiography by Florence Bird.* Toronto: Clarke: Irwin & Company Limited, 1974.

Bix, Amy. *Inventing Ourselves Out of Jobs? America's Debate Over Technological Unemployment 1929–1981*. Baltimore: The Johns Hopkins University Press, 2000.

Bluck, Sherna Berger. *Rosie the Riveter Revisited: Women, The War, and Social Change*. Boston: Twayne Publishers, 1987.

Bothwell, Robert and William Kilbourn, *C.D. Howe: A Biography*. Toronto: McClelland and Stewart, 1979.

Brownmiller, Susan. *Against Our Will: Man, Women and Rape*. New York: Simon & Schuster 1975.

Buddle, Melanie. *The Business of Women: Marriage, Family and Entrepreneurship in British Columbia, 1901–1951*. Toronto: University of British Columbia Press, 2010.

Bumstead, J.M. *The Peoples of Canada: A Post-Confederation History*. Toronto: Oxford University Press, 1992.

Bourgeois-Doyle, Richard I. *Her Daughter the Engineer: A Biography of Elsie Gregory MacGill*. National Research Council Biography Series. No. 3. P.B. Cavers Ed., Ottawa: NRC Research Press, 2008.

_____. *George J. Klein: The Great Inventor*. NRC Press Biography Series No. 2. P.B. Cavers ed. Ottawa: NRC Research Press, 2004.

Brown, Rosemary, *Being Brown: A Very Public Life*. Toronto: Random House, 1989.

Burkowski, Gordon. *Can-Car: A History 1912–1992,* Thunder Bay, Ontario: Bombardier Inc., 1995.

Buss, Helen M. *Mapping Our Selves: Canadian Women's Autobiography in English*. Montréal: McGill-Queen's University Press, 1993.

Cameron, Elspeth and Janice Dickin eds. *Great Dames*. Toronto: University of Toronto Press, 1997.

Campagna, Palmiro. *Requiem for a Giant: A.V. Roe Canada and the Avro Arrow*. Toronto: A Honslow Book, 2003.

_____. *Storms of Controversy: The Secret Arrow Files Revealed.* Third Edition. Toronto: Stoddart Publishing, 1998.

Christie, Nancy. *Engendering the State: Family, Work, and Welfare in Canada.* Toronto: University of Toronto Press, 2000.

Code, Lorraine, ed. *Encyclopedia of Feminist Theories.* Reprint 2000. New York: Routledge, 2002.

Constant, Edward W. II. *The Origins of the Turbojet Revolution.* Baltimore: The Johns Hopkins University Press, 1980.

Cook, Ramsay. *The Regenerators: Social Criticism in Late Victorian English Canada.* Toronto: University of Toronto Press, 1985.

Cowan, Ruth Scwartz. *More Work for Mother: The Ironies of Household Technology from the Open Heath to the Microwave.* United States of America: Basic Books, 1983.

Creager, Angela N.H. et al. eds. *Feminism in Twentieth-Century Science, Technology, and Medicine.* Chicago: University of Chicago Press, 2001.

Crean, Susan. *Grace Hartman: A woman for her time,* Vancouver: New Star Books, 1995.

Crowley, Terry. *Agnes MacPhail and the Politics of Equality.* Toronto: James Lorimer & Company, Publishers, 1990.

Crouch, Tom D. *Rocketeers and Gentlemen Engineers: A History of the American Institute of Aeronautics...and what came before.* Reston, VA: American Institute of Aeronautics and Astronautics, 2006.

Damer, Eric and Herbert Rosengarten. *UBC The First 100 Years.* Vancouver: The University of British Columbia, 2009.

Dane, Nazla. *With Enthusiasm and Faith: History of the Canadian Federation of Business and Professional Women's Clubs – La Fédération Canadienne des Clubs de Femmes de Carrières Libérales et Commerciales – 1972–1984.* Book II. Toronto: The Canadian Federation of Business and Professional Women, 1983.

Deakin, Phyllis A. *The History of The International Federation of Business and Professional Women: Volume 1, 1930–1968*. Second Edition. London: International Federation of Business and Professional Women, 1996.

Des Jardins, Julie. *The Madame Curie Complex: The Hidden History of Women in Science*. New York: The Feminist Press, 2010.

Dodd, Dianne and Deborah Gorham, eds. *Caring and Curing: Historical Perspectives on Women and Healing in Canada*. Ottawa: University of Ottawa Press, 1994.

Douglas, Deborah G. *American Women and Flight Since 1940*. Kentucky: The University Press of Kentucky, 2004.

DuBois, Ellen Carol. *Harriot Stanton Blatch and the Winning of Woman Suffrage*. New Haven: Yale University Press, 1997.

Dumont, Micheline. *Feminism à la Québecoise*. Trans. Nicole Kennedy. Ottawa: Feminist Historical Society/Société d'histoire féministe, 2012.

Dunn, Jane. *Virginia Woolf and Vanessa Bell: A Very Close Conspiracy*. London: Virago Press, 2000.

Eggleston, Wilfrid. *National Research in Canada: The NRC 1916–1966*. Toronto: Clarke, Irwin & Company Limited, 1978.

Ellis, Frank. *Canada's Flying Heritage*. Reprint 1954. Toronto: University of Toronto Press, 1981.

Ferguson, Eugene S. *Engineering and the Mind's Eye*. Cambridge, Mass.: The MIT Press, 1993.

Fitzpatrick, Ellen. *Endless Crusade: Women Social Scientists and Progressive Reform*. New York: Oxford University Press, 1990.

Forbes, Elizabeth. *With Enthusiasm and Faith: History of the Canadian Federation of Business and Professional Women's Clubs – La Fédération Canadienne des Clubs de Femmes de Carrières Libérales et Commerciales – 1930–1974*. Book I. Victoria: The Canadian Federation of Business and Professional Women, 1974.

Ford, Anne Rochon. *A Path Not Strewn With Roses: One Hundred Years of Women at the University of Toronto, 1884–1984*. Toronto: University of Toronto, 1985.

Franklin, Ursula. *The Ursula Franklin Reader: Pacifism as a Road Map*. Toronto: Between the Lines, 2006.

Fraser, Sylvia ed. *Chatelaine: A Woman's Place: Seventy Years in the Lives of Canadian Women:* Toronto: Key Porter Books, 1997.

Freedman, Estelle B. *No Turning Back: The History and the Future of Women*. New York: Ballantine Books, 2002.

Freeman, Barbara M. *The Satellite Sex: The Media and Women's Issues in English Canada, 1966–1971*. Waterloo: Wilfrid Laurier Press, 2001.

French, Katherine L. and Allyson M. Poska. *Women & Gender in the Western Past, Volume Two Since 1500*. New York: Houghton Mifflin & Company, 2007.

Friedland, Martin L. *The University of Toronto: A History*. Toronto: University of Toronto Press, 2002.

Friedson, Eliot. *Professionalism: The Third Logic, On the Practice of Knowledge*. Chicago: University of Chicago Press, 2001.

Frize, Monique. *The Bold and the Brave: A History of Women in Science and Engineering*. Ottawa: University of Ottawa, 2009.

Gagnon, Robert. *Histoire de l'École Polytechnique de Montréal 1873–1990: Le Montée des Ingénieurs Francophones*. Montréal: Boréal, 1991.

Gidney, R.D. and W.P. J. Millar, *Professional Gentlemen: the Professions in Nineteenth Century Ontario*, Ontario Historical Studies Series. Toronto: University of Toronto Press, 1994.

Gillett, Margaret, *We Walked Very Warily: A History of Women at McGill*. Montréal: Eden Press Women's Publications, 1981.

Glazer, Penina Migdal and Miriam Slater, *Unequal Colleagues: The Entrance of Women into the Professions, 1890–1940*. New Brunswick, NJ: Rutgers University Press, 1987.

Gleason, Mona. *Normalizing the Ideal: Psychology, Schooling, and the Family in Postwar Canada*. Studies in Gender History. Toronto: University of Toronto Press, 1999.

Gluck, Sherna Berger. *Rosie the Riveter Revisted: Women, The War, and Social Change*. Boston: Twayne Publishers, 1987.

Gorham, Deborah. *Vera Brittain: A Feminist Life*. Cambridge, Mass.: Blackwell Publishers, 1996.

Griffiths, N.E.S. *The Splendid Vision: Centennial History of the National Council of Women of Canada, 1893–1993*. Ottawa: Carleton University Press, 1993.

Haas, Violet B. and Carolyn C. Perrucci eds. *Women in Scientific and Engineering Professions*. Rexdale: John Wiley & Sons Canada, 1984.

Hamilton, Nigel. *Biography: A Brief History,* Cambridge: Harvard University Press, 2007.

Hamilton, Roberta. *Setting the Agenda: Jean Royce and the Shaping of Queen's University*. Toronto: University of Toronto Press, 2002.

Hansen, James R. *Engineer in Charge: A History of the Langley Aeronautical Laboratory, 1917–1958*. The NASA History Series. Washington, D.C.: NASA, 1986.

Harding, Sandra. *The Science Question in Feminism*. London: Cornell University Press, 1986.

Hatch, Sybil E. *Changing Our World: True Stories of Women Engineers*. Reston, Virginia: The American Society of Civil Engineers, 2006.

Heilbrun, Carolyn G. *Writing a Woman's Life*. New York: W.W. Norton & Company, 1988.

Hill, Lawrence. *Women of Vision: The Story of the Canadian Negro Women's Association, 1951–1976*. Toronto: Umbrella Press, 1996.

Hughes, Helen MacGill, *News and the Human Interested Story,* Reprint 1940. New Brunswick, NJ: Transaction Books, 1981.

_____. *News and the Human Interest Story, University of Chicago Sociological Series,* Chicago: University of Chicago, 1940.

Jain, Devaki. *Women, Development, and the UN: A Sixty-Year Quest for Equality and Justice. United Nations Intellectual History Project Series.* Bloomington: Indiana University Press, 2005.

Kealey, Linda, ed. *A Not Unreasonable Claim: Women and Reform in Canada, 1880s-1920s.* Toronto: University of Toronto Press, 1979.

Kealey, Linda and Joan Sangster. *Beyond the Vote: Canadian Women and Politics.* Toronto: University of Toronto Press, 1989.

Keller, Evelyn Fox. *Reflection on Gender and Science.* 10th Anniversary Edition. Reprint 1985. New Haven: Yale University Press, 1995.

Keshen, Jeffrey A. *Saints, Sinners, and Soldiers: Canada's Second World War.* Vancouver: UBC Press, 2004.

Kinnear, Mary. *In Subordination: Professional Women, 1870–1970.* Montréal: McGill-Queen's Press, 1995.

Kinney, Jeremy R. *Airplanes: The Life Story of a Technology, Greenwood Technographies Series,* Westport, Connecticut: Greenwood Press, 2006.

Kirton, Jonathan Grenville. *Canadian Car & Foundry Aircraft Production at Fort William on the Eve of World War II.* Thunder Bay: Thunder Bay Historical Museum Society Inc., 2009.

Knowles, Valerie. *First Person: A Biography of Cairine Wilson Canada's First Woman Senator.* Toronto: Dundurn Press, 1988.

Kohlstedt, Sally Gregory ed. *History of Women in the Sciences: Readings from Isis.* Chicago: The University of Chicago Press, 1999.

Korinek, Valerie. *Roughing it in the Suburbs: Reading Chatelaine Magazine in the Fifties and Sixties.* Toronto: University of Toronto Press, 2000.

LaMarsh, Judy. *Judy LaMarsh: Memoirs of a Bird in a Gilded Cage.* Toronto: Pocket Books, 1970.

Lancaster, Jane. *Making Time: Lillian Moller Gilbreth – A Life Beyond "Cheaper by the Dozen".* Boston: Northeastern University Press, 2004.

Landsberg, Michele. *Writing the Revolution.* Ottawa: Feminist History Society/Société d'histoire feministe, 2011.

Langford, John W. *Transport in Transition: The Reorganization of the Federal Transport Portfolio, Canadian Public Administration Series,* ed. E. Hodgetts, Montréal: McGill-Queen's Press, 1976.

Langston, Nancy. *Toxic Bodies: Hormone Disruptors and the Legacy of DES.* New Haven: Yale University Press, 2010.

Lewis, S.P. *Grace: The Life of Grace MacInnis.* Madeira Park, BC: Harbour Publishing, 1993.

Lucena, Juan C. *Defending the Nation: U.S. Policymaking to Create Scientists and Engineers from Sputnik to the 'War Against Terrorism'.* New York: University Press of America, Inc., 2005.

Lunardini, Christine. *What Every American Should Know About Women's History: 200 Events that Shaped Our Destiny.* Holbrook, Massachusetts: BOB ADAMS, INC., 1994.

Lynes, Neanette, *The Factory Voice: A Novel.* Regina: Coteau Books, 2009.

Lyzun, Jim. *Aviation in Thunder Bay.* Thunder Bay: Thunder Bay Historical Museum Society Inc., 2006.

MacGill, Elsie. *My Mother the Judge: A Biography of Judge Helen Gregory MacGill.* Reprint 1955. Toronto, PMA Books, 1981.

Mackenzie, David. *ICAO: A History of the International Civil Aviation Organization.* Toronto: University of Toronto Press, 2010.

_____. *Canada and International Civil Aviation, 1932–1948.* Toronto: University of Toronto Press, 1989.

Macpherson, Kay. *When in Doubt Do Both: The Times of My Life.* Toronto: University of Toronto Press, 1994.

McCreery, Christopher. *The Order of Canada: Its Origins, History, and Development.* Toronto: University of Toronto Press, 2005.

McLeod, Thomas H. and Ian McLeod. *Tommy Douglas: The Road to Jerusalem.* Calgary: Fifth House Ltd., 2004.

McGuign, Dorothy Gies. *A Dangerous Experiment: 100 Years of Women at University of Michigan*, Michigan: Centre for Continuing Education of Women, 1970.

McIlwee, Judith Samson and J. Gregg Robinson. *Women in Engineering: Gender, Power and Workplace Culture.* New York: University of New York, 1992.

McKenzie, Judith. *Pauline Jewett: A Passion for Canada.* Montréal & Kingston: McGill-Queen's University Press, 1999.

McKillop, A.B. *Matters of Mind: The University in Ontario: 1791–1951.* Toronto: University of Toronto Press, 1994.

McMillen, Sally G. *Seneca Falls and the Origins of the Women's Rights Movement.* Toronto: Oxford University Press, 2009.

Marble, Alan Everett and Verilea D. Ellis. *The House That Sexton Built: A Century of Outstanding Graduates.* Tantallon, N.S: Four East Publications, 2007.

Marcus, Alan I., ed. *Engineering in a Land-Grant Context: The Past, Present and Future of an Idea.* West Lafayette, Indiana: Purdue University Press, 2005.

Milberry, Larry. *Aviation in Canada.* Toronto: McGraw-Hill Ryerson, 1979.

Miles, Angela and Geraldine Finn, eds. *Feminism in Canada: From Pressure to Politics.* Montréal: Black Rose Books, 1982.

Millwood, Liz. *Women in British Imperial Airspace, 1922–1937.* Montréal and Kingston: McGill-Queen's University Press, 2008.

Mitchell, Margaret. *No Laughing Matter: Adventures, Activism & Politics.* Vancouver: Granville Island Publishing, 2008.

Molson, K.M. and H.A. Taylor. *Canadian Aircraft Since 1909.* Stittsville, ON: Canada's Wings, Inc., 1982.

Newman, Jacquella and Linda A. White. *Women, Politics, and Public Policy: The Political Struggles of Canadian Women.* Toronto: Oxford University Press, 2006.

Oldenziel, Ruth. *Making Technology Masculine: Men, Women and Modern Machines in America, 1870–1945.* Amsterdam: Amsterdam University Press, 1999.

Parker, Richard. *John Kenneth Galbraith: His Life, His Politics, His Economics.* Toronto: HarperCollins Publications Ltd., 2006.

Parkin, J.H. *Aeronautical Research in Canada, 1917–1957: Memoirs of J.H. Parkin.* Volumes 1 & 2. Ottawa: National Research Council Canada, 1983.

Peckham, Howard H. *The Making of The University of Michigan, 1817–1992.* 175th Anniversary Edition, Margaret L. Steneck and Nicholas H. Steneck eds. Ann Arbor: University of Michigan, 1996.

Pierson, Ruth R. *They're Still Women After All: The Second World War and Canadian Womanhood.* Toronto: McClelland and Stewart, 1986.

Pietilä, Hilkka. *The Unfinished Story of Women and the United Nations.* NGLS Development Dossier. New York: UN Non-Governmental Liaison Service, 2007.

Prentice, Alison et. al. *Canadian Women: A History.* Second Edition. Scarborough: Nelson Thomson Learning, 1996.

Rebick, Judy. *Ten Thousand Roses: The Making of a Feminist Revolution.* Toronto: Penguin Canada, 2005.

Roathchild, Joan, ed. *Machina Ex Dea: Feminist Perspectives on Technology.* New York: Pergamon Press, 1983.

Robbins, Wendy, Meg Luxton, Margrit Eichler and Francine Descarries. *Minds of Our Own: Inventing Feminist Scholarship and Women's Studies in Canada and Québec, 1966–1976.* Waterloo: Wilfrid Laurier University Press, 2008.

Robinson, Jane. *Bluestockings: The Remarkable Story of the First Women to Fight for an Education*. London: Penguin Books, 2010.

Rooke, P.T. and R.L. Schnell. *No Bleeding Heart: Charlotte Whitton a Feminist on the Right*. Vancouver: University of British Columbia Press, 1987.

Rossiter, Margaret. *Women Scientists in America: Before Affirmative Action 1940–1972*. Volume 2. Baltimore: The Johns Hopkins University Press, 1995.

_____. *Women Scientists in America: Struggles and Strategies to 1940*. Volume 1. Baltimore: The Johns Hopkins University Press, 1982.

Rowley, Hazel. *Franklin and Eleanor*. New York: Picador, 2010.

Sangster, Joan. *Transforming Labour: Women and Work in Postwar Canada*. Toronto: University of Toronto Press, 2010.

Schiebinger, Londa. *Has Feminism Changed Science?* Cambridge: Harvard University Press, 1999.

Sergio, Lisa. *A Measure Filled: The Life of Lena Madesin Phillips: Drawn from her Autobiograph*. Reprint 1972. United Kingdom: IFBPW, 1989.

Sharpe, Robert J. and Patricia I. McMahon. *The Persons Case: The Origins and Legacy of the Fight for Legal Personhood*. Toronto: University of Toronto Press, 2008.

Sheffield, Suzanne Le-May. *Women and Science: Social Impact and Interaction*. New Brunswick: Rutgers University Press, 2006.

Snow, C.P. *The Two Cultures: And a Second Look – An Expanded Version*. Reprint 1959. Cambridge: Cambridge University Press, 1969.

_____. *The Two Cultures and the Scientific Revolution*. Cambridge: Cambridge University Press, 1960.

Stephen, Jennifer A. *Pick One Intelligent Girl: Employability, Domesticity and the Gendering of Canada's Welfare State, 1939–1947*, Toronto: University of Toronto, 2007.

Stewart, Greig. *Shutting Down the National Dream: A.V. Roe and the Tragedy of the Avro Arrow*. Toronto: McGraw-Hill Ryerson Limited, 1988.

Strong-Boag, Vernoica and Anita Clair Fellman eds. *Rethinking Canada: The Promise of Women's History*. Toronto: Copp Clark Pitman, 1991.

Taylor, Margaret Allen and John Claridge Taylor. Eds. *The History of the International Federation of Business and Professional Women, Volume II, 1968–1995*. London: International Federation of Business and Professional Women, 1996.

Toman, Cynthia. *An Officer and a Lady: Canadian Military Nursing & The Second World War*. Vancouver: UBC Press, 2007.

Trescott, Martha Moore, ed. *Dynamos and Virgins Revisited: Women and Technological Change in History*. New Jersey: The Scarecrow Press, Inc., 1979.

Tye, Diane. *Baking As Biography: A Life Story in Recipes*. Montréal & Kingston: McGill-Queen's Press, 2010.

Valverde, Marianna. *The Age of Light, Soap, and Water: Moral Reform in English Canada, 1885–1925*. Toronto McClelland & Stewart Inc., 1991.

Vance, Jonathan F. *High Flight: Aviation and the Canadian Imagination*. Toronto: Penguin Canada, 2002.

Vickers, Jill et al. *Politics as if Women Mattered: A Political Analysis of the National Action Committee on the Status of Women*. Toronto: University of Toronto Press, 1993.

Vincenti, Walter G. *What Engineers Know and How They Know It: Analytical Studies from Aeronautical History*. Baltimore: The Johns Hopkins University Press, 1990.

Ware, Susan. *Still Missing: Amelia Earhart and the Search for Modern Feminism*. New York: W.W. Norton & Company, 1993.

Westfall, William. *The Founding Moment: Church, Society, and the Construction of Trinity College*. Montréal & Kingston: McGill-Queen's University Press, 2002.

White, Richard. *The Skule Story: The University of Toronto Faculty of Applied Science and Engineering, 1873–2000*. Toronto: University of Toronto Press, 2000.

Wilks, Brian. *Browsing Science Research at the Federal Level in Canada: History, Research Activities, and Publications*. Toronto: University of Toronto Press, 2004.

Witz, Anne. *Professions and Patriarchy*. London: Routledge, 1992.

Woolf, Virginia. *A Room of One's Own*. Reprint 1929. New York: First Harvest Edition, 1989.

ARTICLES

Abir-am, Pnina G. and Dorinda Outram. "Introduction". eds. Pnina G. Abir-am and Dorinda Outram. *Uneasy Careers and Intimate Lives: Women in Science 1789–1979. Lifes of Women in Science,* Ann Hibner Koblitz ed., New Brunswick, NJ: Rutgers University Press, 1987, p. 1-16.

Ainley, Marianne Gosztonyi. "Introduction." *Despite the Odds: Essays on Canadian Women and Science*. Marianne Gosztonyi Ainley, ed., Montréal: Véhicle Press, 1990, p. 17-21.

Arscott, Jane. "'More Women': The RCSW and Political Representation, 1970." in *Women and Political Representation in Canada*. Women's Studies Series Number 2, Manon Tremblay and Caroline Andrew, eds., Ottawa: University of Ottawa Press, 1998, p. 145-168

_____. "Twenty-five Years and Sixty-five Minutes After the Royal Commission on the Status of Women". *International Journal of Canadian Studies*. 11 (1995), p. 33-58.

Aschaiek, Sharon, Nicole Axworthy and Michael Mastromatteo. "Engineering in the Next 10." *Engineering Dimensions.* (July/August 2007), p. 54-64.

Backhouse, Constance. "Introduction", in *Feminist Journeys/Voies Féministes.* Marguerite Andersen ed., Ottawa : Feminist Historical Society, 2010, p. 24-29.

Barber, Leslie A. "U.S. Women in Science and Engineering, 1960–1990: Progress Toward Equality?" *Journal of Higher Education.* Volume 66, Number 2, (March/April 1995), p. 213-234.

Bégin, Monique. "The Canadian Government and the Commission's Report", in *Women and the Canadian State/Les femmes et l'état canadien.* Caroline Andrew and Sandra Rodgers eds., Montréal & Kingston: McGill-Queen's Press, 1997, p. 12-26.

_____. "The Royal Commission on the Status of Women: Twenty Years Later." in *Challenging Times: The Women's Movement in Canada and the United States.* Constance Backhouse and David H. Flaherty, eds., Montréal: McGill- Queen's University Press, 1992, p. 21-38.

Bird, Florence. "Reminiscences of the Commission Chair", in *Women and the Canadian State/Les femmes et l'état canadien.* Caroline Andrew and Sandra Rodgers, eds., Montréal & Kingston: McGill-Queen's Press, 1997, p. 185-196.

Bix, Amy Sue. "Engineering National Defense: Technical Education at Land-Grant Institutions during World War II." in *Engineering in a Land-Grant Context: The Past, Present and Future of an Idea.* Alan I. Marcus, ed., West Lafayette, Indiana: Purdue University Press, 2005, p. 105-133.

_____. "From "Engineeresses" to "Girl Engineers" to "Good Engineers": A History of Women's U.S. Engineering Education". *NWSA Journal.* 16(1) (Spring 2004), p. 27-49.

_____. ""Engineeresses" Invade Campus: Four Decades of Debate Over Technical Education". *IEEE Technology and Society Magazine.* (Spring 2000), p. 20-26.

_____. "Feminism Where Men Predominate: The History of Women's Science and Engineering Education at MIT". *Women's Studies Quarterly*. (2000), 1&2, p. 24-45.

Black, Naomi. "The Canadian Women's Movement: The Second Wave." In *Changing Patterns: Women in Canada*. Sandra Burt et. al. eds., Toronto: McClelland & Stewart Inc., 1993, p. 151-176.

_____. Introduction to *My Mother the Judge,* by Elsie Gregory MacGill. Reprint 1955. Toronto: PMA Books, 1981, p. xi-xxiv.

Brandt, Gail Cutherbert. "'Pigeon-Holed and Forgotten': The Work of the Subcommittee on the Post-War Problems of Women, 1943." *Histoire sociale – Social History*. Volume XV, Number 29, (May 1982), p. 239-259.

Brodie, Janine. "The Great Undoing: State Formation, Gender Politics, and Social Policy in Canada." in *Western Welfare in Decline: Globalization and Women's Poverty*. Catherine Kingfisher ed., Philadelphia: University of Pennsylvania Press, 2002, p. 90-110.

_____. "Canadian Women, Changing State Forms, and Public Policy." in *Women and Canadian Public Policy*. Janine Brodie ed., Toronto: Harcourt Brace & Co., 1996, p. 1-28.

Buddle, Melanie. "'You Have to Think Like a Man and Act Like a Lady': Business women in British Columbia, 1920–80." *BC Studies*. Number 151, (Autumn 2006), p. 69-95.

Burr Margadant, Jo. "Introduction: Constructing Selves in Historical Perspective" In *The New Biography: Performing Femininity in Nineteeth-Century France*. Jo Burr Margadant ed. Berkeley: University of California Press, 2000, p. 1-32.

Burt, Sandra. "The Canadian Advisory Council on the Status of Women: Possibilities and Limitations". In *Women and Political Representation in Canada. Women's Studies Series* Number 2. Manon Tremblay and Caroline Andrew eds., Ottawa: University of Ottawa Press, 1998, p. 115-144.

Carstairs, Catherine and Nancy Janovicek. "Introduction: Productive Pasts and New Directions". In *Feminist History in Canada: New Essays on Women, Gender, Work, and Nation,* Catherine Carstairs and Nancy Janovicek eds., Vancouver: UBC Press, 2013, p. 3-22.

Clow, Barbara. "'An Illness of Nine Months' Duration': Pregnancy and Thalidomide Use in Canada and the United States", in *Women, Health, and Nation: Canada and the United States Since 1945,* eds. Georgina Feldberg, Molly Ladd-Taylor, Alison Li, and Kathryn McPherson. Montréal & Kingston: McGill-Queen's University Press, 2003, 45-66.

Cowan, Ruth Schwartz. "Foreward: Musings About the Woman Engineer as Muse". In *Crossing Boundaries, Building Bridges: Comparing the History of Women Engineers 1870s-1990s.* Annie Canel et. al., eds., Amsterdam: Harwood Academic Publishers, 2000, p. xiii-xvi.

Douglas, Deborah G. "The End of 'Try-and-Fly": The Origins and Evolution of American Aeronautical Engineering Education through World War II". In *Engineering in a Land-Grant Context: The Past, Present and Future of an Idea.* Alan I. Marcus ed., West Lafayette, Indiana: Purdue University Press, (2005), p. 77-104.

Eberts, Mary. "'Write It For the Women': Doris Anderson, the Changemaker". *Canadian Woman Studies / les cahiers de la femme.* Volume 26, Number 2, (2007), p. 6-13.

Fingard, Judith. "College, Career, and Community: Dalhousie Coeds, 1881–1921". In *Youth, University and Canadian Society: Essays in the Social History of Higher Education.* Paul Axelrod and John G. Reid eds., Kingston and Montréal: McGill-Queen's University Press, 1989, p. 26-46.

_____. "Gender and Inequality at Dalhousie: Faculty Women Before 1950". *Dalhousie Review,* (1984–85), 64(4), p. 687-703.

Franklin, Ursula. "Will Women Change Technology or Will Technology Change Women?" In *The Ursula Franklin Reader: Pacifism as a Map.* Toronto: Between the Lines, 2006, p. 243-256.

Fraser, D. "Elsie Gregory MacGill: Aeronautical Engineer." *Archivist.* 14, (January-February 1987), p. 8-9.

Freeman, Barbara M. "Framing Feminine/Feminist: English-language Press Coverage of the Hearings of the Royal Commission on the Status of Women in Canada, 1968". *International Journal of Canadian Studies.* 11 (1995), p. 11-32.

Greif, Moniko. "Women Engineers in Western Germany: Will We Ever Be Taken For Granted?" In *Crossing Boundaries, Building Bridges: Comparing the History of Women Engineers 1870s-1990s.* Annie Canel, Ruth Oldenziel and Karin Zachmann eds., Amsterdam: Harwood Academic Publishers, 2000, p. 279-282.

Guppy, Neil, Doug Balson and Susan Vellutini. "Women and Higher Education in Canadian Society". In *Women and Education: A Canadian Perspective.* Janke Gaskell and Arlene Tigar McLaren eds., Calgary, Alberta: Detselig Enterprises, 1987, p. 175-192.

Haussman, Melissa. "Of Rights and Power: Canada's Federal Abortion Policy 1969–1991". In *Abortion Politics, Women's Movements, and the Democratic State: A Comparative Study of State Feminism.* Dorothy McBride Stetson ed., *Gender and Politics.* Series Editor: Karen Beckwith. New York: Oxford University Press, 2001, p. 63-86.

Heap, Ruby. "Fighting the 'Corset of Victorian Prejudice' Women's Activism in Canadian Engineering during the Pioneering Decades (1970's-80s)." In *Feminist History in Canada: New Essays on Women, Gender, Work, and Nation,* eds. Catherine Carstairs and Nancy Janovicek, (Vancouver: UBC Press, 2013), p. 218-236.

_____. "Introduction: Women and Gender in Canadian Science, Engineering, Medicine". *Scientia Canadensis.* Volume 29. Number 2, (2006), p. 3-15.

_____. "'The only girl in such a big class': Women Students at the University of Toronto's Faculty of Applied Science and Engineering during the 1920s and the 1930s". *Scientia Canadensis* Volume 29. Number 2, (2006), p. 45-73.

_____. Writing Them into History: Canadian Women in Science and Engineering Since the 1980s." *Out of the Ivory Tower: Feminist Research for Social Change*. Andrea Martinez and Meryn Stuart eds., Toronto: SUMACH Press, 2003, p. 49-67.

_____. "Physiotherapy's Quest for Professional Status in Ontario, 1950–80". *Canadian Bulletin of Medical History*. 12, (1995), p. 69-99.

Heap, Ruby and Ellen Scheinberg. "'Just one of the gang': Women at the University of Toronto's Faculty of Applied Science and Engineering, 1939–1950". In *Learning to Practice: Professional Education in Historical and Contemporary Perspective*. Ruby Heap, Wyn Millar and Elizabeth Smyth eds., Ottawa: University of Ottawa Press, 2005, p. 189-211.

Hocker-Drysdale, Susan. "Sociologist in the Vineyard: The Careers of Helen MacGill Hughes and Everet Charrington Hughes". In *Creative Couples in the Sciences*. Helena M Pycior, Nancy G. Slack and Pnina G. Abir-am eds, *Lives of Women in Science*. Ann Hibner Koblitz ed., New Brunswick, NJ: Rutgers University Press, 1996, p. 220-231.

Hornig, Lilli S. "Foreword". In *Journeys of Women in Science and Engineering: No Universal Constants?* Susan A. Ambrose ed., Philadelphia: Temple University Press, 1997, p. ix-xiii.

_____. "Professional Women in Transition". In *Women in Scientific and Engineering Professions*. Violet B. Hass and Carolyn C. Perrucci eds., Rexdale: John Wiley & Sons Canada, 1984, p. 43-58.

Hubbard, Ruth. "Should Professional Women be Like Men?" In *Women in Scientific and Engineering Professions*. Violet B. Hass and Carolyn C. Perrucci eds., Rexdale: John Wiley & Sons Canada, 1984, p. 205-211.

Hughes, Helen MacGill. "Wasp/Woman/Sociologist". *Society*, (July/August 1977), p. 69-80.

"Introduction". In *Challenging Professions: Historical and Contemporary Perspectives of Women's Professional Work*. Elizabeth Smyth et al., eds., Toronto: University of Toronto Press, 1999, p. 3-22.

"Introduction: The Context of Learning to Practise". In *Learning to Practise: Professional Education in Historical and Contemporary Perspective"*. Ruby Heap, Wyn Millar and Elizabeth Smyth eds., Ottawa: University of Ottawa Press, 2005), p. 1-11.

Jenson, Jane. "Competing Representations: The Politics of Abortion in Canada". In *Women and the Canadian State/Les femmes et l'état canadien*. Caroline Andrew and Sandra Rodgers eds., Montréal & Kingston: McGill-Queen's Press, 1997, p. 291-305.

Kemp, David D. "Can-Car Re-Tools for Victory Hurricane." *The Beaver.* (June/July 1992), p. 24-32.

Keshen, Jeffrey. "Revisiting Canada's Civilian Women During World War II." *Histoire social/Social History.* 20(60), (1997), p. 239-266.

Lerman, Nina E., Arwen P. Mohun, and Ruth Oldenzie, "The Sholders We Stand On/The View from Here: Historiography and Directions for Research". In *Gender & Technology: A Reader*. Nina E. Learnman et al., eds., Baltimore: The Johns Hopkins University Press, 2003, p. 425-449.

Little, Margaret Hillyard. "Claiming a Unique Place: The Introduction of Mother's Pensions in British Columbia". In *Rethinking Canada: The Promise of Women's History*. Third Edition. Veronica Strong-Boag and Anita Clair Felman eds., Toronto: Oxford University Press, 1997, p. 285-303.

Lucena, Juan C. "Women in Engineering: Politics in the Making of a Statistical Category". *IEEE Technology and Society Magazine.* (Spring 2000), p. 6-14.

McPherson, Kathryn. "First-wave/second-wave feminism". In *Encyclopedia of Feminist Theories*. Reprint 2000. Lorraine Code ed., New York: Routledge, 2002, p. 208-210.

Mack, Pamela E. "What Difference Has Feminism Made to Engineering in the Twentieth Century?" In *Feminism in Twentieth-Century Science, Technology, and Medicine*. Angela N.H. Creagor et al., eds., Chicago: University of Chicago Press 2001, p. 158-161.

Martin-Neilson, Janet. "The Very Model of a Modern Engineer: Education and Status at the Engineering Institute of Canada, 1925–1932". *Scientia Canadensis*. 30(1) (2007), p. 53-73.

Merritt, Susan E. "Elsie MacGill (1905–1980): Aeronautical Engineer". In *Her Story III: Women From Canada's Past*. Susan E. Merrit eds., St. Catherines: Vanwell, 1999, p. 180-193.

Millar, W.P.J. and R.D. Gidney. "'Medettes': Thriving or Just Surviving? Women Student in the Faculty of Medicine, University of Toronto, 1910–1951". In *Challenging Professionals: Historical and Contemporary Perspectives on Women's Professional Work*. Elizabeth Smyth et. al., eds., Toronto: University of Toronto Press, 1999, p. 215-233.

Millar, Wyn, Ruby Heap and Bob Gidney. "Degrees of Difference: The Students in Three Professional Schools at the University of Toronto, 1910 to the 1950s". *Learning to Practice: Professional Education in Historical and Contemporary Perspective*. Ruby Heap, Wyn Millar and Elizabeth Smyth. Ottawa: University of Ottawa Press, 2005, p. 155-187.

Molson, Kenneth M. "World War Two Aircraft Production in Canada: A Reminiscent Look at the Unprecedented Growth of a Key Industry in A Country Newly at War". *CAHS Journal* (Winter 1992), p. 138-147.

Mossman, Mary Jane. "Bertha Wilson: 'Silences' in a Woman's Life Story". In *One Woman's Difference: Justice Bertha Wilson*. Kim Brooks ed., *Law and Society Series*. W. Wesley Pue ed., Vancouver: University of British Columbia Press, 2009, p. 297-316.

Morris, Cerise. ""Determination and Thoroughness" The Movement for a Royal Commission on the Status on Women in Canada". *Atlantis*. Volume 5. Number 2, (Spring 1980), p. 1-20.

O'Neil, Maureen and Sharon Sutherland. "The Machinery of Women's Policy: Implementing the RCSW". In *Women and the Canadian State/ Les femmes et l'état Canadien*. Caroline Andrew and Sandra Rodgers eds., Montréal & Kingston: McGill-Queen's Press, 1997, p. 197-219.

Oldenziel, Ruth. "Multiple-Entry Visas: Gender and Engineering in the US, 1870–1945". In *Crossing Boundaries, Building Bridges:*

Comparing the History of Women Engineers, 1870s-1990s. Annie Canel, Ruth Oldenziel and Karin Zachmann eds., Amsterdam: Harwood Academic Publishers, 2000, p. 11-49.

Oldenziel, Ruth, Annie Canel and Karin Zachmann. "Introduction: Crossing Boundaries, Building Bridges: Comparing The History of Women Engineers, 1870s-1990s". In *Crossing Boundaries, Building Bridges: Comparing the History of Women Engineers, 1870s-1990s.* Annie Canel, Ruth Oldenziel and Karin Zachmann eds., Amsterdam: Harwood Academic Publishers, 2000, p. 1-10.

Paltiel, Freda. "Quest for Equality". In *Our Own Agendas: Autobiographical Essays by Women Associated with McGill University.* Margaret Gillett and Ann Beer eds., Montréal & Kingston: McGill-Queen's University Press, 1995, p. 111-120.

Perrucci, Carolyn C. "Central Issues Facing Women in the Science-Based Professions". In *Women in Scientific and Engineering Professions.* Violet B. Hass and Carolyn C. Perrucci eds., Rexdale: John Wiley & Sons Canada, 1984, p. 1-16.

Prentice, Alison. "Women Becoming Professional Scholars: Historians and Physicists". In *Learning to Practise: Professional Education in Historical and Contemporary Perspective.* Ruby Heap, Wyn Millar and Elizabeth Smyth eds., Ottawa: University of Ottawa Press, 2005, p. 213-238.

Prentice, Alison. "Three Women in Physics". In *Challenging Professions: Historical and Contemporary Perspectives on Women's Professional Work..* Elizabeth Smyth et al., eds., Toronto: University of Toronto Press, 1999, p. 119-140.

Pursell, Carroll. "'Am I a Lady or an Engineer?' The Orgins of the Women's Engineering Society in Britain, 1918–1940". In *Crossing Boundaries Building Bridges: Comparing the History of Women Engineers, 1870s-1990s.* Annie Canel et al., eds., Amsterdam: Harwood Academic Publishers, 2000, p. 51-73.

Quinn, Patrick J. "One of Ours: Claudette MacKay-Lassonde, P.Eng., 1948–2000". *Engineering Dimensions.* (July/August 2000), p. 15.

Riegler, Natalie. "Some Issues to be Considered in Writing of Biography." *CBMH/BCHM.* Volume 11. (1994), p. 219-227.

Ruby, Claudia. "Transformer le monde par la critique littéraire : regard stylistique sur les chroniques radiophoniques de Jeanne Lapointe", Recherches féministes, Volume 24, Number 1, (2011), p. 101-118.

Sabia, Laura. "Fiercely Feminist". In *A Fair Shake: Autobiographical Essays by McGill Women.* Margaret Gillett and Kay Sibbald eds., Montréal: Eden Press, 1984, p. 358-375.

Sangster, Joan. "CHR Forum: Invoking Experience as Evidence". *The Canadian Historical Review.* 92, 1 (March 2011), p. 137.

Septer, Dirk. "Fairchild's Underrated Husky: The F-11 Never Fully Realized its Potential as a Bushplane." *CAHA Journal.* (Fall 1997), p. 110-116.

Sissons, Crystal. "Elsie Gregory MacGill: Feminist and Advocate for Social Change". *Atlantis.* Volume 34. Number 2, (2009), p. 48-57.

_____. "Engineer and Feminist: Elsie Gregory MacGill and the Royal Commission on the Status of Women, 1967–1970." *Scientia Canadensis.* Volume 29, Number 3, (2006), p. 74-97.

Smith, Helen and Pamela Wakewich, "'I Was Not Afraid to Work' Female War Plant Employees and Their Work Environment". In *Canadian Environments: Essays in Culture, Politics and History,* Canadian Studies No. 2. Serge Jaumain ed., Series Ed. Robert C. Thomsen and Nanette L. Hale, Brussels: P.I.E. – PETER LAND S.A., 2005, p. 229-247.

_____. "Beauty and the Helldivers": Representing Women's Work and Identities in a Warplant Newspaper". *Labour/Le Travail.* Number 44, (Fall 1999), p. 71-107.

_____. "Representations of Women and Wartime Work in The Canadian Car and Foundry Company Newspaper, *The Aircrafter*". *Papers & Records.* (1997), p. 64-77.

Stephen, Jennifer A. "Balancing Equality for the Post-War Woman: Demobilising Canada's Women Workers After World War Two". *Atlantis*, Volume 32 Number 1, (2007), p. 122-132.

Strong-Boag, Veronica. "'Ever a Crusader': Nellie McClung". In *Rethinking Canada: The Promise of Women's History*. Third Edition. Veronica Strong-Boag and Anita Fellman eds., Toronto: Oxford University Press, 1997, p. 271-284.

Strong-Boag, Veronica and Anita Clair Fellman eds. "Introduction". In *Rethinking Canada: The Promise of Women's History*. Third Edition. Veronica Strong-Boag and Anita Fellman, eds., Toronto: Oxford University Press, 1997, p. 1-10.

"The Unmarried Woman Artist: Emily Carr". In *Framing Our Past: Canadian Women's History in the Twentieth Century*. Sharon Anne Cook, Lorna R. McLean and Kate O'Rourke eds., Montréal & Kingston: McGill Queen's Press, 2001, p. 45-46.

Tillotson, Shirley. "Human Rights Law as Prism: Women's Organizations, Unions, and Ontario's Female Employees Fair Remuneration Act, 1951". *Canadian Historical Review*. LXXII, (1991), p. 532-557.

Trescott, Martha M. "Women Engineers in History: Profiles in Holism and Persistence". In *Women in Scientific and Engineering Professions*. Violet B. Hass and Carolyn C. Perrucci eds., Rexdale: John Wiley & Sons Canada, 1984, p. 181-204.

Trofimenkoff, Susan Mann. "Feminist Biography." *Atlantis*, Volume 10, Number 2, (Spring 1985), p. 1-9.

Tronrud, Thorold J. "Building the Industrial City". In *Thunder Bay From Rivalry to Unity,* Thorold J. Tronrud and A. Ernest Epp eds., Thunder Bay: The Thunder Bay Historical Museum Society, Inc., 1995, p. 99-119.

Turnbull, Lorna. "A Way of Being in the World". In *One Woman's Difference: Justice Bertha Wilson*. Kim Brooks ed., *Law and Society Series*. W. Wesley Pue ed., Vancouver: University of British Columbia Press, 2009, p. 246-261.

Vickers, Jill. "The Intellectual Origins of the Women's Movement in Canada". In *Challenging Times*. Constance Backhous and David H. Flaherty eds., Montréal: McGill-Queen's University Press, 1992, p. 39-60.

Wakewich, Pamela. "'The Queen of the Hurricanes': Elsie Gregory MacGill, Aeronautical Engineer and Women's Advocate". In *Framing Our Past: Canadian Women's History in the Twentieth Century*. Sharron Anne Cook, Lorna R. McLean and Kate O'Rouke eds., Montréal & Kingston: McGill-Queen's Press, 2001, p. 396-401.

Walden, Keith. "Hazes, Hustles, Scraps, and Stunts: Initiations at the University of Toronto, 1880–1925". In *Youth, University and Canadian Society: Essays in the Social History of Higher Education*. Paul Axelrod and John G. Reid eds., Montréal and Kingston: McGill-Queen's University Press, 1989, p. 94-121.

Warren, (Milstead), Vi. "Flying with the ATA: A Girl Air Transport Auxiliary Pilot Recalls Her Wartime Experiences". As told to Arnold Warren. *CAHA Journal*, (Fall 1999), p. 84-112.

Wisnioski, Matthew H. "'Liberal Education Has Failed': Reading Like an Engineer in 1960s America". *Technology & Culture*, 50(4), (October 2009), p. 753-782.

Zachmann, Karin. "Mobilizing Womanpower: Women, Engineers and the East German State in the Cold War". In *Crossing Boundaries, Building Bridges: Comparing the History of Women Engineers 1870s-1990s*. Annie Canel, Ruth Oldenziel and Karin Zachmann eds., Amsterdam: Harwood Academic Publishers, 2000, p. 211-252.

THESES

Briggs, Catherine. "Fighting for Women's Equality. The Federal Women's Bureau, 1945–1967: An Example of Early "State Feminism" in Canada." Doctoral Dissertation. Waterloo: University of Waterloo, 2001.

Cummings, Judith. "The Report of the Royal Commission on the Status of Women: A Liberal Feminist Analysis." Masters Thesis. Ottawa: Carleton University, 1991.

Hodgetts, John Edwin. "Royal Commission of Inquiry in Canada: A Study in Investigative Technique." Masters Thesis. Toronto: University of Toronto, 1940.

LaPierre, Paula J.S. *The First Generation: The Experience of Women University Students in Central Canada.* Doctoral Dissertation. Toronto: University of Toronto [OISE], 1993.

Martin-Neilson, Janet. "In Principle but not in Practice: Professional Engineering Organizations in 20th Century Canada." Masters Thesis. Toronto: University of Toronto, 2006.

Morris, Cerise. "No More Than Simple Justice: The Royal Commission on the Status of Women and Social Change in Canada." Doctoral Dissertation. Montréal: McGill University, 1982.

Sissons, Crystal. "Elsie Gregory MacGill: Engineering the Future and Building Bridges for Canadian Women, 1918–1980". Doctoral Dissertation. Ottawa: University of Ottawa, 2008.

Speers, Kimberly Marie. "The Royal Commission on the Status of Women: A Study of the Contradictions and Limitations of Liberalism and Liberal Feminism." Masters Thesis. Kingston: Queen's University, 1994.

PRESENTATIONS

Heap, Ruby and Crystal Sissons. "Retracing Paths to Advance Future Journeys: Creating Bridges Between Engineering and Social Sciences" at the Canadian Committee on Women and Engineering +20 National Workshop, University of Ottawa, Ontario, April 29, 2011. http://projectccwe.files.wordpress.com/2011/05/crystal-sissons.pdf (Accessed November 11, 2012).

Sissons Crystal. Invited Lecture, "Flying, Feminism and Fearlessness" for the Canadian Aeronautics and Space Institute, Ottawa Branch, Women in Aerospace Then and Now at The University of Ottawa, March 1, 2012.

_____. "Women in Science and Engineering on the Radar: The Canadian Federation of Business and Professional Women and Women in STEM" Presentation at Women's Worlds 2011, July 5, 2011, Ottawa, Ontario.

_____. "Three Pioneering Feminist Canadian Engineers" at The International Symposium of Women and Gender Studies – Where Do We Stand? Paris, France, September 15, 2011.

_____. "Elsie Gregory MacGill: Pioneering Woman Engineer & Feminist" at the Women in Science and Engineering (WISE) Wine and Cheese, Carleton Branch, Ottawa, Ontario, April 30, 2008.

WEBSITES & MULTIMEDIA

"1975–2006 Ontario Building Code Amendment History". Available at: http://www.obc.mah.gov.on.ca/Page106.aspx (Accessed February 5, 2008).

"AFFESTIM", http://www.affestim.org/ (Accessed April 19, 2011).

Archives of Ontario, Archives Descriptive Database, "Elsie Gregory MacGill fonds": http://ao.minisisinc.com/scripts/mwimain.dll/144/ARCH_DESC_FACT/FACTSDESC/REFD+F+4526?SESSIONSEARCH (Accessed January 25, 2013).

"Business and Professional Women – BPW Canada", www.bpwcanada.ca (Accessed February 2, 2013).

"BPW Ontario History", http://www.bpwontario.org/about-bpw/history.html (Accessed April 2, 2011).

"Canadian Coalition for Women in Engineering, Science, Technology and Trades" www.ccwestt.org (Accessed February 2, 2013).

"Canadian Car & Foundry National Historic Site of Canada", *Thunder Bay Business*, (July 2012), 9. Available at: issuu.com/northsuperior/docs/business_july_2012black , (Accessed July 14, 2012).

"Canadian Centennial Medal: Background", http://archive.gg.ca/honours/medals/hono4-cent_e.asp (Accessed March 19, 2011).

Canadian Federation of University Women. "CFUW History", www.
cfuw.org/en-ca/aboutus/cfuwhistory.aspx (Accessed March 11, 2012).

"Chapter XVI. Status of Women. Convention on the Political Rights
of Women". Available at: http://untreaty.un.org/temp/WEBBACKUP_
OLD/final/ts2/newfiles/part_boo/xvi_boo/xvi_1.html (Accessed
December 7, 2007).

Constance Backhouse. "Law: Sexual Assault Cases Researched:" www.
constancebackhouse.ca (Accessed February 3, 2013).

"Convention on the Political Rights of Women". http://untreaty.un.org/
ENGLISH/bible/englishinternetbible/partI/chapterXVI/treaty1/cop
(Accessed August 7, 2007).

"De Havilland DHC-2 Beaver" The Canadian Aviation and Space
Museum, http://www.aviation.technomuses.ca/collections/artifacts/
aircraft/deHavillandCanadaDHC-2Beaver/ (Accessed January 26, 2014).

"Department History" Michigan Aerospace Engineering, Michigan
University, www.engin.umich.edu/aero/about/aero/history (Accessed
August 15, 2014).

Dormer Ellis, "BPW Canada: Times Have Changed" An address
presented at BPW Canada Convention, June 19, 2010, Horseshoe
Valley, Ontario, http://www.bpw-international.org/latest-news-top/
bpw-news/bpw-latest-news/615-canada-times-have-changed-by-dormer-
ellis (Accessed April 3, 2011).

"Fairclough, The Right Hon. Ellen Louks, P.C., C.C., O.Ont.,
L.L.D, F.C.A.", Parliament of Canada, http://www.parl.gc.ca/
parlinfo/Files/Parliamentarian.aspx?Item=d7fdad8e-4c2b-4c9a-9d74-
154e592f19d7&Language=E&Section=ALL (Accessed January 18, 2014).

Fairmont Royal York Hotel, "Hotel History", www.fairmont.com/
royal-york-toronto/hotelhistory/ (Accessed November 12, 2012).

Highlands Digitalization Project, "The Agnes Macphail Website", www.
greyhighlandspubliclibrary.com/AgnesMacphail/ACM_Home_Page.
htm (Accessed November 12, 2012).

"Heritage CanCar Airport Hawker Hurricane Monument Proposal – Vesa Peltonen", *NetNews,* (June 16, 2012). http://netnewsledger.com/2012/06/16/heritage-cancar-airport-hawker-hurricane-monument-proposal-vesa-peltonen/ (Accessed July 14, 2012).

Soroptimist International "History". http://soroptimistinternational. org/html/history.htm (Accessed December 3, 2007).

IFBPW "BPW International's Resolutions: Education: Training, Technical, and Vocational Guidance": Encourage Women to Receive and Countries to Offer Training (1953), http://www.bpw-international. org/BPW-Previous/publications/resolutions-edu-training.htm#1953 (Accessed April 10, 2011).

IFBPW, "BPW International's Resolutions, Equal Pay for Work/ Value of Work", http://www.bpw-international.org/BPW-Previous/ publications/resolutions-equality-equal-pay.htm#1959 (Accessed April 10, 2011).

"ILO Convention C-100". http://www.ilo.org/ilolex/cgi-lex/ratifce. pl?C100 (Accessed August 7, 2007).

"In Memoriam: Rose Sheinin (Née Shuber)", *Concordia University Journal,* Volume 4, Number 13, April 2, 2009. http://cjournal. concordia.ca/archives/20090402/in_memoriam_rose_sheinin_nee_ shuber.php (Accessed August 24, 2012).

"INWES International Network of Women Engineers and Scientists", www.inwes.org (Accessed February 2, 2013).

LAC, "Old Messengers, New Media: The Legacy of Innis and McLuhan", http://www.collectionscanada.gc.ca/innis-mcluhan/030003-1000-e.html (Accessed March 12, 2012).

"LaMarsh, The Hon. Julia Verlyn (Judy), P.C., O.C., Q.C., B.A." The Parliament of Canada, http://www.parl.gc.ca/Parlinfo/Files/ Parliamentarian.aspx?Item=5794257d-84e7-4451-af19-35e0cfc6ccaa&Language=E&Section=ALL (Accessed January 18, 2014).

"The Lone Flower Rona Alexandra Hatt Wallis (BaSC '22), 1901-1982)" http://blogs.apsc.ubc/ca/making a difference/ January 25, 2011 (Accessed October 8, 2011).

Marsh, James. "Mackenzie Valley Pipeline", *The Canadian Encyclopedia*, http://www.thecanadianencyclopedia.com/en/article/mackenzie-valley-pipeline/ (Accessed February 1, 2014).

The New Canadian Air and Space Museum, "Avro Canada CF-105 Arrow", http://www.casmuseum.org/avro_cf105_arrow.php (Accessed January 28, 2013).

Northwestern Ontario Aviation Heritage Centre. http://www.noahc.org/ (Accessed February 3, 2013).

"Our Elsie", The Toronto Business and Professional Women's Club, http://www.bpwtoronto.com/hp_2.html (Accessed March 12, 2011).

"Order of Canada: Ursula Martius Franklin, C.C., O. Ont., Ph.D., LL.D, F.R.S.C." www.gg.ca/honour.aspx?id=3073&t=12&ln=Franklin (Accessed October 13, 2012).

Villeneuve, Denis. "Polytechnique", Remstar Media Producers and Alliance Films, 2009, 77 minutes.

"Procedures related to FIPPA Requests". http://www.fippa.utoronto.ca/Page16.aspx (Accessed 21 June 2006).

"Producer's Biography", Empowerkids.com J. Gary Mitchell Film Company, http://www.empowerkids.com/html/ProducersBio.htm (Accessed January 24, 2014).

Quota International "History", http://www.quota.org/gtku/aq.hist.htm (Accessed December 3, 2007).

"Queen Elizabeth II Silver Jubilee Medal: Background", http://archive.gg.ca/honours/medals/hono4-qesj_e.asp (Accessed March 19, 2011).

Saxberg, Kelly. *Rosies of the North*. National Film Board of Canada, 1999. Documentary. 46m30s.

"Spotlight on Women in Science and Engineering (WISE)". Reprinted from *The Link*, February/March 1999, 2. Permission PEO. http://wise_professional.homestead.com/files/Wise_in_spotlight.txt, (Accessed August 26, 2007).

Stairs, Denis. "Colombo Plan". *The Canadian Encyclopedia Historica.* http://www.thecanadianencyclopedia.com/index. cfm?PgNm=TCE&Params=A1ARTA0001771 (Accessed December 12, 2007).

"Stevenson, Victor" *Obituaries, The Chronicle Journal* Tuesday, August 12, 2008. http://chroniclejournal.com/includes/datafiles/print. php?id=128119&title=STEVENSON%20Victor (Accessed June 13, 2010).

Struthers, James. "Great Depression". *The Canadian Encyclopedia.* http://thecanadianencyclopedia.com/index.cfm (Accessed August 3, 2007).

The Toronto Business and Professional Women's Club, "Her Story", http://www.bpwtoronto.com/herstory.html (Accessed November 6, 2012).

"The Toronto Business and Professional Women's Club: Very Important Members", http://www.bpwtoronto.com/hp_1.html (Accessed March 26, 2011).

"Through Adversity, 1920–1939", *Corrections Canada: An Interactive Timeline,* Correctional Service Canada, http://www.css-scc.gc.ca/history/1920/third_e.shtml (Accessed December 8, 2007).

"Seneca: History", www.senecac.on.ca/about/history.html (Accessed January 27, 2013).

Zonta International, "About Zonta International", http://www.zonta. org/whoweare.aspx (Accessed January 25, 2014).

ACKNOWLEDGEMENTS

This book owes its genesis and realization to many people who have stood by me and offered strength, guidance, and assistance beyond what I could have ever expected. It has been a long and at times very frustrating journey, which I never could have completed alone. The fact that you are holding this book in your hands means that a once distant dream is now a solid reality.

Of the many specific people who deserve my sincere gratitude, I must start with my husband, Teva Vidal. He has always believed in me, the importance of Elsie's story, and that I could complete this book. He encouraged me even when I questioned and doubted myself. He has read and edited multiple drafts of this book. Moreover, he has never tired of discussion on this topic, despite the fact it has consumed so much of my time and energy. Teva, my thanks for your love, support and motivation simply cannot be expressed in words.

I am also very indebted to Drs. Lorna Marsden and Constance Backhouse. Lorna has been an enthusiastic supporter from the first time that I contacted her for an interview about Elsie, and it was she who put me in touch with Constance and the encouraging members of the Feminist History Society. Constance has patiently and persistently supported me during the uncertainties of the post-doctoral world, through regular meetings, and mentorship. Her dedication to the recognition and celebration of Canadian women's history is truly inspiring. Constance also opened other doors of support including that of the Marion Dewar National Capital Region

Women's History Book Club. To each of the members of the book club I give my thanks for your support, the invigorating discussions, new perspectives, sources, fun, laughter – and of course the food!

As with any project, this one has evolved considerably during its production. Along the way, articles based on this research have been published in *Scientia Canadesis* and *Atlantis*.[1] I am grateful to the anonymous peer reviewers of these publications and of this book whose questions and comments have significantly improved its composition. I am also indebted to the editorial guidance and assistance from Dr. Diana Majury and Jennifer Penney as we worked toward the final manuscript. Diana provided steady encouragement and support and Jennifer's keen eye helped make the text more readable while also challenging me with insightful questions and suggestions. Diana has also been a guide in the midway transition to working with Margie Wolfe and her engaging team at Second Story Press.

Dr. Ruby Heap guided my progress on this project throughout my graduate years. She has always seen the final product in book format, and provided ongoing enthusiasm as I continued working toward that end. Her mentorship and friendship set the foundation for this book's completion. Many thanks as well go out to Dr. Ann Denis, Dr. Janice Ahola-Sidaway, Donatille Mujawamariya, and Dr. Monique Frize who have never failed to enquire on my progress and celebrate the milestones, no matter how small, as they occurred.

The ongoing encouragement from my first history professors at Lakehead University is something truly precious to me. Regularly, on visits home to Thunder Bay I would meet with Dr. Helen Smith, Professor Vic Smith, and Dr. Pam Wakewich. Over coffee we discussed women's history, Elsie, and life in general. These meetings offered insightful ideas and perspectives as I muddled through the vast source material. Dr. Ronald Harpelle and Kelly Saxberg also provided some initial source material that has proven to be invaluable and offered ongoing encouragement along the way. I would also like to sincerely thank my inspirational history teacher at Hammarskjold High School, Roy Piovesana. His dedication, enthusiasm, and attention to detail fueled my interest in the study of history into a real passion.

Research and writing of this nature requires long hours and

dedication. I have lost track of how many visits I have made to the Library and Archives of Canada, but the Commissioners always reminded me when I had been away too long! Being welcomed regularly by smiling faces and humourous banter helped even the long hours fly by. The staff in the reading rooms was always ready and willing to help whenever needed, and their assistance is much appreciated. My thanks also goes out to all those who assisted me at the Archives of Ontario, the Northwestern Ontario Aviation Heritage Centre, the University of Toronto Archives, the Thunder Bay Historical Museum, and the City of Vancouver Archives.

I would also like to gratefully acknowledge the early financial support of this work during my doctoral studies provided by the Ontario Graduate Scholarship (OGS) and the Social Sciences and Humanities Research Council of Canada (SSHRC), without which the latter stages would not have been possible.

One of the interesting things about engaging in a journey of this nature is the people who you meet along the way. Both individuals and groups have supported me by providing much needed information, resources, and venues where I could share my evolving work. Elsie's life twinned the worlds of engineering and feminism and it is from those same worlds that I acknowledge assistance and encouragement from l'Association de la francophonie à propos des femmes en science, technologies, ingénierie et mathématiques (AFFESTIM), the Canadian Aeronautical and Space Institute (CASI), the International Network of Women Engineers and Scientists (INWES), Natural Sciences and Engineering Research Council of Canada's (NSERC) Chairs for Women in Science and Engineering, the members of the Elsie MacGill Northern Lights Award, and Women and Science and Engineering (WISE), both Ottawa and Carleton University Chapters. It is my hope that this book will give you back a bit of your history and in some small way assist you in your efforts to encourage women to seriously consider the sciences and engineering as a future possibility for their own life paths.

My thanks is also due to the encouraging forum provided by the Canadian Science and Technology Historical Association, where I presented various papers on Elsie's story.

The members of the Canadian Federation of Business and

Professional Women of Canada (BPW Canada) have provided me with important research support and resources, as well as a window into the world in which Elsie lived by welcoming me into their ongoing work. The members of BPW Canada's former Virtual Club and BPW Ottawa have provided an important sounding board and tolerated my increasing lack of time in the final stages of this book's production. In particular, Kathy Laing has always encouraged me with her enthusiasm and insight into the corporate knowledge of BPW Canada. Our many extended visits and road trips have warmed my heart and renewed my spirit with the energy to keep moving forward. I am also very grateful to the International Federation, and especially former international president Liz Benham, who made documents on the international history available for my consultation.

I also sincerely appreciate the time invested by each person who was willing to meet with me whether over the phone or in person for interviews about Elsie's life. I would especially like to acknowledge Ann Soulsby and Victor Stevenson who were very supportive of my work, and looked forward to seeing it in print, but passed away before this was possible. This book has benefited from the support and encouragement of Elsie's nieces, Helen Brock and Elizabeth Schneewind, who provided precious insights and photographs to add further nuance to this account of their aunt's life. Sincere gratitude is also due to Dr. Monique Bégin, Dr. Naomi Black, Dr. Dormer Ellis, Dr. Ursula Franklin, Wendy Lawrence, Cathleen Morrison, Liz Neville, and Brigid O'Reilly.

Family and friends have given me more reasons than I can count to keep going and helped me laugh when I wanted to cry. Their understanding of numerous periods where I was simply unavailable on account of the work to be done, as well as their insistence on breaks to ensure I did not become buried under paper and books are priceless gifts and very much appreciated.

My parents have been a source of much support over the years. Not only have they listened to the ongoing saga of the work and tolerated my bringing work on visits home or to the family camp, but they also managed the fine art of sitting around file boxes and piles of books in my cramped living room without spilling a glass of wine! On a more serious note, they also provided me with important research assistance. Their daily scouring of Thunder Bay's *Chronicle Journal* has kept me abreast of developments related to aviation history in the city, and my father even attended a meeting on Hawker Hurricanes in my stead. Because of his assistance that night, he was able to put me in touch with Victor Stevenson, who I interviewed on my next trip home. Mom and Dad, I promise, this time, I *really* am done!

My brother Darren and my sister-in-law, Kora Kamps, have endured their share of "Elsie talk," and their support has been much appreciated. Even my nieces Eva and Ella have heard about Elsie, and soon the newest addition to the family, Dustin, will hear about her too. While it might be a while before you will understand who she is, please know that this work is in part dedicated to all of you. May your own futures be as ongoing as the horizon!

My in-laws Antoinette and Jean-Louis Vidal encouraged me and celebrated my work even before we officially became family. The many incredible meals and necessary time away from my work that they provided re-energized me more times than I can count. Jean-Louis, while you were not able to see this project completed, your enthusiasm touched my heart and this book is dedicated in part to your zest for life and desire to make every moment count, something you had very much in common with Elsie.

Maeva Vidal's enthusiasm and Luke Graham's curiousity about the ongoing process and their joint support have helped me to keep on track while maintaining my sense of humour. Thank you both for believing in me!

Thank you Uncle Gary for your copy of Can Car's history, it has been well-used and consulted!

Linda and Thomas Dean have watched out for me in more ways than one, and have become family. Regular shopping trips, meals, barbecues, and coffees have lead to a deep and blessed friendship. Heather and Jean-Marc Maxwell, who initially provided me with friendship and shelter upon my arrival in the National Capital Region, were crucial supports when this journey was only a thought.

I have been sincerely privileged to have the strong support of friends both new and old who have stood by me as I told another Elsie story, or waited patiently for me to emerge from my self-imposed hermitage with a new draft. Please know that I appreciate your understanding and patience beyond measure and that simply your interest in my efforts has meant the world to me! I would especially like to thank: Natasha Blitvic, Aggie Casselman, Lina Chapman, Mary Dawood, Anthony and Leigh Di Mascio, Heather Haslam-Smith, Wendy Haché, Debra Hauer, Dalice Kelln, Anna Koolstra-Kelley, Lisa Krupa, Mélanie and Cory Matieyshen, Katie Rollwagen, Amber Sigurdson, Andrea Shalay, Matthew Diegel and Kaja Ranta, Joan and Dick Powers, Judy and Larry Warwick, Janis and Leo Zrudlo, Dr. Barton Beglo and the members of St. Peter's Lutheran Church. Any omissions to this list are simply due to memory and not intention.

I also owe my thanks for the understanding and support provided by my all of my work colleagues who watched me disappear on a regular basis into my office at lunch time to cram in a few more revisions while eating a hurried lunch, or checked-in regularly on my progress over coffee. Many thanks especially to Madeleine Allard, Éric Bastien, Éric Bergeron, Wafa Bitar, Jacques Critchley, Theressa Degn, Anna Engman, Renée Gibbins, Luc Lebrun, Christiane Nkolo, Mika Oehling, Hélène Plourde, Stephanie Robertson, Gianni Rossi, Heather Sams, Ian Thiesson, Jocelyne Tremblay, Anna Torgerson, Adam Yake, and Gail Zboch. Your daily humour and support has made this process less stressful.

Finally, I must thank Elsie Gregory MacGill. She has been both a challenge and an inspiration to me over the past years. While historical accounts can never fully represent the life of an individual, I hope that this book may shed some further light onto the formidable woman she was.

PHOTO CREDITS

Cover: Courtesy of Elizabeth Schneewind and Helen Brock/ Thunder Bay Historical Museum, Hurricane, 984.78.56

Page 12: City of Vancouver Archives, Reference Number: AM54-S4-2: CVA 371-117

Page 13: City of Vancouver Archives, Reference Number: AM54-S4-: Port P376.2

Page 14: Courtesy of Elizabeth Schneewind and Helen Brock

Page 17: Courtesy of Elizabeth Schneewind and Helen Brock

Page 18: Courtesy of Elizabeth Schneewind and Helen Brock

Page 19: City of Vancouver Archives, Reference Number: AM54-S4-2: CVA371-119 Date: 1933

Page 24: University of Toronto Archives, Engineers attempting to raid University College, Digital Image No: 2001-15-54MS, Original Item No: B1993-0007/001(04), Creator: H.M. Scheak

Page 25: University of Toronto Archives, Trinity College Women's Residence, St. George St., May 1925. Digital Image No: 2004-30-3MS, Original Item No: A1965-0004 [60.45]

Page 27: University of Toronto Archives, Faculty of Applied Science Class Photo, 1927, Accession No. B2009-0030/P

Page 33: Library and Archives Canada, PA-200745: Elsie Gregory MacGill, Accession No: 1983-237 NPC

Page 36: Courtesy of Elizabeth Schneewind and Helen Brock

Page 40: Courtesy of Elizabeth Schneewind and Helen Brock

Page 44: University of Toronto Archives, Kenneth F. Tupper, 1949?, Digital Image No: 2001-24-1MS, Original Item No: A1978-0041-022(29), Creator: Milne Studios

Page 46: Library and Archives Canada, PA-148380: Elizabeth Gregory MacGill 'Elsie' – Aeronautical Engineer and Feminist, April 1938, Box 05655, Credit: Polyphoto/Library and Archives Canada

Page 48: Courtesy of Elizabeth Schneewind and Helen Brock

Page 49: City of Vancouver Archives, Item: Port P1140.1 – [Helen Gregory MacGill, Ll.D.] Reference Code: AM54-S4-: Port 1140.1, Date: [193-?]

Page 51: Courtesy of Elizabeth Schneewind and Helen Brock

Page 53: Library and Archives Canada, PA-148465: L. to R. David Boyd, Brian Sheaver, Elsie MacGill and Mary Boyd watching flight of Hurricane aircraft at Canadian Car and Foundry Co. flying field, Date: 1941, Place of Publication: Fort William, ON, Accession No: 1983-237 NPC

Page 54: Thunder Bay Historical Museum, Aerial view of Can Car close-up, 977.113.83

Page 56 top: Thunder Bay Historical Museum, Hurricanes in production at Can Car, 984.78.54

Page 56 bottom: Thunder Bay Historical Museum, Hurricane, 984.78.56

Page 59: Courtesy of Elizabeth Schneewind and Helen Brock

Page 61: Library and Archives Canada, MG31-K7 Volume 16, File 7: Queen of the Hurricanes, Elsie MacGill: Comic Book c. 1940s; "Queen of the Hurricanes: Elsie Gregory MacGill", True Comics, Number 8 (January 1942), 17-21

Page 64: Thunder Bay Historical Museum, Can Car Floor, 984.1.180

Page 68: Thunder Bay Historical Museum, Helldivers coming off the line at Can Car, 988.1.46

Page 69: Courtesy of Elizabeth Schneewind

Page 82: Courtesy of Elizabeth Schneewind/Photographer Arthur Kay, Toronto, Ontario

Page 90: University of Toronto Archives, Charles Hamilton Mitchell, ca. 1940, Digital Image No: 2001-15-29MS, Original Image No: A1974-0008-P015(04)

Page 104: Photos by Crystal Sissons

Page 107: Photo by Crystal Sissons

Page 115: Courtesy of Ann Soulsby

Page 136: Library and Archives Canada, *The Business and Professional Woman*/October 1963/AMICUS 90450/p.1

Magazine of the Canadian Federation of Business and Professional Women's Clubs of Canada (BPW Canada)

Page 141: Library and Archives Canada, *The Business and Professional Woman*/July-August 1964/AMICUS 90450/pp.4-5

Magazine of the Canadian Federation of Business and Professional Women's Clubs of Canada (BPW Canada)

Page 143: Courtesy of Elizabeth Schneewind

Page 168: Photo by Crystal Sissons

Page 204: Courtesy of Ann Soulsby. Photo by John Evans Photography Ltd., 519 Sussex Drive, Ottawa, No. 693945

Page 205: Courtesy of Ann Soulsby

Page 206: University of Toronto Archives, Elsie Gregory MacGill, Digital Image No: 2008-8-2MS, Original Image No: A1978-0041 (09) [731145-26], Creator: Robert Lansdale, Copyright: University of Toronto

Page 215: Courtesy of Ursula Franklin

Page 216: Photo by Crystal Sissons

Page 217: Courtesy of Anna Pangrazzi, President and Director of Sales, Elsie Gregory MacGill Northern Lights Award

Page 218: Svenja Hansen © Parks Canada

Page 270: Author photo by Chris Power

ABOUT THE AUTHOR

Crystal Sissons is an independent historian and works at the Social Sciences and Humanities Research Council of Canada in Ottawa. She completed her Master's and Ph.D. in history at the University of Ottawa, after finishing undergraduate degrees in history and education at Lakehead University in Thunder Bay, Ontario. Crystal is also active in a number of organizations, including the Business and Professional Women's Club of Ottawa within BPW Canada.